THE ULTIMATE HALLOWEEN MOVIE EXPERIENCE

THE ULTIMATE HALLOWEEN MOVIE EXPERIENCE

MICHAEL MYERS: THE MAN, THE MONSTER, THE MADNESS

BY

SCOTTY MCCOY

PHOTOGRAPHS BY

KIM GOTTLIEB-WALKER

FOREWORD BY

JAMIE LEE CURTIS

EDITED BY

CHARLES F. ROSENAY

INAUGURAL VOLUME IN THE AMERICAN HORROR FILM CLASSICS SERIES

BearManor Media

2022

The Ultimate Halloween Movie Experience

© 2022 *Scotty McCoy*.

All rights reserved.

No portion of this publication may be reproduced, stored, and/or copied electronically (except for academic use as a source), nor transmitted in any form or by any means without the prior written permission of the publisher and/or author.

Published in the United States of America by:

BearManor Media

4700 Millenia Blvd.
Suite 175 PMB 90497
Orlando, FL 32839

bearmanormedia.com

Printed in the United States.

Typesetting and layout by BearManor Media

ISBN—978-1-62933-963-4

Table of Contents

Dedication	3
Foreword	5
Jamie Lee Curtis	5
Ana Alicia	8
Stacey Nelkin	10
A Word from the Author	12
Scotty McCoy	12
Interviews with *Halloween* Principles	15
Sandy Johnson	18
Ana Alicia	24
Alan Howarth	29
Stacey Nelkin	35
Sasha Jenson	43
Kathleen Kinmont	48
Jeffrey Landman	53
Daniel Farrands	63
Tom Proctor	69
Christopher Durand	76
Gary J. Clayton	82
Daeg Faerch	87

Dee Wallace	89
Ken Foree	96
Photo Gallery	98
Trivia Section	101
Halloween (1978)	101
Halloween II (1981)	116
Halloween III: Season of the Witch (1982)	133
Halloween 4: The Return of Michael Myers (1988)	151
Halloween 5: The Revenge of Michael Myers (1989)	167
Halloween 6: The Curse of Michael Myers (1995)	184
Halloween H20: 20 Years Later (1998)	203
Halloween: Resurrection (2002)	220
Halloween (2007)	238
Halloween II (2009)	256
Halloween (2018)	274
Halloween Kills (2021)	293
Halloween Mashup	312
Answer Key	337
Acknowledgements	358
Social Media Lounge	360

Dedication

I dedicate this book to my dad, Scott G. McCoy, who, on September 14, 2016, was diagnosed with a rare, aggressive form of brain cancer known as Glioblastoma. Sadly, he passed away on August 8, 2021, due to intracranial hemorrhage, after having beaten cancer which wasn't his cause of death. He was given 1 ½ years to live, and he made it one month shy of five years! RIP dad. I miss and love you!

Foreword

Jamie Lee Curtis

"Laurie Strode," *Halloween* (1978)

I was new to filming. I hadn't filmed anything prior. I got the role because my mom, Janet Leigh, was in the 1960 slasher film *Psycho* (1960), and I was nervous to film my first movie that was also a slasher. After the first day of filming, I got a call from John Carpenter. I was terrified he was going to fire me. After all, I was a new actress with no prior experience, and I felt like my first day on set wasn't good. I met with John, and he told me I did a terrific job on set for the first day of filming and the rest was history. We made history. *Halloween* (1978) made history. We have ten films in the *Halloween* (1978) franchise, and it is all because of a genius film director, John Carpenter.

A group of young adults who weren't that experienced with acting was the main cast. There was me, along with Nancy Kyes and P.J. Soles as the main stars. Then there was Donald Pleasence, God bless his soul. Unfortunately, Donald has passed away; however, he was a major reason for *Halloween*'s (1978) success. If it weren't for John Carpenter spending extra money on Donald, I don't know if *Halloween* (1978) would've been a huge success. Then there was Brian Andrews and Kyle Richards, who played the two kids being babysat. They were tremendous child actors and they brought in the element of spookiness of Michael Myers: no one is safe, not even children. Charles Cyphers was great as well. He was a great actor who brought the feeling that Donald's character was crazy, but he also might be right.

Michael Myers, as a character, is supposed to be this evil human being that doesn't care who or what he kills. John Carpenter, along with the signature theme song, made Michael into a historical figure every October and a legendary, iconic character that is everyone's dream to be for Halloween. Debra Hill, who dated John back during filming, who unfortunately passed away from cancer, was the first ever Michael Myers. Many people say Will Sandin is the first Michael as a boy, which he was, but Debra Hill played Michael's arm when grabbing for the kitchen knife. So, I must give her credit where credit is due.

The entire cast and crew are ultimately responsible for *Halloween*'s (1978) success, and without *Halloween* (1978), my career would've never even begun. Filming the original in 1978 was a great experience that had me in three of the ten sequels, and then it branched my career into multiple films, including *The Fog* (1980), *Prom Night* (1980), and even Fox's *Scream Queens* (2015).

I want to thank Scotty for reaching out to me to write the foreword to his book, *The Ultimate Halloween Movie Experience, Michael Myers: The Man, The Monster, The Madness* (2022), because this franchise is so successful that it deserves an ultimate book for the ultimate fans. Without the fans, my career never would've taken off to begin with. I could've been in a movie that was a bust, but the fans made the movie so successful that Halloween has never been the same again.

Rick Rosenthal directs Jamie Lee Curtis and Donald Pleasance in *Halloween II* (1981) Jamie Lee Curtis shows off her bruise
– Photos by Kim Gottlieb-Walker

Ana Alicia

"Nurse Janet," *Halloween II* (1981)

Rick Rosenthal and his wife, Nancy Stevens, were two talented members of my then acting class with Milton Katselas. I first realized that Rick was an up-and-coming director when he approached me in class and asked if I would be interested in auditioning for a film he was directing, *Halloween II* (1981). I was humbled and excited to be considered for this, which would be my first theatrical film. I had met Jamie Lee Curtis a year prior while we were both sitting on a wall at Universal Studios waiting to meet with the head of Universal contract players, Monique James. Jamie and I were one of the few remaining contract players, as these players were about to become a thing of the past. She was lovely, fresh, and authentic. I admired those qualities about her, and still do, along with her professionalism and work ethic.

When I watched *Halloween I* (1978) in preparation for my audition, I was impressed by the way John Carpenter crafted a film that was terrifying while actually incorporating little graphic violence. He created the terror in the audience's imagination through skilled choice of music, camera angles, and cast, led by the very talented Jamie Lee Curtis. Thus, I was thrilled to be auditioning. I don't remember much about the audition other than Rick's ability to put one at ease immediately, bringing out the best in his actors.

Shooting was exciting and quite enjoyable, as the cast and crew followed the lead of its director, Rick, all being generous and dedicated. The moment that stands out the most for me is the day of my eye injury, which gratefully turned out quite well. There was a desk a bit too close to a pad on which I was supposed to fall backwards during my death scene. During the first take, as I fell back supposedly dead after a lethal injection into my eye, all one hears in the outtake is "oh shit" coming from the dead body, as I hit the same eye on the corner of the desk. The next thing heard was Rick saying, "cut," followed by the actress (me), saying "can't you use it?," as I touched the blood running down my eye. Rick said with a calm glint in his eye, "though I appreciate your dedication, we can't, we have to take care of you." This was followed by sending me immediately to the ER where I received 12 stitches.

A few days later I continued to shoot, but as you can imagine all camera angles had to be directed at the right side of my face, as my left side was very swollen and had stitches. One of those scenes was the cafeteria scene with Leo Rossi and Lance Guest. If you look closely, you can see the strategy that was used to keep the swelling off camera.

When I went to the screening of *Halloween II* (1981), I thought Rick, the crew and the cast had done a great job. I also thought quietly to myself, "I hope when I have children, I won't regret doing a horror film." I never realized that by the time I would have children old enough to watch horror, the violence in this film would be nothing compared to the film violence of their day.

When I was being interviewed by Scotty McCoy for his book and blog, it was so much fun remembering all the wonderful people that had worked on that film. Thank you, Scotty, for asking me to be a part of your book, and a heartfelt thanks to director Rick Rosenthal for believing in me, and to all YOU fans that assured the film's success.

Stacey Nelkin

"Ellie Grimbridge," *Halloween III: Season of the Witch* (1982)

I've given so many interviews and done so many podcasts for *Halloween III* (1982), that are all in the public domain, that I honestly have nothing new to share about it.

It truly has been "the gift that keeps on giving" as NONE of us anticipated its cult status decades later. When it came and went from the theaters within days, I thought that this was just another film that I've been in that won't really help further my career.

Decades later, I am honored to meet all the wonderful fans who express appreciation and understanding of the movie. It's those fans who have created its status as a cult film and have made all of us involved in the film still relevant! I am eternally grateful for that.

Adrienne Barbeau reminded me at an event that she and I met decades ago in an elevator in a building that we both frequented in Brentwood. At the time, she was married to John Carpenter, who was in the process of producing *Halloween III* (1982). She said that she told him that she met this "cute" actress and asked me to bring her my pic and resume, which I guess I did.

Around the same time, Ron Walters, a terrific make-up artist, with whom I had worked while co-starring in *The Last Convertible* (1979) had been hired to be the makeup artist for *Halloween III* (1982), and he kept mentioning to me that they hadn't found the lead female actress.

At the time, my career was flourishing, and I wasn't interested in doing a horror film, especially because I can't watch them as I have a very low threshold for fear (I can't ride roller coasters either) - but Ron kept mentioning it as the weeks went past.

Finally, I asked my agent at CAA to get me a copy of the script and I LOVED the character I was considered for – Ellie Grimbridge. My agents set up a reading and as I walked in my door after the audition, my phone was ringing with my agent telling me that I got the part. Shooting began only a few days later.

Working with Tom Atkins and Tommy Lee Wallace and the amazing late Debra Hill was a highlight. They were all creative, fun loving, and professional people. I am grateful that I still get to see Tom A. and sometimes Tommy Lee at the Horror conventions.

To say that I have been pleasantly surprised by the film's recent cult status is an understatement!!

It's all quite surreal . . . and lots of fun!!

A Word from the Author

Scotty McCoy

McCoy's Headshot

I started my life in the horror industry back in 1996 at the age of six years old. Yes, six years old. I know, quite young to start your venture into the horror industry, but it happened, and it forever changed my life. The first horror film I ever saw at six years old was *Friday the 13th Part 7: The New Blood* (1988). After seeing that, I was mesmerized and in love with that film, to the point of needing to go and see all the *Friday the 13th* (1980) films that were out at the time, which the most recent back then was *Jason Goes to Hell: The Final Friday* (1992). I then went and saw all the *Halloween* (1978) films, all the *A Nightmare on Elm Street* (1984) films, and so on.

Ever since my journey into horror, I have done multiple things up to this very day. I have interviewed, as of this moment, more than

150 celebrities, most of whom come from the horror and slasher movie genres. I have created original video content for YouTube, and I have written and published three horror trivia books, including *The Ultimate Friday the 13th Trivia Book* (2016), *The Ultimate Halloween Trivia Book* (2017), and *The Ultimate Halloween Trivia Book, 2nd Edition* (2018). I have had the honor of being on various podcasts, web shows, radio shows, and have even met horror fans from around the world at conventions and signings. I even started my very own horror indie film company, Gravestone Films, which has released our first feature film, *Samhain* (2020), as well as a direct-to-YouTube short fan film titled *Friday the 13th: Dead Before Dusk* (2020) and our second full feature film, *72* (2022), is also available.

I have done so much in my young adult life, which, after being told by my peers in high school that I cannot do it -— since I suffer from ADHD, OCD, Bipolar Disorder, and Tourette's syndrome — made me even more motivated to become a success and prove all my peers wrong. Now, these same peers ask for my autograph and a picture with me. They pay for my movies and books. They now talk to me as if I am "something," but I always was something, just not in their eyes until I was in the public eye. Regardless of the bullying and taunting, I fortunately become someone of importance. My advice to anyone who is suffering the same criticisms, ridicules, and bullying from anyone, whether it be your friends, family, strangers, or just acquaintances, is simple: don't let them win and get the satisfaction. If you have passion, if you are motivated, and if you have goals, do everything in your power to make them come true and live your dreams. You can do anything and everything if you put your mind to it. You will fail, but just try again. I have and look where I am now! I am signed by 3iBooks with books that are published, have a film company, two college degrees, a successful YouTube channel, and have a full-time job with the US Coast Guard. If I can do this, so can you! Don't quit; just continue and succeed. I have said that my haters are my motivators. The same can apply to you, as well. If you fall, you get back up. I have faith in everyone to accomplish their dreams if they don't quit and keep on keeping on. You got this! Trust me. I love you all and thank you for your utmost love and support. I hope to meet you all someday, and, until then, be good people!

Interviews with *Halloween* Principles

The interviews in this section have been conducted by Scotty McCoy (author) and his guests, all of whom are associated with the *Halloween* (1978) franchise in some way, shape, or form. The interviews were personally conducted by Scotty and transcribed word for word. See the disclaimer on the next page for all details regarding the interviews.

Thank you to all the guests that have agreed to an interview with me. It is truly appreciated!

Entire cast and crew of *Halloween II* (1981). Photo by Kim Gottlieb-Walker

DISCLAIMER

ALL OF THE GUESTS THAT WERE INTERVIEWED FOR *SLASHER SCOTTY* (2016) AND/OR *THE ULTIMATE HALLOWEEN MOVIE EXPERIENCE, MICHAEL MYERS: THE MAN, THE MONSTER, THE MADNESS* (2022). HAVE CONSENTED AND ACKNOWLEDGED THAT THE INTERVIEW WAS RECORDED FOR PURPOSES TO BE USED BY SCOTTY IN ANY WAY HE SEES FIT AND CAN USE THEM FOR PUBLICATION IN BOOKS, PODCASTS, AND/OR ANY FORM OF MEDIA, EITHER ONLINE OR OFFLINE, AND THEY EXPECT NO COMPENSATION IN RETURN FOR THEIR INTERVIEWS BEING PUBLISHED OR MADE PUBLICLY AVAILABLE. SCOTTY WAS INFORMED BY ANY GUESTS THAT EXPECT COMPENSATION FOR PUBLISHED AND RELEASED INTERVIEWS, AND IN TURN, HAS EITHER A. DECLINED THE INTERVIEW OR B. HAS CONDUCTED THE INTERVIEW IN A WAY THEY AGREE TO FOR NO MONETARY VALUE. ANY GUEST WHO REQUESTED MONETARY VALUE HAS NOT HAD THEIR INTERVIEWS PUBLISHED IN *THE ULTIMATE HALLOWEEN MOVIE EXPERIENCE, MICHAEL MYERS: THE MAN, THE MONSTER, THE MADNESS* (2022). ALL GUESTS HAVE AGREED, EITHER IN WRITING OR ORALLY, THAT THE INTERVIEWS CAN BE USED IN A WAY THAT SCOTTY SEES FIT, AS LONG AS IT DOES NOT SLANDER THE GUEST IN ANY WAY, SHAPE, OR FORM.

THE ENTIRE TEXT OF THE INTERVIEWS HAS BEEN TRANSCRIBED FROM ITS ORIGINAL SOURCE AND HAS NOT BEEN ALTERED IN ANY WAY, SHAPE, OR FORM. NOTHING WAS REMOVED, ADDED, OR ENHANCED FROM THE INTERVIEWS. SCOTTY AND HIS TEAM, INCLUDING THE PUBLICATION AND LITERARY TEAM, ARE NOT

RESPONSIBLE FOR ANYTHING THAT WAS MENTIONED BY THE GUEST THAT MAY BE INACCURATE AS ALL CONTENT TRANSCRIBED WAS VERIFIED AND CONFIRMED TO HAVE BEEN SPOKEN BY THE GUEST THEMSELVES.

THE INTERVIEWS, AS WELL AS THE CONTENTS OF THIS ENTIRE BOOK, IS UNDER COPYRIGHT OF SCOTTY MCCOY AND HIS RESPECTIVE PUBLISHING AND LITERARY TEAM. ANY COPYING, RE-RELEASING, PUBLISHING, DISTRIBUTING, POSTING (EITHER IN BOOKS, ONLINE (SUCH AS WEBSITES, SOCIAL MEDIA, FORUMS, BLOGS, OR ANY OTHER ONLINE SOURCES), RECORDING, PLAGIARISING, OR CLAIMING OWNERSHIP OR CREDIT IN ANY WAY, SHAPE, OR FORM OF ANY OF THE INTERVIEWS ON THE FORTHCOMING PAGES, AS WELL AS ANY CONTENT OF THE PREVIOUS PAGES, IS STRICTLY PROHIBITED AND CAN AND WILL RESULT IN CRIMINAL AND/OR CIVIL PENALTIES TO THE FULLEST EXTENT OF THE LAW.

Sandy Johnson

"Judith Myers," Halloween (1978)

Scotty McCoy: Hello, Sandy. How are you doing?
Sandy Johnson: I am doing great! Thank you so much for inviting me to chat about *Halloween* (1978)!

Scotty McCoy: Not a problem at all. For those unfamiliar with your background, how did you get your start into acting?
Sandy Johnson: I got my start into acting as a student in school, middle school to be exact, and I was in drama, choreography, and dance, that sort of thing, and then I got into community theater, started taking acting classes when I still lived in the Hollywood area, and then when I was in *Playboy*, I started getting calls for other roles. So, I kind of came up through school.

Scotty McCoy: Awesome! We know you played Judith Myers in *Halloween* (1978). What was your audition like for that role, which later became an iconic part of the franchise?
Sandy Johnson: The audition was really interesting, as it wasn't in a studio or anything. It was in one of the houses that we were going to be filming *Halloween* (1978) in. There were several people at the table, and they were asking me questions and to read some lines. They also asked me to scream, which was interesting in a regular neighborhood (laughs). After I did all of that, they said "Thank you very much. We'll let you know once we come to a decision." Shortly after, maybe the next day or so, my agent called me and told me that I was cast as Judith Myers.

Scotty McCoy: That's amazing! But being known for Judith Myers, even though you're only on screen briefly, it's such an iconic role in today's history. How does it affect your personal life in today's world all these years after you did the film?

Sandy Johnson: If I am at a convention, then yes, they do. However, if I am walking down the street, not really, no. Which is good at times because I can still have a private life (laughs).

Scotty McCoy: What about back when the movie was released, were you ever bombarded by paparazzi or fans then?

Sandy Johnson: Honestly, no. Let me tell you why. It's because *Halloween* (1978) never started out that way. It was just one of those low budget independent horror films. It wasn't, at the time, the staple it is today. The lines to see it were just normal compared to the new ones that come out in today's era. There wasn't even a really big premiere or anything for it. I mean, we all went to go and see it together at the theater, but it wasn't a huge deal. It really took a long time for it to actually become this cult classic that had this huge fan base right away. It took time to develop and then it ultimately gained its fan base as time went on.

Scotty McCoy: We do know that Will Sandin played the role of Michael Myers as a child, but he wasn't in the scene where you died at his hands. Who was playing the role of the young Michael Myers in the POV scene where you get killed?

Sandy Johnson: The reason why Will didn't do the scene was because he was a young child and I was topless and it wasn't appropriate for a child to be seen doing murder, at least not back in 1977 or 1978 when we filmed the movie. And Debra Hill had little, tiny hands and she was a very hands-on person on set, and she was the one that you see grab the knife, pick up the mask, and stab me to death.

Scotty McCoy: Speaking of Debra Hill, what was it like working with her?

Sandy Johnson: She was very nice. Very friendly. She was also very business-like; she knew what she wanted and worked with us to get the scene to what she wanted. Both she and John Carpenter were very hands on and just knew what they wanted and how they wanted it.

Scotty McCoy: Was the knife that Debra used a real knife or a prop knife?

Sandy Johnson: I believe it was a real knife.

Scotty McCoy: Did she have the mask on when using the knife?

Sandy Johnson: Yes, right when she picked up the mask, she would put it on and she wore it for the rest of the scene. It just was able to set the mood for the scene and so she can get into character.

Scotty McCoy: Did she have a camera that was used behind the mask to mimic young Michael Myers POV through the mask's eyeholes?

Sandy Johnson: Actually, no. The eyehole POV shot was all done in post-production when the film was completed and taken to the editing room.

Scotty McCoy: Was the on-set atmosphere spooky at all? Like, did it feel all suspenseful when you were filming your scenes?

Sandy Johnson: I would say yes, primarily because, unlike on a real set, there weren't a lot of people in the room with me. It wasn't a big room, and it was dark. I couldn't really see those who were in the room, but I could hear them coming up the stairs, going down the stairs, coming from around the corner, and things like that. So, it did become sort of creepy as things would just creep up on you, especially when you are trying to get into the mental state of practicing your performance and trying to remember everything you were supposed to do and were told to do.

Scotty McCoy: What was John Carpenter like as a director?
Sandy Johnson: He explained his vision really well and how the mood of the scene should flow. He even imitated the direction he wanted me to face for the scene. And he was a nice guy.

Scotty McCoy: What was your most memorable moment of filming *Halloween* (1978)?
Sandy Johnson: The most memorable, hmm, I would have to say when I was upstairs, humming to myself, and brushing my hair, it was all nice and quiet, and then I had to turn around and a knife was coming at me. That whole scene was so suspenseful, so I enjoyed every aspect of it.

Scotty McCoy: What was the best part of filming *Halloween* (1978)? And what was the worst?
Sandy Johnson: The most fun part about filming *Halloween* (1978) was the downstairs scenes. It was fun and playful, plus my boyfriend was good looking (laughs). The worst part would have to be the blood pellets that I had to smash against my chest would stain my skin, so they had to be scrubbed off in between takes to keep with the continuity.

Scotty McCoy: Oof! So, you had to smash the blood pellets into yourself when performing your death scene?
Sandy Johnson: Yes. I had pellets on the inside of my hands so when I slapped my hands into my chest, they would break. If you go back and watch *Halloween* (1978), look closely and you'll be able to see I am slapping my chest.

Scotty McCoy: I am going to have to go back and watch that now (laughs). We know and already established that *Halloween* (1978) was such a low budget film. What was the environment like due to it being made on such a low budget? Was it stressful? Was it easy? Was it fast paced?

Sandy Johnson: It was very fast paced. It wasn't stressful, it was actually really fun. But it was very busy because they were still fixing up the house from the scenes that they already shot since those scenes the house was dilapidated. But for my scenes, the house had to look new and lived in. So, they were quite busy putting on the finishing touches to the house which made the environment pretty fast paced to be in.

Scotty McCoy: Have you seen all of the other *Halloween* (1987) films in the franchise? And, if so, which one did you like the most and which one did you like the least?

Sandy Johnson: I hadn't seen any of the other films until about six or seven months ago from the time we are conducting this interview. I realized that I should see them all as I'm a part of that franchise, but I still have yet to see *Halloween III: Season of the Witch* (1982) and Rob Zombie's *Halloween* (2007) and its sequel, *Halloween II* (2009). I do plan on seeing *Halloween III: Season of the Witch* (1982), but I am not into heavy gore, so I'll probably not see the Rob Zombie films. I really did like them all, but if I had to choose, I would say either *Halloween II* (1981) or *Halloween* (2018). I also enjoyed *Halloween H20: 20 Years Later* (1998).

Scotty McCoy: The last question I have for you is simple. Are there any social media accounts or Websites that fans can keep up to date on your career, keep in touch with you, or even buy some merchandise of yours?

Sandy Johnson: I am on Facebook at The Real Sandy Johnson. Instagram, I am on there as unicornsandyj. I got that name from my agent who was looking for me for years and years and then he randomly came across me and said I was like his unicorn, a mythical, magical creature (laughs). So, he always calls me his unicorn. I also do have a website where fans can buy autographed photographs, send me things that can be signed, they can watch my videos and podcast interviews, etc. The website's link is unicornsandyj.com. And I don't have a Twitter or a Snapchat or any of those other sites.

Scotty McCoy: Awesome. I thank you so much, Sandy, for taking the time out of your schedule to join me for this interview.
Sandy Johnson: Thank you for having me. I thoroughly enjoyed doing the interview and hope to meet you at a convention one day.

Ana Alicia

"Nurse Janet," *Halloween II* (1981)

Scotty McCoy: Hi Ana, how are you doing today?
Ana Alicia: I am doing wonderful Scotty! Thank you for having me!

Scotty McCoy: Not a problem at all. Going all the way back, how did you get your start into acting?
Ana Alicia: (Laughs) Okay! We're going there (laughs)! Where do you want me to start? Age 3, 11, 13, 18, 21, or 28? These are the key periods of my acting life.

Scotty McCoy: Start right from the beginning (laughs)!
Ana Alicia: Alright! At age 3, I began dancing for my dad. He made me feel like I was the world. I would dance for all of his friends, which I would say was my first venture into the entertainment world. Then, at age 9, I would dance for all my mother's friends to the song from the film *Goldfinger* (1964). At age 11, someone came into my English class, and they asked if anyone would like to fill in for a competition play, as the girl had dropped out and that you need to learn the lines in one night as the play starts tomorrow. I don't know why I even raised my hand, but I did, and the play was called *Marriage-Go-Round* (1958), and then the next day I was in front of hundreds of students and judges at this school competition show.

    The role was that of a Swedish girl, and I had to do a Swedish accent and all for this part. I did well and this shy girl that was always behind books got thrown into the acting department. From that point on, I have done things like *Our Town* (1938) and the teacher, Mrs. Card, took interest in me. That was the beginning of all of it.

Then, by the time I graduated high school, I had done all the musicals where I'd always play the vixens by the age of 17. After high school, it was a done deal that I'd go to Wellesley College for school to become a lawyer, which I did, and the first three months of being at Wellesley, there was a play titled *Miss Sympathy* (1970), and I auditioned and got the lead. I came home during summer break and there's this new dinner theater opening up in El Paso. They heard of me and called me. They asked me if I would want to get paid $500 a week to do all the plays at night and it was only from 7:00 to 10:00 at night. I ended up leaving Wellesley and gone on to work at this dinner theater to get my Equity Card and also got to work with people, such as Dana Andrews, and all the stars would come into this dinner theater from TV shows, like *Gilligan's Island* (1964) and *The Beverly Hillbillies* (1962), and even Gavin MacLeod came in. I was supposed to go to Law School, but before I did that, I decided to check out Los Angeles at 20 years old. I would take my LSAT while I am here. While doing that, I am going into different agent's offices saying, "I got no pictures and I am nobody, but could you represent me!" All the agents would slam their door in my face. I eventually got signed by a guy named Carlo Salvorado and he got me my first job as a lead on a soap opera. And that's how it all started!

Scotty McCoy: What was your audition like for *Halloween II* (1981)?
Ana Alicia: Well, Rick Rosenthal, who was in my acting class, and his wife, Nancy Stephens, who he was just dating at the time, also was in our acting class. He directed the film. And he asked me to come out to read for the part and I did. He already knew he wanted me. It was just a formality for those producers that didn't know me. Funny thing is that most of the people in the film were in the acting class,

me, Nancy Stephens, Leo Rossi, Gloria Gifford, and Lance Guest. I got the role, of course, and I thought after I accepted, "Oh my God! I am going to be in a horror film! What are my children going to think one day when they see me in a horror film?" Then, once sanity reached my head, I thought that I'm going to do my first little movie with my good friend, Rick, and then I signed on to do it.

Scotty McCoy: What did you think when you saw it for the first time?
Ana Alicia: When I first saw it in theaters, I was traumatized and thought to myself, "My children, one day, what are they going to say seeing me in this!" I thought about the blood, and there was barely any blood to begin with compared with today's tropes in horror films and being involved in this slasher film.

Scotty McCoy: Have your children seen the film?
Ana Alicia: My daughter was 13 and my son was 11, a proper age to show your children horror films, and I showed them it. I never even told them I was an actress. So, I sat them down to watch this. What I thought at the time was this horrible, horrible horror film titled *Halloween II* (1981), and after it was over, they were like "That's it? That's what you were carrying on about? That was all the horror you were going on about?" (Laughs) It was like by the time they grew up, things were more horrific to watch and much bloodier and gorier.

Scotty McCoy: What was your death scene like?
Ana Alicia: When shooting my death scene, when Dick Warlock, who played Michael Myers, put the retractable syringe in my head, and I was supposed to fall down, I hit my head off the corner of some object, possibly a desk. It was more like my eye. And the rest of the shoot, I had this big bump on my eye. I was bloody, bleeding everywhere. Rick called for a cut and asked if I was okay, and I went

to the hospital and got some stitches. When I was lying on the floor, I told Rick to hurry and get a shot of the blood by my eye to use as it was real blood and could've been good footage, but he never used it. So, if you notice in a lot of scenes that I am in, particularly when we are in the break room and Leo Rossi's character keeps cursing; they are shooting it from the side where my eye isn't bruised because of continuity purposes (laughs).

Scotty McCoy: What was the best part about filming *Halloween II* (1981)? And what was the worst?
Ana Alicia: It was pretty cool getting to watch Jamie work. She is a top-notch actress, so seeing her work was brilliant. The worst would have to be nearly dying when acting in my death scene (laughs), although it does make for a good story over 30 years later.

Scotty McCoy: Are there any crazy stories from filming *Halloween II* (1981)?
Ana Alicia: I met someone, can't say who, but I met someone, and we went onto his plane, and we did upside down loops in the sky. It was fun, really fun, but dangerous too (laughs).

Scotty McCoy: What was it like working with Dick Warlock?
Ana Alicia: He's super sweet. Super nice guy. It's funny because he carries his mask everywhere (laughs).

Scotty McCoy: How was Rick Rosenthal as a director?
Ana Alicia: He was great. He's a genius director, great producer, and wonderful human being.

Scotty McCoy: So, what was it like being the cause for Mr. Garrett's death scene?
Ana Alicia: Don't you put that death on me (laughs). I didn't know how to work that damn walkie talkie, plus I had to get back to work (laughs).

Scotty McCoy: Because of the new timeline in *Halloween* (2018), if asked to reprise the role of Nurse Janet, would you?

Ana Alicia: At this point in my life, I would do almost, and yes that's almost, anything. Not anything, but almost anything. Because it is one of those things that it's either now or never. Life is too short to not do things that can make you happy. So, yes, I absolutely would!

Scotty McCoy: Well, there you have it. We would have you back in *Halloween* (1978) if asked. Listen to her Jason Blum (laughs). Thank you, Ana, for joining me for this interview.

Ana Alicia: (Laughs) Absolutely. The pleasure was all mine!

Alan Howarth

Musical Composer/Sound Designer, Halloween II (1981) through 6 (1995)

Scotty McCoy: Good afternoon, Alan. How are you doing this fine afternoon?
Alan Howarth: I'm doing wonderful, Scotty. Thank you for having me here to do this amazing interview with you for your book and podcast!

Scotty McCoy: Not a problem at all. The honor is truly mine.
Alan Howarth: Well, thank you!

Scotty McCoy: It's the truth. You were the musical composer and sound designer for *Halloween II* (1981) through *Halloween 6: The Curse of Michael Myers* (1995). But before you got those gigs, you had to get involved with becoming a musical composer and sound designer. How did that all get started and come about?
Alan Howarth: It honestly wasn't planned at all. It was one of those "you know somebody that knows somebody that knows somebody" situations. At first, I was in Cleveland, and I was a rock and roll guy. I played in some of the most popular bands at the time. We were produced by a guy named Bill Simsdick, who later went on to produce bands like The Eagles. At that time, I was always drawn to synthesizers and equipment, that kind of stuff, and I then started a little synthesizer shop in Cleveland. Through that I met a Jazz band called Weather Report where I became their keyboard synthesizer

guy. That ended up getting me to Los Angeles and another Ohio buddy of mine, who also moved out to Los Angeles, was working for Paramount Pictures and he would make copies of tapes and stuff like that for them. Two guys named Steve Flick and Richard Anderson needed someone who knew about synthesizers and my buddy, Pat, overheard them and mentioned to look into his buddy Alan who works for Weather Report. They looked at him and asked if it was the one at 7:00 or 11:00, as they're thinking about meteorology. They took my number, and I went down to meet up with them, and they said that they are working on *Star Trek: The Motion Picture* (1979).

That was the time that *Star Trek* (1966) was no longer going to be on TV but turned into movies. They were looking for sound designers, which, at the time, was just someone that made special sound effects without any fancy title. I auditioned and they asked me to make a sound of the Starship Enterprise going from Warp 1 to Warp 7. I made them the sound effect, which ended up being the sound of the Enterprise. I would later be doing *Star Trek 1* (1979) through 6 (1991), as I was the Enterprise guy so if they needed anything to do with hardware then I was brought back in for that.

Scotty McCoy: How did you happen to meet John Carpenter?
Alan Howarth: The picture editor from *Star Trek: The Motion Picture* (1979) was a guy by the name of Todd Ramsey, and his next movie was *Escape from New York* (1981). I'd been giving him my tapes to promote myself, and he worked with John Carpenter and said that he thinks John and I would get along great. So, he arranged John and me to meet up at my little *Star Trek* (1966) dining room studio in Glendale and we just sat around, played sounds, and we talked. He then said "Yeah, let's do it." Now I am a composer! So, I owe a lot of gratitude to John Carpenter.

Scotty McCoy: How did you get involved with *Halloween II* (1981) then?

Alan Howarth: You know, Scotty, this is very interesting. After *Escape from New York* (1981) wrapped up, John was busy doing *The Thing* (1982) and he messaged me and told me that the studio called and want to do a sequel on *Halloween* (1978) titled aptly, *Halloween II* (1981), and he put me in charge of the score and music and sound for that film, while he worked on *The Thing* (1982) and wrote some of *Halloween II* (1981). I ended up starting with *Halloween II* (1981) and ended up doing *Halloween III: Season of the Witch* (1982), *Halloween 4: The Return of Michael Myers* (1988), *Halloween 5: The Revenge of Michael Myers* (1989), and *Halloween 6: The Curse of Michael Myers* (1995) as the other guy so to speak. I used John's score as the model and just made it more gothic; changed the texture up a bit.

Scotty McCoy: *Halloween III: Season of the Witch* (1982) is an entirely different film that the rest of the franchise, especially the two that came before it. How did that come about and how did the score get affected?

Alan Howarth: Well, John came back to the studio because he wanted to play. The score itself holds up rather well. We all know that the film, however, gets bashed because there is no Michael Myers in it. Carpenter's idea was to break away from Michael Myers and just do these typical Halloween-themed movies with an anthology-like setting that each film will have a different Halloween-related theme. John, after *Halloween III: Season of the Witch* (1982) tanked due to the absence of Michael Myers, had enough of it, and he handed over all of the rights to Mustapha Akkad.

Scotty McCoy: What was it like collaborating with John Carpenter on *Halloween III: Season of the Witch* (1982)?

Alan Howarth: He brought in the latest records, LPs as they were called, and played the "Tangerine Dream" music, and he was very pleased with the music we had done for *Escape from New York* (1981), and he said to me "Alan, this is going to be really easy. All we have to do is rip ourselves off!" The first queue we dialed up was what we called "Chariots of Pumpkins," which was used in the chase scene in the beginning of the movie. That was the first queue, and then we just used that to keep sequencing the movie's score and John would keep nodding and saying "Yeah, that's cool, that's cool!"

Scotty McCoy: At the time of *Halloween III: Season of the Witch* (1982), not having Michael Myers, did you think that fans would react negatively to it?

Alan Howarth: As far as Carpenter was concerned, Michael Myers was killed, officially dead, at the end of *Halloween II* (1981). He then wanted to do this anthology-related theme of Halloween events. It was first *Halloween III: Season of the Witch* (1982), and then there were talks of it being *Halloween 4: Samhain* (1983), and so on and so forth. By the end of it all, the producers saw everyone wanting Michael Myers back and not having this idea, John was like, "good luck," and he moved onto other stuff. The franchise grew with Michael Myers at the helm of it as the killer he's known as today. John does admit now, though, that he was wrong and there was still more life in Michael Myers (laughs).

Scotty McCoy: Why didn't you come back to do *Halloween H20: 20 Years Later* (1998) and *Halloween: Resurrection* (2002)?

Alan Howarth: At this point, it was mostly brought down to being a regime change. New director, the film editor wanted to score it, and he did score it orchestrally, and it got tossed out and went back to the *Scream* guy and there was a creative moment there, and I'm kind of glad I missed it as I would've just done what I always have done and used the original score as a backbone and build upon it.

Scotty McCoy: What was the most difficult when making any of the sound bits or music for the *Halloween* (1978) films?
Alan Howarth: The one that was the most challenging was *Halloween 6: The Curse of Michael Myers* (1995). The reasoning is because the director made his own version of *Halloween* (1978), but the Weinsteins were involved, and once we finally finished the first version, which later got released as the *Producer's Cut* (1995), I'd finished scoring the entire movie once and the Weinsteins wanted the music amped up, more exciting, scarier, more everything. So, I had to go back and add a lot of rock and roll to the score and in the end, I scored that one movie twice. So, it was a challenge as I had to outdo myself one more time. It came out good, but it was a challenge. It's hard to score a film once, but to do it twice and update the score you just did to be as they said "better." It can become quite a challenge and frustrating.

Scotty McCoy: Which *Halloween* (1978) film that you worked on was your favorite?
Alan Howarth: *Halloween III: Season of the Witch* (1982) was the most fun, in its own way. Out of the Michael Myers *Halloween* (1978) films, I'd have to say for me the big experience was *Halloween 4: The Return of Michael Myers* (1988) because that was the first time I was cut loose. The only time I was actually given direction was when Mustapha Akkad called me up and said that he needs to hear the *Halloween* (1978) theme song every time he sees Michael Myers on the screen. He then said, "Other than that, go for it!"

Scotty McCoy: To kind of piggyback on your favorite, which one of the *Halloween* (1978) films was the least favorite to work on?
Alan Howarth: I always had fun (laughs). But seriously, to answer the question, I'd have to say *Halloween 5: The Revenge of Michael Myers* (1989), as the director wanted to go back to the roots of *Halloween* with the piano, so he basically tied me down instead of cutting me loose like I was with *Halloween 4: The Return of Michael Myers* (1989). That's an unfun part about being a composer. You want to be told "You are great, go for it!" Not, "Do this, that, and the other, this way, that way, and the other way!" He was the "Yes, No" guy. The director. The man who had the final say. I had to do what he wanted to get the film done the way he envisioned it. So, I did what I was told, but it isn't as fun when you are a composer and told to do it "This way" instead of "Have fun and do it the way you see it working best because you are the composer, and you are really talented at what you do and great at making musical art."

Scotty McCoy: Did you see the *Halloween* (2018) film?
Alan Howarth: I have not seen it. I would like to, and I heard it's good. And the next one, *Halloween Kills* (2021). And then another after that. So, the franchise is moving along rather well and swimmingly.

Scotty McCoy: Alan, those are some great stories and answers to the questions about your time working with the *Halloween* (1978) franchise.
Alan Howarth: Thank you, Scotty. I had fun and had a blast to discuss *Halloween* (1978). It truly is an iconic gem that, at the time, was never even thought of becoming a holiday cult classic with such an amazing fan base and following.

Stacey Nelkin

"Ellie Grimbridge," *Halloween III: Season of the Witch (1982)*

Scotty McCoy: Good afternoon, Stacey. Thank you for joining me for this interview! I am so glad we can make this happen.

Stacey Nelkin: Me too. I am more than happy to do this interview, Scotty. So, thank you for having me!

Scotty McCoy: Tell us what's the story on your start? How did you get your start into acting?

Stacey Nelkin: Oh, my goodness! Great question (laughs). Going all the way back there (laughs). My initial impetus to become an actress was to look for love from, you know, male role models and figures because I grew up in a very dysfunctional family. My parents were divorced, and my dad was a drug addict. I used to watch TV and I would pretend that, you know, if it was Dr. Joe Gannon from the medical center or one of those people were rescuing me and I'd put myself in those kinds of situations. I'd act them out and do all that stuff. When I was 9, I was starting to get lead roles in all the school plays and that continued when I grew up in New York City. So, when I was 14, it was easy to get a manager and I got a manager, went on auditions practically every single day, and then didn't get a job for two years. Finally, on my 16th birthday, I literally landed two national commercials and got into the Screen Actors Guild and didn't stop working for many, many years. O, that's how it all started.

Like a lot of actors and actresses, you know a deficit coming from a void. Anybody who goes into that business has to have some kind of issue because it's a very crazy, crazy business. So, it kind of replicates the family that I grew up in. I think for a lot of my peers and colleagues, it was a similar situation, as well.

Scotty McCoy: That's very interesting, yet also very sad to know that kind of stuff happens.
Stacey Nelkin: Yeah, it really is. But it unfortunately happens to a lot of those in Hollywood.

Scotty McCoy: I know it's been quite a long time (laughs), but what was your audition like for *Halloween III: Season of the Witch* (1982)?
Stacey Nelkin: You probably heard this before because you are the expert on the *Halloween* (1978) films, but my boyfriend at the time, who later became my fiancé, but we broke up, Perry King, was living with Ron Walters, who was a makeup artist that we both knew from *The Last Convertible* (1979), which was a miniseries that we both did, and we met for the first time there and then fell in love. Perry wound up leaving his wife and moved in with Ron temporarily. Ron had already been hired to do the makeup on *Halloween III: Season of the Witch* (1982), and he was telling us all about the project. They needed a female lead and couldn't find anyone, and he kept saying, "Stacey, why don't you do it?" It didn't really interest me at the time, and then I finally got a copy of the script, and I loved the character, and by this point, they were really desperate. They were like a week away from shooting and they still hadn't cast Ellie Grimbridge. I went in, read the lines with Tom Atkins, and I had so much fun. Literally, as I was walking in the door from the audition, the phone was already ringing, and it was my agent that said I got the job. I was like "Awesome!" I mean, those things never happened, right? If I had not heard from Ron, I'd have never had the opportunity to do the film.

Scotty McCoy: That's so awesome! So, we all know Ellie Grimbridge is turned into an android by the end of the film and eventually killed off by Dr. Dan Challis. How was your death scene filmed and prepped?

Stacey Nelkin: I went to the studio where they did a casting of my head, which I like to call the "Death Mask" because it is kind of a harrowing experience since you can only breathe through a straw that is placed up your nostrils. Your eyes are covered, your mouth is covered, and everything is closed in your nose, except for the nostrils, of course. If you are the tiniest bit claustrophobic, which I think we all are to a certain extent, it can be quite a horrific ordeal. They then made a cast of my head, and then made a plaster replica of my arm, because both my head and arm come off at the end of the movie. The way they actually shot the scene was amazingly brilliant because it was good old-fashioned filmmaking, you know, without the use of CGI or green screen effects, which most films use one or both of those options nowadays. Back when we were filming *Halloween III: Season of the Witch* (1982), they had a body double for me, who was exactly my size and wearing the same outfit I had been wearing for probably a month at that time as it was the same outfit that I wore throughout the whole end of the movie.

They had built on the soundstage a platform that was covered with grass, and it had a hole and a knit on the top that was big enough for somebody to slip underneath, about two feet between the top and the bottom of it. I slipped underneath and stuck my head up through this little hole, so my body double was lying two feet, three feet, whatever it was away from me with grass covering where there was another hole where her head went down so she could breathe, and it was like a little whack-a-mole (laughs). My head was sticking up and I am looking over across the grass and there is my body, and it was a very, very trippy experience. It was so cleverly done!

Scotty McCoy: That's so wild! Your co-star was Tom Atkins. What was it like working with him?

Stacey Nelkin: Oh, Tom. I love Tom. He was great and he was so professional, funny, outspoken, and gracious. A total gentleman.

Scotty McCoy: You obviously have a sex scene with Tom in the film, what was that like?

Stacey Nelkin: One of our first scenes we filmed was the love scene and he just put me so at ease. He was just a classy, easy going guy. And a very generous actor. I loved working with him because most actors can be, you know, a little eager, maniacal, and all of that, but he was just so earthy and made me feel so comfortable during the scenes that most people would feel uncomfortable doing.

Scotty McCoy: That's awesome he was so easy going, classy, and just an all-around great guy! It sure makes filming much easier.

Stacey Nelkin: Absolutely!

Scotty McCoy: *Halloween III: Season of the Witch* (1982) was directed by Tommy Lee Wallace. How was he as a director for this film?

Stacey Nelkin: Oh my God, he was great. Very easy to work with. He had a vision in mind but was extremely open to everybody else's thought process on the film. It was his first film that he directed, and he was just terrific at it!

Scotty McCoy: That's great to hear! Part of being involved with the horror industry and in mainstream horror films, such as *Halloween* (1978), is circulating the convention scene and meeting the fans. Do you participate and make appearances at conventions?

Stacey Nelkin: Do I do conventions? You bet I do! I've been doing them for the last ten years or so, at least. I am just blown away by the response over the years that *Halloween III: Season of the Witch* (1982) has gotten from the fans. It is incredible and they all know the movie backwards and forwards, sideways, and better than any of the cast and crew does.

Scotty McCoy: The fans really are the best. Without them, there would be no convention appearances from the stars of these films that we all love.
Stacey Nelkin: Absolutely right! The fans are so appreciative, and you know a lot of them have the same questions, such as "Do you think Ellie was a robot the whole time?" You know, those kinds of things. We get to have discussions and it's just fantastic to see what a cult classic this film has become over the years.

Scotty McCoy: That's amazing to hear. This film gets a lot of bad negativity with the exclusion of Michael Myers, so the fact that it is getting its much overdue appreciation is phenomenal to hear!
Stacey Nelkin: I completely agree. I think if they didn't keep it under the *Halloween* title, the film would've still had a complete and utter appreciation from the start. With it being titled *Halloween III* (1982) and not just titled *Season of the Witch* (1982), it was immediately associated with Michael Myers being in it, and that wasn't the case. But it is subtitled as *Season of the Witch* (1982) and there are no witches in the film, unless you count the mask, so there's that, as well.

Scotty McCoy: That's a really good point. To those people that say *Halloween III: Season of the Witch* (1982) shouldn't be included in the *Halloween* (1978) franchise, do you have any lasting words to them on why they may be misinformed?
Stacey Nelkin: Everyone is obviously entitled to their opinions, and I'd never want to change someone's opinion to why they feel the way they do. That said, you have your die-hard *Halloween* (1978) fans

where they want Michael Myers and if there is no Michael Myers, then they won't even give the film a fighting chance. This film, on its own, is more science fiction than horror. It's more along the lines of *Invasion of the Body Snatchers* (1956) and that's why it's found its following because there are a lot of people who like movies that are not just gratuitous thrillers and full of nudity and scare the crap out of you. These kinds of films actually make you think a little bit and people come away very pleased nowadays, especially when they go into the film now knowing there is no Michael Myers, so it isn't like a shock factor of "Wait! Where was Michael at?" At conventions, many, many people come up to us and say this is their favorite *Halloween* (1978) film out of the entire franchise. Others, not so much enjoy the film but thank us for being part of the family anyways. Even the jingle of the song was fun (laughs)!

Scotty McCoy: Speaking of the song, how iconic is that song in this film?
Stacey Nelkin: When you hear about the movie *Halloween* (1978), any of the films, you think of the iconic musical soundtrack by John Carpenter. I think the jingle to "London Bridge is Falling Down" on the commercial is our own special and iconic soundtrack and it made the film special!

Scotty McCoy: I love the song. I hear it, it is in my head for days (laughs). On another note, for those fans that say Michael Myers isn't in the film, he actually is. Do you know where he is in the film, Stacey?
Stacey Nelkin: When Tom's character is in the bar?

Scotty McCoy: Absolutely! When fans say to me that Michael Myers isn't in the film, he may not be the main antagonist, but he is technically in the film. He's on the television screen in a commercial of the original *Halloween* (1978) film when Dr. Dan Challis, played by Tom Atkins, is in the bar, and then the *Halloween* (1978) jingle comes on right after when the bartender changes the channel.

Stacey Nelkin: That's a very interesting take on it. I'll have to use that one when I have fans mention it to me at conventions (laughs).

Scotty McCoy: Good stuff (laughs). What was the best part about filming *Halloween III: Season of the Witch* (1982)? And what was the worst?

Stacey Nelkin: I'll start with the worst. It was the morning of the love scene, and it was very cold. In those days, they didn't have spray body makeup, you know, those machines that they do like spray tanning. It was a cold sponge and I had to get sponged all over my body for the makeup for the camera and it was just so cold. I couldn't get warm, I think I was also anxious about having to be semi-nude on screen with the whole world watching when the film releases, but that would have to be the worst.

The best would have to be the friendships I have made. I loved Debra Hill, and Tommy Lee Wallace and I were close. I became dear friends with Tom Atkins. The rest of the cast, the crew of the film, everyone, and it was a lovely experience that I made lifelong friends. Dan O'Herlihy was so extremely talented, but there was no attitude on the set. It was just kind of one of those rare experiences where people are actually decent human beings and not having these large egos and being total divas. That's always a treat when you get to work on a show or film with that kind of environment. There were a few sour grapes I have worked on in future and past films, but this one, everyone was just simply amazing, and it made the job that much more enjoyable and memorable.

Scotty McCoy: Speaking of memorable moments, were there any from your time filming *Halloween III: Season of the Witch* (1982)?

Stacey Nelkin: There were a couple, but the primary one that comes to mind is the way they did the practical effects. The special effects being done practically and not by any artificial means, for lack of a better word, was amazing and just seeing old-fashioned filmmaking being done right before your eyes, from casting my head, plastering my arm, creating the set for the scenes that need to be filmed so they can implement the special effects, and then making the magic happen when filming the scenes. It was really what they call "movie magic!"

Scotty McCoy: I think that'll do it, Stacey. I truly appreciate it that you took the time out of your schedule to come on and discuss some *Halloween III: Season of the Witch* (1982)!
Stacey Nelkin: I am more than happy to discuss it with you. Thank you very much for having me!

Sasha Jenson

"Brady," Halloween 4: The Return of Michael Myers (1988)

Scotty McCoy: Sasha, the man of the hour, thank you for joining me!
Sasha Jenson: Absolutely, thank you for having me. I know it is late on the East Coast, so I am glad you were able to stay up and accommodate my rapid and busy schedule.

Scotty McCoy: Of course! I am honored to have you here with me and talk about Michael Myers and your experiences filming *Halloween 4: The Return of Michael Myers* (1988).
Sasha Jenson: What better way to do an interview on *Halloween* (1978) than doing it literally five days before the Halloween season.

Scotty McCoy: That's what makes it super exciting. Let's start off with a more basic and generic question and tell us about how you get your start into acting.
Sasha Jenson: I am a Los Angeles kid. My dad was a character actor and so I kind of grew up not knowing any better. My dad played the heavy forever. He started in *Chinatown* (1974) with Jack Nicholson, and my dad was "the heavy" and he ended up playing that guy forever in every Clint Eastwood movie and a bunch of Clint's movies, he was great at playing the bad guy. He loved getting shot, getting killed, and fighting everyone.

Scotty McCoy: That sounds awesome! Regarding *Halloween 4: The Return of Michael Myers* (1988), what was your audition like?

Sasha Jenson: I honestly don't remember the audition at all. I do remember saying to myself that when you're auditioning for a movie with a "4" next to it, it's like you're shopping at the 99 cents store looking for items to be on sale (laughs).

Scotty McCoy: So, were expectations low on the film doing well?

Sasha Jenson: Well, kind of, yes. We expected this to end up going straight to video, not even being in the theaters. Especially with how poorly *Halloween III: Season of the Witch* (1982) did, we didn't expect this film to do good, no matter how much they promoted and hyped up Michael Myers' return. The audience in the last film felt gypped and they had to garner back the audiences' trust.

Scotty McCoy: That makes total sense, though. And we know you got to work with Kathleen Kinmont, as well. I had interviewed her, and she wanted me to tell you that she says hi.

Sasha Jenson: (sighs) Oh Kathleen. Such a wonderful woman.

Scotty McCoy: What was it like working with her?

Sasha Jenson: It was great. We attended high school together and I believe I first saw her at the airport heading to Utah, which is how we found out we were doing this film together. And she's gorgeous, very stunning. I had to do a make out scene with her, which was so unnatural because we have like fifty people in the room watching us, a director telling us what to do, and a camera right in our faces. On top of the fact that she's beautiful, it made for a very intimidating scene.

Scotty McCoy: That's understandable, but she's not your only co-stars you interacted with on camera. You also had big scenes with Ellie Cornell, as well as worked with Danielle Harris. How was it working with them?

Sasha Jenson: Danielle was a child, she was literally petrified on set because it was this scary man in a costume, but she did great and her real fear, which wasn't acting, came off great for the scenes she's in. She literally put the next film on her back and was the star of it. Ellie was amazing. We became friends and still are friends to this day. She and I had instant chemistry and I believe it paid off on screen. I even saved her and Danielle from Michael, dying in the process (laughs).

Scotty McCoy: Speaking of that, how was your death scene filmed and prepped?

Sasha Jenson: That's a funny story, Scotty. We were on set for that scene, and George P. Wilbur, who played Michael, knew my dad and was like "Oh that's Jenson's kid," when he first saw me on set. Anyways, Dwight Little, the director, said we need to kill this kid. It wasn't in the script. It just said, "Brady dies," but no indication on how. So, George and I choreographed a fight scene since my dad did a lot of those scenes. He then lifted me up, while I was on this tall teeter totter, and he crushed my neck. The blood capsule in my mouth was supposed to ooze out of my mouth, but I was choking on the blood in the capsule and decided to just spit it out and I figured they were going to make me redo the scene or they were going to cut that out of the film, but in the end, they kept it and it made sense of the scene itself. The funny thing is that I am the only one to realize what happened with the capsule and how it was choking me during the scene.

Scotty McCoy: That's funny (laughs). So, which part of filming *Halloween 4: The Return of Michael Myers* (1988) was the best? I'd have to think being on set of this film would be awesome.

Sasha Jenson: I'd have to say the authenticity of the film. They turned this little town in Utah into a total spooky season. With the decorations of the houses to the fall leaves and the foliage around the town and everything in between, they really made this film have the atmosphere it needed to be an authentic *Halloween* (1978) film. And the house that we were in had such a spooky vibe to it. The aura of the house just made filming the scenes with Michael Myers that much more intriguing and fun.

Scotty McCoy: I love when it feels like the film's season on set. It comes off great on screen for the viewing audience, but it also comes off as authentic for the actors involved which gets them more in the spirit of the film they are shooting.
Sasha Jenson: You are right. It made it more scary, more frightening, more suspenseful, and had a thrill to it that you must be there to even begin to describe.

Scotty McCoy: That's amazing! What did you first think of the script when you read it?
Sasha Jenson: That it was simply going to be a scary movie. I knew it was frightening from the script, but I also knew that it was the fourth film, and it was coming off the train wreck of the previous film, so I personally thought that it was going to be a straight-to-video type of release, but I will admit when I am wrong, and boy, am I glad to have been wrong about the success of the film.

Scotty McCoy: I'm glad it was a success too, as it is one of my favorites in the franchise. Well, let's end this interview on a somber note. You didn't have many scenes with Donald Pleasence, who played the iconic and legendary, Dr. Sam Loomis. Did you interact with him at all behind-the-scenes and hear any stories of his?
Sasha Jenson: We did talk a little bit, but it was more of a "he showed up on set, did his business and performed his scenes, and then was

gone" type of situation. It's his third *Halloween* film he did, and from what I heard, he was telling stories more on the next film's set than he did ours, but he was more of a professional than he was a socialist. He showed up and just did what he had to do and left. He didn't really want to socialize or joke around, but he was probably one of the most professional, yet kindest gentlemen I have ever met too.

Scotty McCoy: That's awesome to hear. Rest in peace Donald Pleasence. I thank you Sasha so much for taking out the time of your very busy schedule to discuss some *Halloween* (1978) with me, especially a few days before the actual holiday.
Sasha Jenson: I thank you for reaching out and having me talk to you about such a prolific franchise.

Kathleen Kinmont

"Kelly Meeker," Halloween 4: The Return of Michael Myers (1988)

Scotty McCoy: Good afternoon, Kathleen. Thank you for taking the time out of your busy schedule to join me for an interview.
Kathleen Kinmont: You are so very welcome, Scotty. Thank you for reaching out with me to chat about *Halloween 4: The Return of Michael Myers* (1988).

Scotty McCoy: Don't mention it. I am totally fangirling right now (laughs).
Kathleen Kinmont: (Laughs) Now you have me blushing!

Scotty McCoy: (Laughs) For the first question, let everyone know how you get your start in the acting industry?
Kathleen Kinmont: Well, my mother is an actress, or was an actress I should say, as she passed away last November. But she was an actress for many, many years before I came along, and I was actually born on a television show when she was doing *The Joey Bishop Show* (1961). So, it was always around me. I think it was like a family business and she showed me what it looked like and how she responded to the calls. Her career was just an overall influence on me and that had a lot to do with me wanting to break into the business. Besides, I really like performing and being on stage where people watch you perform. That's how you really know you have it in you. A lot of actors are shy people and there's a part of me that

is very private, so I feel like it is the perfect opportunity to explore the human condition on a deeper level and psychologically, it's been such an incredible journey to be an actor. I get to play so many different parts and I delve into so many different character minds that I just have been truly grateful for all the different avenues that this industry has brought me.

Scotty McCoy: Interesting. Your mom would be so proud of how you continue to shine in the industry too.
Kathleen Kinmont: Thank you for saying that!

Scotty McCoy: Not a problem. We know *Halloween* (1978) is such an iconic franchise, and with Michael Myers being brought back into the folder after *Halloween III: Season of the Witch* (1982) was met with negativity, it really entered a new format story wise. Your character was such a villainess with being with Brady when he was with Rachel, and I absolutely did love the "Cops do it by the book" nightgown?
Kathleen Kinmont: (Laughs) That's funny, I sell those makeshift nightgowns at conventions, and they sell like hotcakes. Regarding Kelly, it was fun playing her. I gave her a little bit of an irony and sense of humor because that character is mean from the get-go. Her opening line was just such a shutdown to Wade, telling him to "fuck off" when he was trying to score. This kid didn't even have any game, he was just like "I want to get in the water" and I hit him with such a massive smack down and was like a shark.

Scotty McCoy: Exactly. About your audition for *Halloween 4: The Return of Michael Myers* (1988), what was that like?
Kathleen Kinmont: It was straightforward. I believe the director, Dwight H. Little, was in the room and some of the producers. I remember going back more than once, maybe twice, and I got the call quickly. It was neat finding out that Sasha Jenson was cast as

Brady because he and I already knew each other from school, which was great because when we got to Utah, it was like "Oh my God." He took my best friend to the prom, and we were just pals. It was funny because I said to him when I first saw him in Utah, "So, cool. I got to make out with you. Let's start practicing." (Laughs)

Scotty McCoy: (Laughs) That's funny that you must practice making out. But to make sure the chemistry is right, and that the scene goes as planned, it must be done.
Kathleen Kinmont: Exactly, right. It is a totally unnatural experience, and it can also be very hard on relationships. You need to have a superhuman or meta-human amount of trust in your partner, and I did have a boyfriend at the time, who was completely trusting and understanding of the situation at the time, which was a sigh of relief and something I didn't have to worry about with added stress.

Scotty McCoy: Well, that's good at least. Your death scene, although bloodless, is one of my favorite deaths in the *Halloween* (1978) franchise. How was it filmed and prepped?
Kathleen Kinmont: It was a brilliant piece of engineering. I have an intense amount of respect for stunt people, stunt coordinators, and all the technical things that they do to make these scenes look realistic, but also keep the actors safe. For this scene, I did the entire stunt myself. They put me in a harness, and they had a wire that went out of the back of the flannel shirt that I was wearing, so they had a hole in the back of the flannel shirt and a zip wire attached. They also had a hole drilled into the doorway for the door that I was swinging on and they placed a 10-speed bike seat drilled into that door. They took full measurements of my body before all this, such as my leg height, so they know where it would be comfortable enough for me to get up on it as they wanted my legs and feet dangling as I have been lifted off the ground and impaled to the door. The bike seat was very uncomfortable and then during the stunt scene, I was

pulled from the zip wire onto the door, with a padding used so I wouldn't smash my head.

Scotty McCoy: Wow, that's crazy yet amazing. Were you nervous at all when performing this?
Kathleen Kinmont: I wasn't nervous, no. But I was uncomfortable, and my internal juices and organs kept becoming squished for how many takes we had to do (laughs).

Scotty McCoy: Was it fun doing your stunt? Could it have been dangerous?
Kathleen Kinmont: All stunts are dangerous, yes, but it was fun outside of the uncomfortableness I had felt. At least I wasn't climbing and falling off roofs of houses like Ellie and Danielle had to (laughs).

Scotty McCoy: (Laughs) Speaking of Ellie and Danielle, what was it like working with them? What about with Donald Pleasance, Sasha Jenson, and Beau Starr?
Kathleen Kinmont: I hadn't seen Donald Pleasance much on set, he was this old-school British actor and was the utmost professional man I have met so he was just kind of there to work and leave. He told us about some stories during lunch of his experiences filming, which was neat though. Ellie was great, as was Sasha. So was Beau. The whole cast was amazing. Danielle was a child, so she wanted to hang out and be part of the "gang" so to speak. In our big, luxurious hotel, I went swimming with Danielle, I'd play with her, stuff like that. Made sure she felt as equal as the older cast members. We all had a blast filming for sure!

Scotty McCoy: What was the best part about filming *Halloween 4: The Return of Michael Myers* (1988)? And what was the worst?
Kathleen Kinmont: The best part was having to improvise. I was originally supposed to say, which was scripted for me to say, "Get

lost, Wade," when he was supposed to try and score with me. But Dwight, the director, told me to say, "Fuck off, Wade," and I tried so hard to not laugh and he only gave me one chance to try that improvising scene. Once and done. Then, we had to move on. So, I did it and it went well. The scene where, right after, Brady and his friend are laughing at Wade being rejected was all real because of the improvising scene I did since they weren't expecting me to say that, as it wasn't scripted. The worst part had to have been when filming wrapped as it was so much fun, and we became instantly like family.

Scotty McCoy: Was it scary on set?
Kathleen Kinmont: Yes, it was. It felt scary, it felt like Halloween time. It was winter when we were filming, but it felt like it was autumn. It was ominous, and I even explored the house when everyone went on lunch, which was creepy, as well.

Scotty McCoy: That's amazing, though. The last question I have for you is when you first got the script, what were your initial thoughts?
Kathleen Kinmont: I thought it was a scary film. A psychopathic stalker is stalking people and then kills them, this is shit you see on the news. This is a real-life scenario. These situations happen. So, yes, it felt extremely scary and real, which was a reason why I was glad I had signed up for the film.

Scotty McCoy: I thank you for joining me, Kathleen. It's truly been an honor for me to conduct this interview with you.
Kathleen Kinmont: It's been fun, I had a blast.

Jeffrey Landman

"Billy Hill," Halloween 5: The Revenge of Michael Myers (1989)

Scotty McCoy: Hello, Jeffrey. Thank you for joining me for this interview. It's an honor to have you discuss some *Halloween 5: The Revenge of Michael Myers* (1989) with me!
Jeffrey Landman: No, Scotty, thank you for inviting me to chat with you.

Scotty McCoy: The honor and pleasure is truly mine!
Jeffrey Landman: Well, thank you for saying that!

Scotty McCoy: The first question I have for you is a generic start so the fans reading this can get to know more about your start in the industry. With that said, how did you get your start into acting?
Jeffrey Landman: I always wanted to be a performer from a very young age. I know we are talking about something right now that I did when I was ten, it's like, "You were already young, how can it be something you wanted to do at a 'young age,'" but I am talking about a very, very young age. I'd always had an interest and my mother just sort of started me on my path and took me to an open call that she heard about on television for the new *Mickey Mouse ClubHouse* (1989), and I went to that audition and got the call back. From there, I got my first agent, and my next audition was for *Les Misérables* (1989) on Broadway, and I just had this passion for performing at such a young, young age and it manifested into a four-decade long career.

Scotty McCoy: That's amazing that at such a young age you practically knew what you wanted to do for the rest of your life.

Jeffrey Landman: It's a rare thing for children to know what they want to do as a child and follow through with that passion. It's something I followed through with and have no regrets. Then getting the role in *Halloween 5: The Revenge of Michael Myers* (1989) and being part of the *Halloween* (1978) family for the rest of my life, well, it's just so surreal and has changed my life forever.

Scotty McCoy: That's amazing. You were amazing as Billy and did a superb job, which I'm sure had to have been important to cast the right child actor for the part. Did you have an audition for *Halloween 5: The Revenge of Michael Myers* (1989)?

Jeffrey Landman: Yes, I had a series of auditions. I believe there were like three total before I got the part.

Scotty McCoy: Awesome, so what were the auditions like?

Jeffrey Landman: I was living in New York at the time and appearing on Broadway as part of *Les Misérables* (1989) and I was just brought into an audition and was put on tape. I believe mostly what they were looking for in the audition process was to see if I could convincingly put across the stuttering right. So, that was mostly what the focus was on during the auditions. I was then put on tape with the casting director and then a couple of weeks later, I was in Salt Lake City, Utah, where I was filming the movie.

Scotty McCoy: We know you weren't the only child star in *Halloween 5: The Revenge of Michael Myers* (1989), but Danielle Harris was also in the film. What was it like working with her?

Jeffrey Landman: Oh boy, she was wonderful. Still is too. You know there was a lot of pressure put on her as she's the lead of this movie. She carried this film and was the main protagonist. She was always wonderful to me, and we spent a lot of time together. We were brought to Salt Lake City a week before the rest of the cast for rehearsals, and she was just wonderful. She was teaching me things as I'd never been on a film set before, so I didn't know how things worked. She was showing me this new world that I have been so inexperienced with, and she was just great with it. Her performance in the movie is also fabulous and watching her perform was amazing. I love to be around her so I can just soak up the energy she would give off and when performing alongside her, I'd feed off her and follow her lead, if you will.

Scotty McCoy: Do you keep in touch with Danielle?
Jeffrey Landman: Not really, no. I see her maybe once a year or so at conventions and sometimes I may have run into her at a bar once or twice in Los Angeles, but she's a mom and it's hard to remember with today's technological advances, but back then we had no cell phones or emails to easily keep in touch with everyone you worked with, and there certainly wasn't any form of social media either. Nowadays, it's super easy to reach out to someone to send fan mail or even interview them for a podcast, but back then, there weren't even podcasts, it was all tabloids, talk shows, and whatnot. Plus, we were roughly ten to eleven years old when we filmed *Halloween 5: The Revenge of Michael Myers* (1989) and lived in different states, so it wasn't until we were older, and things became more modern on when we would run into each other.

Scotty McCoy: Piggybacking off of the convention comments you mentioned, do you do conventions often?
Jeffrey Landman: I could get booked in a lot more than I do, and I had to turn some down because I am a working actor and have prior obligations that I cannot get out of, unfortunately. I do love doing them and I have done some and have some others in the works that I'll be attending if scheduling permits. I was part of the 40 years documentary for *Halloween* (1978) in Pasadena, California. And

you will be seeing me on the convention circuits, it just has to align with my schedule because as an actor. Once I book a gig, it's about the film I booked, and I cannot get out of it to do a convention. Unfortunately, that's the way it works, but its part of showbiz.

Scotty McCoy: Did you ever interact with the iconic and legendary Donald Pleasence behind-the-scenes or off set?
Jeffrey Landman: I filmed a lot of scenes during the daytime that ended up on the infamous cutting room floor and some of it involved scenes that I had with Donald Pleasence. He was wonderful, an absolute gem. Very patient with us, knowing full well that we are children and not adult, trained, experienced actors. He sat with us for dinners and told all these amazing and wonderful stories about his long and illustrious career. Unfortunately, I was just ten years old, and I didn't have any real grasp on what or who he was at the time. I wish I could certainly go back in time and be at that dinner table now as an adult and take it all in, but he was ultimately a wonderful human being. I think some of the older cast members had more experiences with him because obviously we were just children, but I still feel so grateful to have met and worked with him because obviously and unfortunately, he passed away during the filming of *Halloween 6: The Curse of Michael Myers* (1995), so I feel very lucky that not only did I get to be in a *Halloween* (1978) movie, but I got to be in a *Halloween* (1978) movie with Donald Pleasence.

Scotty McCoy: Absolutely. I couldn't say it better myself. Such a blessing to have acted alongside the late, great Donald Pleasence!
Jeffrey Landman: Agreed. A moment I'll treasure and remember the rest of my life.

Scotty McCoy: How was Dominique Othenin-Girard as a director?
Jeffrey Landman: He was wonderful, very talented, and knew exactly how he wanted the film to be done. Remember, this film

was rushed. The script wasn't even completely done by the time we started filming, so as director, he had his work cut out for him. One great thing I can say about Dominique is that he was very aware that Danielle and I were kids. And because he was the director and they are the ones at the top of the totem pole, so to speak, on set in terms of an authority figure, he made sure that everyone was really aware of that fact and went out of their way to make sure that we were taken care of, and I truly appreciated that.

Scotty McCoy: Were you afraid of Don Shanks when he was in costume as Michael Myers?
Jeffrey Landman: We were children, so of course it was daunting especially with the scenes we had to do. But again, spit balling back to the last question about Dominique, he was great and made sure that Don took off the mask as much as he possibly can so we, as children, felt more comfortable because, let's be honest, he's a tall man in a mask and jumpsuit, chasing us around as if he's going to kill us. So, that also meant a lot because he made sure we weren't afraid and were taken good care of.

Scotty McCoy: I love hearing stories like that. How did you feel about Billy having a stutter? Was it challenging to pull off?
Jeffrey Landman: I loved the decision being made to give my character the stutter because it really deepened my performance and allowed me to sort of grasp the big picture of the movie. Not just what I was doing right because, if Billy didn't have the stutter, he would be like one of those basic, generic two-dimensional characters and just "another kid" in the film at the clinic. But with the added stutter, it brought a whole new dimension to the character, and it brought out all of my talents as an actor, especially as a child actor, to bring this character to life. And a big part of the stutter had to do with the idea that Jamie was unable to communicate and the one person she could communicate with was Billy, who also

had trouble communicating. So, I personally believe it aligned well with the characters of Billy and Jamie, and not just enhanced Billy's character development.

Scotty McCoy: Speaking of being a child actor, what was it like being a child actor in such a demand industry?

Jeffrey Landman: It's kind of hard to answer that type of question because I don't know any differently. I am a child actor, so it's hard to compare it if you have never done it before as I always have done it and then grew into an actor as an adult. My childhood, for sure, was bizarre and strange. Being a child in show business, it changes your whole life. Especially when you book something as big as *Halloween 5: The Revenge of Michael Myers* (1989). It's not like being in the first *Halloween* film, I was in the fifth one, so it already had this huge following. So, it changes your life. Your social life, your educational life, making friends, etc. I do know I was passionate about it, so I didn't think about the enormity of it, per say, I was just happy to be working and doing what I love to do, and I was very lucky in my career that I always sort of landed these amazing projects that were high profile. I had difficult roles, but then again, it challenged me as an actor, and I always succeeded. You know you're going to be challenging yourself when you do Broadway or when you are cast in a movie, it's not easy to craft the art of acting and bring a person, or character, to life that isn't your true persona.

Scotty McCoy: Good answer! What was the best part about filming *Halloween 5: The Revenge of Michael Myers* (1989)? And what was the worst?

Jeffrey Landman: I got to say the worst first because it was something I'll truly always remember (laughs). We shot at night, and it was like April, May, or June, at that time of the year, but it was freezing outside. We were up all night long. We would be on set at six at night and wrap for the night at six in the morning. I remember feeling really exhausted as I had been up all-night filming. It was like Hell on Earth. Just pure exhaustion all night long. Don't get me wrong, it was super exciting too. It was like "Oh my God, I'm filming a *Halloween* (1978) movie," but then it was also like, "I'm ten years old, filming twelve hours from 6 p.m. to 6 a.m., I just want to go to sleep."

The best part was truly getting to be part of something so iconic that is literally a cult following and has such a large and loyal fan base I mean it's thirty years or so later, and we're still talking about not just this film, but the franchise, with new movies being released every couple of years. I don't take that for granted at all, I don't take it lightly that people still want to talk to me about a film I did over thirty years ago. I'm literally part of film history as being in one of the biggest franchises ever and certainly the biggest one in horror, so that is the greatest part and best part about being involved with *Halloween 5: The Revenge of Michael Myers* (1989).

Scotty McCoy: Awesome, awesome. What is your most memorable moment while filming?
Jeffrey Landman: I'd have to say the car chase sequence. It took two full weeks just to film that scene from start to finish. We shot the film out of order, and we even shot the party sequence out of order, so sometimes it would be the first half of the night you're doing this part of the chase scene and then the second half of the next, you're doing this other part of the chase scene. Plus, in the movie that's the part of the film where stuff really starts to happen so when they were blowing up the car, you know they made sure we were all there on set that day to get that experience and be part of it.

Scotty McCoy: That was a super impactful scene. I absolutely loved it. You unfortunately didn't get to work with Ellie Cornell, who played Rachel Carruthers in the film. Did you ever get to meet her on set?

Jeffrey Landman: I did meet her, yes. But I didn't work with her. I do know that she was killed off very early on in the movie. And then when they had to reveal her corpse, they had to fly her back out to film that scene, as well. But I haven't spoken to her much, as I was ten years old at the time and really didn't chit-chat with a lot of the adults that weren't part of my scenes.

Scotty McCoy: We know your character was wearing a pirate costume as it was Halloween, after all. Was that your idea to wear the pirate costume or was that initially in the script?

Jeffrey Landman: The Halloween costumes were all designated in the script, and we know right from the start of filming that I would be a pirate and Jamie would be the princess. There was some costume switching though that did happen from what was originally written in the script.

Scotty McCoy: Oh yeah? Enlighten us? Why was the costume switching and who did it involve?

Jeffrey Landman: (Laughs) Originally, Tina, played by Wendi Kaplan, was supposed to be the devil and Tamara Glynn's Samantha was going to be the French maid. They changed it, however, because they didn't want the good girl to be the devil and Tina was the ultimate good girl, so to speak, as she was like this heroine in the film and ends up sacrificing herself and dies to protect Jamie.

Scotty McCoy: Very interesting. Speaking about Wendi Kaplan, what was it like working with her?

Jeffrey Landman: Oh, she was wonderful. We didn't have many on screen scenes together, maybe two or three total. I think most of the ones we did film together, along with ones I filmed with Donald Pleasence, ended up getting cut and left on that cutting room floor. But after she sacrificed herself for Jamie, it was like "What the fuck!?" Where will this movie go now?

Scotty McCoy: And boy the movie did go there! Danielle as Jamie, a child, was fighting off Michael. Granted there were cops aiding her, and, of course, Dr. Loomis puts the final nail in Michael's coffin for this movie, but it was a very interesting way to go with making Danielle, a ten-year-old child, be your final girl!

Jeffrey Landman: Absolutely! It was risky, and they did shoot a scene with stabbing Danielle's leg when she was in the laundry chute, but that got cut because of it being too graphic. Like, who wants to see a kid get stabbed in the leg? But, if you watch some later scenes, you see the blood there which wasn't removed and messed with some continuity because of reshoots. But when you watch *Halloween 4: The Return of Michael Myers* (1988), it's Jamie and Rachel, but Rachel does a lot of the protecting. Rachel is dead here, Tina is dead now, the cops are being easily dispatched of, and Loomis is out of commission until the very end, so it was literally a fight for survival for a ten-year-old girl and I believe Danielle pulled it off and did a phenomenal job.

Scotty McCoy: I couldn't agree more, even if I wanted to (laughs). What was the environment like on set?

Jeffrey Landman: It sort of did feel like it was really Halloween season, even though it was late Spring and early Summer when we were filming. I guess a lot of that had to do with the decorations and costumes and what not. I had a lot of fun filming it, and everyone in the cast had a great time. There wasn't a lot of stress or anything like that. We were there to work, but still had fun. It was an overall amazing experience that I'll forever remember and cherish for the rest of my life.

Scotty McCoy: That's awesome. Any stories from behind-the-scenes that you'll always remember that you'd like to share?

Jeffrey Landman: I remember they had parties when we weren't filming that only "adults can attend" (laughs). So, Danielle and I couldn't go to the hotel rooms where they were having these types of parties. It was funny because we both wanted to go, but obviously couldn't. I'm not entirely sure what happened, but thinking back to it, there was probably drinking, maybe hooking up with each other, things children shouldn't be exposed to (laughs).

Scotty McCoy: (Laughs) That's interesting. Being a child on set, was there schooling?
Jeffrey Landman: Yes, actually. We had a three-part trailer. I would have the part on the left, Danielle had the part on the right, and then the middle part of the trailer was our schooling where we had a private teacher that would come on set. When we weren't filming, they would give us our education as it is law for children to attend school, and if they were working as an actor out in Los Angeles, the law required us to be taught on set outside of our work schedule.

Scotty McCoy: That's great to know, and I guess that'll wrap up this interview. I truly thank you Jeffrey for clearing your schedule to make this interview happen and we can dive deep and headfirst right into *Halloween 5: The Revenge of Michael Myers* (1989).
Jeffrey Landman: I had a blast, Scotty. Thank you for reaching out and making this happen.

Daniel Farrands

Screenwriter, Halloween 6: The Curse of Michael Myers (1995)

Scotty McCoy: Hey, Daniel. I truly appreciate you joining me for an interview for you to discuss your love of *Halloween* (1978) and your time spent writing *Halloween 6: The Curse of Michael Myers* (1995).
Daniel Farrands: Hey, thank you so much for having me, Scotty. I am truly appreciative of you reaching out to me to discuss some *Halloween* (1978), as well.

Scotty McCoy: The honor is truly mine. I must ask you though, how you got your start into filmmaking and screenwriting?
Daniel Farrands: It initially started as a dream as a child where I wrote a letter to Frank Mancuso Jr., when he was the guy producing the *Friday the 13th* (1980) films, I believe they were on *Friday the 13th Part 3* (1982). He wrote me a letter back telling me as a child my age to never give up on my dreams as my visions for the *Friday the 13th* (1980) franchise was exceptional, and that's kind of where it took off.

Scotty McCoy: How old were you when you wrote to Frank Mancuso Jr.?
Daniel Farrands: I was 14 years old.

Scotty McCoy: That's awesome to have some ambition so young. I'm assuming you weren't 14 when you wrote *Halloween 6: The Curse of Michael Myers* (1995)? (Laughs)

Daniel Farrands: I wasn't, but close (laughs). You want to hear the story?

Scotty McCoy: Yeah, absolutely. How did you get your start with writing *Halloween 6: The Curse of Michael Myers* (1995)?

Daniel Farrands: Well, I started out the same way I did at 14. I wrote a letter to Moustapha Akkad and told him all about my passion for the *Halloween* (1978) franchise and how I'd write the next film. I just finished seeing *Halloween 5: The Revenge of Michael Myers* (1989) in theaters, so I knew what I would want to do. In 1990, when I was 19 years old, I got a call from Ramsey Thomas, who was a producer on *Halloween 5: The Revenge of Michael Myers* (1989), and he told me they were actively seeking writers for the sixth *Halloween* (1978) film and that Moustapha Akkad wanted to meet with me. I went to his office, it was huge: a large desk, all the film posters surrounding him, and this big, powerful man smoking a pipe sitting behind the desk in a large, king-like chair. I gave him a copy of this *Halloween Bible* (1990) that I had with all the film's storylines and timelines, character descriptions, biographies, background, death scenes, and family relations, and everything from cities and towns, such as Russellville, Haddonfield, and the Lost River Drive-In. He looked at me and just said, "Uh huh, thank you," and it was over. I walked out of his office and thought to myself that he hated me. A few years passed and it was 1994 and he called me and asked to meet up with me. I did and he told me that he wanted me to write the sixth film if I can pitch to him an idea that would make sense for the sixth film. I was shocked he even remembered me from years ago and he always kept my *Halloween Bible*. He asked me what I envision *Halloween 6* (1995) to be about, which at the time didn't even have a subtitle title, and you know what I said?

Scotty McCoy: What did you say to him?

Daniel Farrands: I remember everything I heard and read from John Carpenter's pitch to him back in 1977, and that was "Boogeyman killing babysitters," which completely lit up his eyes. So, my pitch to him was "*Rosemary's Baby* (1968) meets *Halloween* (1978)." His eyes lit up and he uttered, "I love it! Write me a script and get me it." So, I wrote up a 35-page script and he told me that I wrote him two movies, to cut it in half, so I technically had written up *Halloween 6* (1995) and *Halloween 7* (1998). And then I ended up doing some touch ups based on his input and wrote a full script of *Halloween 6* (1995) which later became *Halloween 6: The Curse of Michael Myers* (1995), based on input from the previous film and how it came over into the current film.

Scotty McCoy: That's so cool, but how did the curse of thorn come into the picture?

Daniel Farrands: It's funny you should ask. I re-watched *Halloween 5: The Revenge of Michael Myers* (1989) and I saw the symbols they had with the tattoo on Michael's wrist. That tattoo, after researching different kinds of witchcraft books, is a thorn tattoo and depending on the way it is facing it is either evil or holy. Obviously, we went the evil route. They had no clue what that tattoo meant when filming it in *Halloween 5: The Revenge of Michael Myers* (1989), nor did they have any clue about half the stuff being filmed, such as the mysterious Man in Black. But as production continued, they added stuff into my script, which didn't turn out so good in the end.

Scotty McCoy: There are two more questions for you to follow up on that. The first being, was your script more so the theatrical version or the producer's cut? And how did you decide to use Dr. Wynn as the Man in Black, since he is vaguely remembered in the first film?

Daniel Farrands: My script wasn't entirely used in either cut. The producer's cut is closer to my script, but the entire ending is totally different. For Dr. Wynn, as a diehard *Halloween* (1978) fan myself, it was a nod to the franchise. I initially had in my script that he was the one to teach Michael to drive. It was a deleted scene in the producer's cut, but ultimately not used in the final footage. I even had a nod to *Halloween III: Season of the Witch* (1982) where the dad, John Strode, after he comes home from work and his wife's dead and he's wanting dinner, that he puts on the television and the Silver Shamrock jingle played, which would've been funny, but ultimately never even considered on being filmed.

Scotty McCoy: That's a shame. That would've been a beautiful tribute too. What about with Dr. Loomis, that character wasn't seen as much as he usually is. Any specific reason for that?
Daniel Farrands: We knew that Donald Pleasence was slowing down. He obviously passed after filming wrapped, but we had no clue he was dying. Just that he was slowing down. He passed during reshoots and if you look closely in the producer's cut, you can see it isn't him being clocked in the back of the head. I had written a lot more for him, including stunt scenes, but it just wasn't able to be done. He was older and couldn't prefer anything remotely close to them. He did call me though before filming started and when he signed on, he said it was the best and scariest *Halloween* (1978) script he has read since the first one.

Scotty McCoy: Was there any thoughts on bringing back Laurie Strode?
Daniel Farrands: Yes, there was. And my first draft had Laurie Strode brought back too in a surprising fashion.

Scotty McCoy: Really? Care to elaborate on what was initially written?
Daniel Farrands: Absolutely! So, in the initial first draft I wrote that turned into "two movies," I had Laurie Strode at the end in a

five-minute cameo played by Jamie Lee Curtis. Jamie Lloyd didn't die in the movie and was close to being killed by Michael until Laurie Strode came out of nowhere to protect her daughter and said "Michael." Michael would turn around and he comes face-to-face with Laurie and the movie ends on a major cliffhanger. There was no plan on even hyping or promoting Jamie Lee Curtis even being involved. It would be that shock factor for fans watching. But Moustapha was like "Get that out of your mind. She will NEVER do it. She is making millions of dollars in Hollywood right now and would never come back and do a *Halloween* (1978) film." So, the idea was completely scrapped and then Jamie Lloyd was killed off relatively early in the film, and of course, by a different actress.

Scotty McCoy: About that, why didn't Danielle Harris come back to film *Halloween 6: The Curse of Michael Myers* (1995)?
Daniel Farrands: If you ever get Danielle for an interview, you can ask her, but I'll give you the scoop from what I know. First off, the studios treated her like fucking garbage. She was asking for more money for the part, but they wouldn't even budge. It was like she wasn't worth it after she was literally carrying the last two films by herself. And at the time of the sixth film, she has established herself as an actress in much bigger roles, including a big guest part in several episodes on *Roseanne*. So, Danielle Harris wasn't a nobody anymore, she was more established. I do love JC Brandy, and I am good friends with her to this day, but Danielle Harris was Jamie Lloyd, and she was replaced and tossed aside like trash, and it ended up backfiring on the film in the end.

Scotty McCoy: Interesting. What was the most stressful part about writing the film?
Daniel Farrands: The time frame I had. I was given a month to write it. We started filming in October and it was now September, and they already had a director, a cast, and a crew and all their jobs

depended on me completing this script in one month so we could start production.

Scotty McCoy: Wow, that is stressful. What about the easiest part?
Daniel Farrands: Writing a movie script is never easy, anyone who says it has never written a proper script before. I'd have to say, if anything, not having to research the films as I already knew everything about them and mention them in my script. I give a nod to Russellville, which was previously mentioned in *Halloween II* (1981). The fact that I was a true fan living a dream to write this film and even wrote a *Halloween Bible* (1990), it just made writing much easier and fun, and even to decrease the stress and pressure of completing a full final draft in a month.

Scotty McCoy: Very true. One last question. You directed the *Crystal Lake Memories* (2013) and *Never Sleep Again* (2010) documentaries. Any chance of us getting a similar documentary on *Halloween* (1978)?
Daniel Farrands: I'd like to, but I don't know what else we can add. There are the makings of all those films on the *Shout Factory* (2020) box set that are no longer available but do sell on eBay for outrageous amounts of money. They also are probably on YouTube, as well. The only thing I think we can do is just get all those documentaries and kind of paste them into one large documentary.

Scotty McCoy: I still think that would be amazing. I thank you Daniel for taking the time out of your busy schedule to join me!
Daniel Farrands: Scotty, the honor was mine. If I may add, please check out both *Ted Bundy: American Boogeyman* (2021) and *Aileen Wuronos: American Boogeywoman* (2021) on various streaming platforms. I directed, produced, and wrote both of those films on notorious serial killers.

Tom Proctor

Motorist, Halloween 6: The Curse of Michael Myers (1995)

Scotty McCoy: Welcome, Tom! Thank you for making time out of your busy schedule to do an interview with me and discuss some of *Halloween 6: The Curse of Michael Myers* (1995).
Tom Proctor: No problem at all, Scotty. Thank you for inviting me to chat and reminisce about such a wonderful film and franchise.

Scotty McCoy: It's truly my honor. Please inform everyone on how you got your start into acting?
Tom Proctor: It's kind of funny. My family and I ran cattle up in the Velcro Mountains in Utah and we got the location wrong. The spot we were supposed to be at was on the other side of the mountain and so we accidentally rode on to the first set and they figured out we were in the wardrobe and thought we were part of the shoot. They were having trouble trying to do a stampede and they were having problems with their horses, and it was obvious that we could solve that problem right away and so that's how it first started. By an accident when I'm running cattle (laughs).

Scotty McCoy: (Laughs) Oh boy! That's funny! What was your audition like for *Halloween 6: The Curse of Michael Myers* (1995)?
Tom Proctor: The casting director was Ross Brown, and he was one of those people that would send people out in tears because everyone's used to the whole "That's very nice. Thank you." Ross was one

of those people that are like "What the fuck are you doing? What the fuck was that?" So, I went in and it's funny because I get it now, in Utah, in a very small town, we had our own idea of what a headshot was and what Hollywood was looking for and to Hollywood, when they came there, we were just ridiculous (laughs). Ross took one look at my headshot and said, "What the fuck is this?" I said, "It's my headshot," and he goes, "Do you want to play Bruno in every fucking movie? This is a horrible headshot!" (Laughs) My headshot was horrible, and I turned around to him and said back, "Says the man that is wearing bright orange tennis shoes with green pants!" I then said, "I'm sorry, but you magically expect me to give a fuck about your opinion?" Nobody else had done that, but I'm more old school, this cowboy-type guy that has an "if you don't like it, then there's two sides of the street and you can walk the other way" mentality. But anyways, Ross needed someone who could do stunt driving because originally in the script the motorist wrecks his truck off the side of the road. The weather eventually got bad and everything that could go wrong was going wrong for the production so the whole stunt driving scene was nixed. My scenes were being pushed back, pushed back, and pushed back even more. So, due to the delays in filming the scene, it just got removed all together. When they rewrote it, the part was limited to where you see me drinking beer, taking a piss on the side of the road, the girl sneaks around and steals my car, and I'm killed in the rainstorm.

Scotty McCoy: Was it a real rainstorm or just special effects?
Tom Proctor: They set up rain machines, but when they did and used it, a blistering cold ring just really hit hard and started blowing things everywhere and the crew couldn't work with it. The scene just wasn't feeling right so they wanted to wait till it was bad weather to shoot.

Scotty McCoy: How did they manage that? How long did you have to wait to film your scenes?

Tom Proctor: Well, once the rain machine stopped working, they just put me on hold until we got a real rainstorm. I said to the P.A., "You know this weather's not going to let up for the next fifteen days, and then it'll be another fifteen days, and you'll never get me into the film." She responded, "No way, once they call for bad weather, we're going to immediately be on set and start filming the scene to get the shot done perfectly." I told her that she could just do a drop in pick up to save the production some money and she responded so ignorantly, "How about you do your job and I'll do mine" and I just waved my hands up and backed off and said, "Alright, that works!"

Scotty McCoy: Wow, that's crazy! So, how long were you on set for?

Tom Proctor: For the fifteen seconds you see me on your screen, they had me on hold for twenty days and had to pay me for all twenty days, but I only worked for three of those days on set.

Scotty McCoy: That's insanity. Your idea you mentioned earlier would've prevented all of that too!

Tom Proctor: It absolutely would've, but they didn't listen to my suggestion and wanted to play "boss man," so they spent more money than they had to, but my pocketbook was saying "Thank you!" (Laughs)

Scotty McCoy: (Laughs) Speaking of your death scene, how was that filmed and prepped?

Tom Proctor: That was probably one of the more fun things that I had to do. I can't remember the name of the SFX guy off the top of my head, but they had to cast the head, and I mean my whole, entire head and part of my body so the spinal cord could come out of the back.

Scotty McCoy: Did you have to re-film the death scene for the Theatrical Cut because the death for the Theatrical Cut is different than in the Producer's Cut of the film?

Tom Proctor: Actually, yes. Originally, my death was just a neck snap/twist to break the neck. You never see the spine come out of my neck. But the Weinsteins wanted more blood, gore, and graphic content so they reshoot the scene where my spine is exposed for the Theatrical Cut of the film and the Producer's Cut is what we originally shot.

Scotty McCoy: That's cool. Do you do any convention appearances to meet the *Halloween* (1978) fans?

Tom Proctor: (Laughs) It's funny, actually. I kept getting calls to go to the conventions. I respond to the guys asking me to come to the conventions, "I think you got the wrong guy. I'm only in the film for like fifteen seconds." They always respond with "I don't think you know the fans, they really give a fuck about everyone in the movie, even if it is for fifteen seconds." I finally went on the 25th anniversary of the film and Sean Clark got a hold of me and said, "Tom, we've been traveling around with your hat and your head, selling headshots to the fan and still got tons of requests for you." I'm shocked that the fans still want to see me.

Scotty McCoy: Do any fans at these conventions notice you from any other horror films you've done in the past?

Tom Proctor: Actually, yes. I have done two different horror films. One with Kevin Kangas called *Fear of Clowns 2* (2007), which I thought no one had ever even seen because it was this little low budget film. There was another that Kevin wrote titled *The Bounty* (1984) and I was in the leading role and Sean Clark told me we're going to go and sign autographs on *The Bounty* (1984), and I said to him, "Did somebody really see that? Do people actually care about this small, low budget/no budget film?" We got to the convention, and it was just surreal. The lines were just crazy, and everyone wanted pictures of me from *The Bounty* (1984) and even from my fifteen seconds in *Halloween 6: The Curse of Michael Myers* (1995) and it really caught me by surprise. When I went to the comic con conventions, especially the one in El Paso, Texas, they had me go there for my part in *Guardians of the Galaxy* (2014) and the most screen snaps that people choose to buy and get autographed is from *Halloween 6: The Curse of Michael Myers* (1995).

Scotty McCoy: That's amazing. It really is. Do you get any emails about people wanting headshots from you?

Tom Proctor: It's funny. I have people from as far as Europe requesting screen stills from *Halloween 6: The Curse of Michael Myers* (1995) and they offer to pay shipping and everything. A lot of it is from the death scene, but then the dialogue, which is really well written and even when it is a couple of lines, if written well, it leaves a lasting and memorable impression on the fans.

Scotty McCoy: What was Joe Chappelle like as a director?

Tom Proctor: He was amazing. He knew exactly what he wanted, and I had watched him give direction to so many people with one line, one word, you know "Can you do it like this?" So, every time on every take of mine he'd say "Tom, that was perfect. No changes. Do it again the exact same way." I kept thinking to myself, "Wow, he either really likes my shit or thinks I suck so bad that I'm not directable" and that's something extremely realistic that goes through the actor's head, especially back in those days when I was just starting off. Actors are not known for being secure with their work and sometimes one line of dialogue is very powerful with the way it is presented and spoken. The dialogue was properly directed by Joe and set up the suspense of Jamie being chased by Michael and that whole truck chase scene; you knew it was powerful with the way Joe was directing as he knew how the scene should be shot to have a more impactful and lasting impression.

Scotty McCoy: Speaking of Michael and Jamie, they were played by George P. Wilbur and JC Brandy respectively. What was it like working with them both?
Tom Proctor: They were both great. JC's performance was impeccable. She really sold the scene well, and George, having played Michael in the past, was great and came with experience.

Scotty McCoy: Did you interact or hang out with the other cast members off set?
Tom Proctor: I did with George Wilbur. I spoke with JC just lightly as there was that situation, we spoke about earlier with the weather being brutal. She was a trooper, any other actress would've been like "Fuck this shit," but she stuck it out and was a true professional. I didn't really mingle though, just a tad with JC and George. Otherwise, I was warming up in my trailer.

Scotty McCoy: The last question I have for you is about your death. With George playing Michael, how did he happen to work with you on making it look as real as possible?
Tom Proctor: The thing with doing death scenes in a movie is the comfortability you have with your co-stars and the need to place trust into someone else's hands. Remember, George is a true and trained professional stuntman. It doesn't mean he won't make any mistakes, but he is trained, and you must place your trust in him. Like when he was snapping my neck, the biggest risk there is that the actor will get carried away and snap too hard. The correct way of doing that is that the actor puts their hand on the victim's face and the victim snaps their own neck around. George was good about that and took the hands along for the ride. And then I must perform

the full stunt, facial expressions, and all, to properly sell it so it looks like he snapped my neck.

Scotty McCoy: That's amazing, it truly is movie magic!
Tom Proctor: That it is. Like we have stunt and fight coordinators on set, and George is a trained stuntman, so there weren't any major risks, but with all stunts, there are still risks, nonetheless.

Scotty McCoy: I couldn't have said it any better myself. I thank you Tom for taking the time out of your busy schedule to do this interview and flashback to the good ol' days of *Halloween 6: The Curse of Michael Myers* (1995).
Tom Proctor: Don't mention it, Scotty. I had fun and a blast discussing this film that, like Michael Myers, will never die (laughs).

Christopher Durand

"Michael Myers," Halloween H20: 20 Years Later (1998)

Scotty McCoy: Oh my God! It's Michael Myers himself. Thank you for joining me on Halloween, Christopher Durand!

Christopher Durand: Absolutely! I am Michael Myers after all! I might as well do an interview on Halloween to discuss some *Halloween H20: 20 Years Later* (1998)!

Scotty McCoy: I am truly appreciative of you stopping by for an interview and diving into some specific details of a truly amazing film in such a classic and iconic holiday franchise.

Christopher Durand: The honor is all mine! I am glad to be here.

Scotty McCoy: How did it all begin? How'd you get your start in stunts and acting?

Christopher Durand: Definitely not through a family line like most actors and stunt performers get their start. I had absolutely no connection to the business at all. My parents were academics, they were physicists. I had a friend in high school, however, who was a phenomenal martial artist, and his mom was an actress. He wanted to use his skills, so we worked on it together and trained. He got his start through his mom introducing him to cool stunt people and then I realized through him that there's this cool business that you can do all these cool stunts, basically get paid to play "Cowboys and Indians," and I just got my start by working up the ranks, sneaking onto soundstages, and just meeting cool people that would refer me to others and it just started from there. With acting, it's basically the same thing as a stuntman, only difference is you are delivering dialogue and fully on camera, whereas in stunts you see the side or back of the stunt performer, so I just started acting through my stunts and it got noticed and from there on, I ended up doing both.

Scotty McCoy: That's a neat way to get involved into two of the best worlds of entertainment. How did you happen to land the role of Michael Myers in *Halloween H20: 20 Years Later* (1998)? Was there an audition process, and, if so, what was that process like?

Christopher Durand: It was the twentieth anniversary of *Halloween* (1978) and, in the past, they always had guys with just a stunt background because Michael had to look intimidating and can do dangerous types of stunts that an actor with no stunt background couldn't perform. But for this anniversary, they wanted a Michael Myers that can do stunts, but also can act with just his body language because he doesn't talk. They needed me to sell it with my eyes in everything that I did. So, they auditioned numerous actors who could do stunts, and by numerous, I mean hundreds and hundreds of them, but they didn't like any of them. They felt they couldn't connect with those actors as the main antagonist of the film. So, they went to Donna Keegan, who was the stunt double of Jamie Lee Curtis, and she knew a few guys that could do the part. She gave Steve Miner and the producers a list of five actors who could perform stunts, people she knew the background of and knew that they could be the ones to do the stunts required for this film. So, they looked at the list and I was one of the names on it, and they reached out to each of us, and they settled with me as they felt I connected the most with the role of Michael and could sell the character and his evilness with just my eyes.

Scotty McCoy: Nice, nice. Speaking of Jamie Lee Curtis, what was it like working with her? How was she on set?

Christopher Durand: It was great working with her. She's a real pro in all aspects of the word. This film was revisiting what started her career. Without *Halloween* (1978), there would be no Jamie Lee Curtis as we know her today, and she has gone on record multiple times stating just that. She is a very hands-on person, meaning she wants to jump in and help whenever and wherever she can and, the thing is, you can't do that because her role is carrying the film. Being the star and performing the role of Laurie Strode, not being a producer, or a writer, or even a director. She loved helping, and though it isn't a bad thing, you have to let everyone do their jobs, just like they let her do her job as an actress and make the movie as Laurie Strode.

Scotty McCoy: Continuing on with the bandwagon of Jamie Lee Curtis as Laurie Strode, did you know that she wasn't going to really kill Michael Myers? Were there plans on having *Halloween: Resurrection* (2002) after *Halloween H20: 20 Years Later* (1998) with Michael switching places with the paramedic?

Christopher Durand: (Laughs) Yes, we knew from the beginning. Jamie wasn't happy because she only brought this story to light and offered to return if she could kill Michael and end the franchise for good. After she signed her contract, she didn't realize that there was a specific contract within the studio and the franchise of *Halloween* (1978) alone that you cannot ever kill Michael Myers. It's forbidden and never can happen because if you kill off Michael, you kill off *Halloween* (1978), because we all know how *Halloween III: Season of the Witch* (1982) turned out when Michael was supposed to be dead. She wasn't happy with the fact that she cannot kill Michael and she couldn't back out due to the contract on her end already being signed, so she had come to a compromise with the studio that she'll "kill" Michael in the eyes of the viewers and get what she wanted, but he won't be dead; he'll have switched places with a paramedic. So, an added scene to be inserted into *Halloween: Resurrection* (2002) was filmed with the flashback scene shown, and then Jamie had to return for the first part of *Halloween: Resurrection* (2002) and her story would end and she would be killed per her wishes because she was done being known as the "*Halloween* (1978) girl."

Scotty McCoy: Interesting! A scene that always gave me chills was your stare down with Jamie Lee Curtis' Laurie Strode in the circular window. What was the process of that? Was that scene something that was as iconic as it was and used in every publicity trailer and still leading up to the film's release?

Christopher Durand: That scene was planned as the first interaction of Michael and Laurie. We knew this going into it and had to make it as memorable and iconic to grab the audience when they watched the trailer. The scenes where I am chasing Josh Hartnett and Michelle Williams and they were screaming for help. I stayed away from them for at least an hour before we filmed it, so they hadn't seen me in a while and showed some legitimate terror. Then, when we come up to that scene of Jamie and I, you can see my goal is to kill this kid and his girl, but then I come face-to-face with this older lady and you watch me tilt my head, and it is my body expression signaling that this is my sister that I have been looking to kill for twenty years. Michael realized this lady is his sister and she never died, and now his goal has changed, and he is on the collision course to kill his sister once and for all.

Scotty McCoy: That's awesome. As I previously have said, that scene always gives me a chill down my spine when I watch it. Which stunt to you was the hardest to perform?

Christopher Durand: Hands down, it's when Laurie hit me with the ambulance. I had to be safe by getting hit with the car, get thrown quite a few feet backwards, and then roll down a hill with the ambulance, which was controlled with a crane, down an embankment and be pinned against a tree. It was fun and safe, we all were fine after it was over, but it was the most technical stunt we had to perform that had a lot of layers to it that could easily injure someone that wasn't careful and didn't listen specifically to what had to be done and when to do it.

Scotty McCoy: It was a very interesting stunt, and I'm sure you all were safe, but damn that looked insane too. Which kill that you performed was your most favorite out of them all?

Christopher Durand: Adam Arkin. He is just a true pro and very talented, with a very talented father too. And with how he shook and convulsed as I stabbed him, he sold it super well. It may have been a scene before that was previously used in a different fashion, but it was also a kill that I believe was sold better by Adam than it has been in the past. I think Adam did amazing and if you also look at me, Adam isn't my intended target. Me killing him was specifically to send a message to Laurie that this is going to be you. As I am killing Adam's character, I haven't removed my eyes from Laurie so you can see that I am telling Laurie that your boyfriend is in the wrong place at the wrong time and your ass is next.

Scotty McCoy: I have never even noticed that! I really think that adds a whole new perspective to his death and what Michael's clear and true intentions truly are. Have you seen *Halloween Kills* (2021) yet?

Christopher Durand: I haven't yet. I have young kids, so it's hard to go out to the movies and see a horror flick because, you know, young kids shouldn't see it, nor could they probably get in given their ages.

Scotty McCoy: Makes sense though. The last question I have for you, Chris, is: if you were offered to return to *Halloween* (1978) as Michael Myers, would you accept?

Christopher Durand: Maybe, but it depends. I had such a great cast working with me and I played an epic Michael Myers in a franchise's twentieth anniversary film, so it would really depend on the script and on the cast and crew attached to the project.

Scotty McCoy: That sounds like a plan! I thank you so much Chris for taking time out of your busy schedule, especially on Halloween, to join me for an interview and talk some Michael Myers and *Halloween H20: 20 Years Later* (1998).

Christopher Durand: You betcha! Happy Halloween, Scotty!

Gary J. Clayton

"Young Michael Myers," *Halloween Resurrection* (2002)

Scotty McCoy: Young Michael Myers is here. Gary Clayton, thank you so much for joining me for this interview!
Gary Clayton: Of course, man. I am honored for my interview with you to be my first interview I have done.

Scotty McCoy: Wow, your first interview? No pressure for me (laughs). Well, I am honored to be the one to conduct your first interview.
Gary Clayton: Thank you for the kind words!

Scotty McCoy: Not a problem at all. For those unfamiliar with you and your work, why don't you tell everyone reading this on how you got your start into the acting industry?
Gary Clayton: I'd be happy to. I was in a casting office where my mom was doing some work as she was part of the film business and had doubled for Jamie Lee Curtis for some time in the *Halloween* (1978) films. They saw me sitting in the casting office and saw how I looked like the kid from the original *Halloween* film, and they said they could use me as a young Michael Myers in *Halloween: Resurrection* (2002) and asked me if I would be interested. They then asked my mom if she'd be okay with it and she agreed. So, everyone was on board, and it went from there.

Scotty McCoy: Did you pursue acting after this?

Gary Clayton: Not for a while after. I retired from acting at the age of 6 (laughs). I did *Halloween: Resurrection* (2002) at 6 years old. I didn't really get into acting until I turned 13 years old. I have done some smaller roles. I was in *Christmas with the Kranks* (2004) and on *Everybody Hates Chris* (2005) so I did some smaller roles in those productions, but I didn't really start diving into acting until 13 and a few days ago, I had an audition for another film that I can't speak about until I hear back if I got the part or not.

Scotty McCoy: Well, good luck on the role you auditioned for. I'm sure you'll get it!

Gary Clayton: Well, thank you for saying that sir.

Scotty McCoy: Don't mention it! You were Young Michael Myers in *Halloween: Resurrection* (2002), but the scene was ultimately deleted from the final print of the film. Do you happen to know why the scene was deleted?

Gary Clayton: It was supposed to be the original opening of *Halloween: Resurrection* (2002). *Halloween: Resurrection* (2002) wasn't even supposed to be a found footage-type of film with reality stars in the Myers house. It was a totally different plot and script. The original plot had a lot of problems with the filmmaking aspect of it. They just chopped out a lot of the film, and my scene was one of them that got left on the cutting room floor. Eventually, they did reshoots after a rewrite of the script and that is where we ended up with the *Halloween: Resurrection* (2002) we have today.

Scotty McCoy: Could you describe the scene to those who haven't seen it?

Gary Clayton: Of course! It was basically a family gathering, or some type of barbecue, and my mom had the camera on me, and I looked distant and evil. I am pushing the camera out of my face, as the signature *Halloween* (1978) theme song played, and it was supposed to give more of a background on Michael Myers as a child.

Scotty McCoy: I think that would've been an interesting place to go because it wasn't until Rob Zombie's *Halloween* (2007) that we got a totally different backstory of Michael Myers, and this storyline or timeline never really dived into the mystic of Michael Myers.

Gary Clayton: The thing that makes Michael so scary and ominous is that he is mysterious. You know he is the embodiment of evil, but don't know why he is evil or why this evil force has chosen him to be the one to kill. It's like he's born without a soul. I think a backstory would be cool, but you still need to have a sense of not knowing who this man is and why he is evil, otherwise he's just a normal killer like Jason Voorhees or Freddy Krueger. Yes, they're scary, but an unknown cause of their actions that make them evil is what would make them even scary, which is what we get with Michael Myers.

Scotty McCoy: Good points, Gary. Where can anyone see this scene at, if at all?

Gary Clayton: The entire deleted scene is available from various channels on YouTube. Just type in the search bar "*Halloween: Resurrection* (2002) Deleted Scene" and you'll find it quite easily.

Scotty McCoy: Have you seen any of the films prior to accepting the role for this movie?

Gary Clayton: Probably not, I know we were speaking prior to the interview for weeks and you mentioned watching horror films at six years old, but I never really got into horror films until my later years in life. I am 26 years old now, and can enjoy them, but as a child, I don't think I'd be getting much sleep.

Scotty McCoy: I'm assuming it's safe to say you saw them all now?
Gary Clayton: I have seen all of them. The only one I originally didn't see was the *Halloween* (2018) reboot, but I have seen that as

of a few weeks ago. And on Halloween this year, I plan on watching *Halloween Kills* (2021) and then going out to a Halloween party with some friends to talk about it. I'm excited to see the new one too, I heard good things about it. I also have the entire box set of *Halloween* (1978) somewhere in my house, but not entirely sure where I put it. I should break it out and have a movie marathon this month for spooky season (laughs).

Scotty McCoy: (Laughs) Which film is your favorite of the franchise?
Gary Clayton: I know I'll get a lot of hate for saying this, but unpopular opinion, my favorite one in the franchise is Rob Zombie's *Halloween II* (2009). I look at it from a filmmaker's point of view though, not just from the character's development or the story arc. He did amazing effects and had amazing cinematography for the film, and I just truly appreciate that effort he put into the making of the film.

Scotty McCoy: Hey, that's your opinion and no one should knock you on what you like?
Gary Clayton: True!

Scotty McCoy: You were a child actor. Were there any challenges in being a child actor?
Gary Clayton: Not really, no. I was in a few things as a kid and was six when I did this film. But I just wanted to be a normal child, and, to do that, I figured it was best to not always be in the limelight. I eventually went into music and started a label there, as well as continued to act, as I got older.

Scotty McCoy: The spotlight can be hard for those that are children and can lead to so many bad paths a lot of actors take.
Gary Clayton: Exactly! Child actors grow up and turn to drugs, alcohol, sex, and become traumatized because they didn't have the

opportunity to live a normal life as a child, and it all starts with the parents, who mostly force the child into the business to be the bread and butter of the household, and that's not right.

Scotty McCoy: I couldn't agree more, Gary. But I truly thank you for taking the time with me to do an interview. I am truly appreciative of you sharing your experiences that a lot of people may not have known about *Halloween: Resurrection* (2002).
Gary Clayton: You're very welcome, bro. I thank you for reaching out and glad we could make this happen.

Scotty McCoy: No problem. Enjoy your Halloween party and have a killer time watching *Halloween Kills* (2021), no pun intended (laughs).
Gary Clayton: You too, man. See ya!

Daeg Faerch

"Young Michael Myers," *Halloween* (2007)

Scotty McCoy: We have a killer right now on the show. Daeg Faerch, who played Michael Myers as a boy for the first half of Rob Zombie's *Halloween* (2007) film. Thank you for joining me, Daeg. How are you doing this evening?
Daeg Faerch: Doing great, man. Thanks for having me. It has been a busy day dealing with some music stuff and my agent in getting me some more acting gigs.

Scotty McCoy: That is awesome. So, how did your start in acting come about?
Daeg Faerch: I have been involved in acting for quite some time now. Ever since I was a small boy. My mom used to be a dancer and she got me involved with show business and the rest is history, as they say.

Scotty McCoy: Nice, so I am assuming your mom is your manager?
Daeg Faerch: She is definitely a *momager*. I have a manager as well, a bad ass one, but my mom is always booking me the gigs I need to further my career and looking over the things to see if they are on the up and up.

Scotty McCoy: So, did your mom look over the *Halloween* (2007) script for you? Or did you both look into it together?
Daeg Faerch: I was young, so my mom just looked into it. It was a cool experience though when I did get onto set.

Scotty McCoy: What was the best part of being on set?
Daeg Faerch: Let us just say, it is pretty cool to get paid to "kill" people (laughs). I hate wrapping a shoot though. That is hard as everyone becomes like family.

Scotty McCoy: So, I am taking it that was the worst part of filming, so to speak?
Daeg Faerch: Yeah, absolutely!

Scotty McCoy: So, why didn't you return for *Halloween 2* (2009)?
Daeg Faerch: I do not like talking about it, but in short, I aged too much and did not look young like in the first film from 2007.

Scotty McCoy: Damn, I am sorry to hear that! How was Rob Zombie as a director?
Daeg Faerch: He was great. He gave us a lot of freedom, something a lot of directors do not do. I am looking forward to seeing his version of *The Munster's* (2022) too.

Scotty McCoy: I am also excited to see that. I thank you Daeg for taking the time out of your schedule to do this interview with me.

Dee Wallace

"Cynthia Strode," *Halloween* (2007)

Scotty McCoy: There's a legend in the house (laughs)! Dee Wallace, it is so nice to connect with you and discuss some *Halloween* (1978) with you!
Dee Wallace: (Laughs) Thank you, Scotty. I am flattered about being called a legend, and I truly thank you for inviting me for an interview to discuss some topics about the Boogeyman himself.

Scotty McCoy: Absolutely! I couldn't be more honored to do this interview with you. On a more personal note, my dad is a huge fan of yours from way back to your time filming *ET: The Extra Terrestrial* (1982).
Dee Wallace: That's very sweet. Tell your dad thanks for being a fan and to "phone home" (laughs).

Scotty McCoy: (Laughs) I absolutely will do that! Your acting career is impeccable. Your résumé speaks for itself. But how did it all begin?
Dee Wallace: Oh my God! I was honestly born this way. Seriously (laughs)! I've been acting and dancing ever since I popped out of my mother's womb (laughs). But professionally, I taught a year of high school, and I wrote a letter to Hal Prince, and he flew me in so I could audition for *A Little Night Music* (1977) in New York, and I stayed and as they say, the rest is history. I started doing a lot of commercials and got all my union cards and stayed for two years, came out to Los Angeles, and just started booking gigs and different roles for various types of films right away.

Scotty McCoy: One letter to a director led to such an illustrious career?

Dee Wallace: What is life without risks and chances? I had nothing to lose and everything to gain, so I figured I'd roll the dice and apparently it paid off!

Scotty McCoy: It certainly has. Not to keep kissing your ass, but it's the truth. You are a legend in the acting industry, and I someday wish to obtain the superstardom that you have succeeded in doing.

Dee Wallace: Don't feed my ego, Scotty (laughs). But seriously, one piece of advice, Scotty. Never give up on your hopes and dreams. The sky's the limit and you reach for the stars, you'll end up achieving all you could ever hope and desire. You may fail along the way, that's normal and life. But if you learn from those failures and get back up and try again, you will, without a doubt, succeed at one of those attempts to make it!

Scotty McCoy: That's awesome advice, Dee. Thank you. What was your audition like for Rob Zombie's adaptation of *Halloween* (2007)?

Dee Wallace: Actually, I did not audition for *Halloween* (2007)!

Scotty McCoy: Wow, you are just that good (laughs). Care to elaborate on how you got cast in the film without auditioning?

Dee Wallace: Yeah, absolutely. Rob Zombie, the director, follows a lot of the horror icons. I might be so bold as to include myself in that (laughs). He saw me in *Cujo* (1983) and *The Howling* (1981) and loved my work. His team sent mine an offer and the script, of course. I also am a huge fan of Rob Zombie's from his work on *House of 1000 Corpses* (2003) and that entire series he worked on. He's really a genius and an icon in his own right. I just really wanted to work with him and it just kind of took on a life of its own and we got to improv a lot and it just was a great experience that I have no regret adding to my filmography.

Scotty McCoy: Speaking about Rob. How was he as a director?

Dee Wallace: Oh, he's great. He knew exactly what he wanted, but he also gives you so much leeway to bring in your own ideas and things like, "Oh, what if we did this?" Or "What if we did that?" Things of that nature. He didn't really mind if you stuck entirely to the script, if the premise of the film wasn't changed too much, so he encouraged improv, which is where you really get a lot of the magic on the screen because everybody is participating in the creativity and that's what makes a brilliant director. Because they give you that leeway and then it makes your job as an actor much more fun, easier, and less stressful.

Scotty McCoy: Your daughter on screen is, of course, Laurie Strode, and she's played by Scout Taylor-Compton. What was it like working with her?

Dee Wallace: Oh my gosh, Scout's like another daughter for me. We've become close friends and she's extremely talented. A very talented young lady. We just clicked right away, like instant chemistry. It really was like a mother-daughter relationship, but also equal actors working together. We had a ton of fun and came up with creative ideas together for our scenes that we shot together on trying something this way and that way and all possible ways to make the scenes more fun, relatable, and entertaining, all at the same time. I'm a big fan of hers, not just a friend, but also a fan. She has earned her spot in Hollywood and is a definite Scream Queen for sure.

Scotty McCoy: What was your most memorable moment while filming *Halloween* (2007)?

Dee Wallace: I must tell you two of them as they are definitely tied as memorable moments that I'll remember for the rest of my life. One of them is the scene where I'm sitting with my on-screen husband on the front steps. All the Halloween kids were walking by, and it was like two in the morning. We were both deathly ill with like 103° fevers. We were improvising pretty much the entire scene. I was just using a lot of the stuff from my daughter and what happened with my daughter on a lot of the Halloween's we shared. The other moment for me that is a very memorable one is something that happened off camera. I'm standing there with Rob and we're waiting for the guys to lighten everything up and I said to him, "Well, what was your favorite film this year?" and he responded back to me, "*Little Miss Sunshine* (2006)!" I looked at him and I went, "Oh Rob, don't tell anybody because it will totally blow your cover!" He just looked at me (laughs), but that's why I love him and working with him. He's super funny and just an all-around great guy to be around. He really brought me joy working on that set, and that story is something I'll always remember and laugh at when I think about it!

Scotty McCoy: (Laughs) That's hilarious. Too funny! Unfortunately, you had to die in the film, and it was just a simple neck snap, but weren't you supposed to have a different death in the film?
Dee Wallace: Actually, yes, I was. You want me to tell you what I was supposed to do?

Scotty McCoy: I sure do! Enlighten me and everyone reading this interview!
Dee Wallace: Originally, when I was killed by Michael, I would've been dying against a bookcase. But three weeks later, the producers called and said they need me to come back onto the set and I said to them that I already was killed off, and they said that Rob wants to kill me better than the way we initially shot. But yeah, instead of being thrown through the table, I was going to be thrown up against the bookcase.

Scotty McCoy: Interesting! Did you do your own stunts when you were brought back to be thrown through a table and walk us through the filming process of shooting your death scene?

Dee Wallace: Once I went back to the set, I would start off by crawling down the hallway. They had a stunt girl that went through the glass table. But after she goes through the glass table, it is just me and Tyler. This is where we were going to do the neck breaking scene. I had to keep telling Tyler that you can really put your arms around my neck. I knew I could hold onto his hand for the scene. He was just so gentle though, like a gentle giant.

Scotty McCoy: The stunt girl really did resemble you during the scene (laughs)!

Dee Wallace: (Laughs) From behind, yes. It was probably because of the wig she was wearing to mock my hair style and color. But if you look closely and pay attention, the entire stunt scene of going through the table is done from the side and behind the body because it's not really me and she doesn't look like me from the front, especially in the face (laughs).

Scotty McCoy: Were you uncomfortable doing the stunt yourself? Or did you just not want to do it? Would you have done it if asked?

Dee Wallace: I wasn't uncomfortable, it was more so the producers that were uncomfortable because their lead actor, who could get really hurt doing this stunt, which is a very true statement and a good point they made. I could've gotten hurt. I'm not a trained stuntwoman. I've taken classes in performing stunts, but I don't do them for a living like Tyler does. But if asked, I totally would've done my own stunt for the film as it does look like a lot of fun and then having the bragging rights after to be able to say, "I did this stunt!"

Scotty McCoy: I tend to agree though. You did the scene beautifully too and really built up the suspense that it was meant to have. Tyler Mane played the Boogeyman himself, Michael Myers. What was it like working with him?

Dee Wallace: He's such a sweetheart. I mean, as I said before, a true gentle giant. The funny thing is for playing a killer, he couldn't be any nicer, even if he tried.

Scotty McCoy: What was the best part about filming *Halloween* (2007)? And what was the worst?

Dee Wallace: Dear Lord, really putting me on the hot seat, Scotty (laughs). The worst part, hmm, honestly, I don't think there was a worst part other than being deathly ill while shooting half of my scenes. Otherwise, it was just super fun. Working with Rob Zombie was just a blast in and of itself. I loved knowing that on set I was always safe and taken care of. So, the best part would just be the fun and safety on set and how it really was a positive experience.

Scotty McCoy: That's amazing to hear! We know you had the porch scenes with your on-screen husband. You had the kitchen scenes with Scout. And that all ended up leading into your death scene. You weren't in the movie a whole lot but made a positive impact that your death ultimately hit close to home. But given the scenes you had to film, how long were you on set to film them all?

Dee Wallace: You know, I think if you put all of the scenes together that I filmed, including reshoots, which includes recreating my death scene entirely, I would say everything that I had to film was compressed into a full week of filming, at most.

Scotty McCoy: Nice! A week of Dee Wallace is an amazing week in my book!

Dee Wallace: (Laughs) Well, thank you for that compliment, Scotty.

Scotty McCoy: Not a problem at all. When you left the voicemail on the answering machine, was that included in the week of filming? How was all of that done? I'm assuming voiceover!

Dee Wallace: Actually, it wasn't a voiceover. It technically was, but it wasn't done with a boom mic and recorders. Rob wanted it to sound real and not a pre-recorded audio that everyone watching can tell was inserted into the film during post-production. It's easy to tell when something was recorded on a set and just placed in the spot it needs to be in. We authentically recorded the clip by having me call onto the phone line where an answering machine picked up and we left a genuine message on the answering machine as if it was our real machine.

Scotty McCoy: It's that simple, eh?

Dee Wallace: Easy as pie! Sometimes the best method of filmmaking is to make a scene seem authentic. It is just as easy as that and sometimes it is staring at you right in the face.

Scotty McCoy: Duly noted! Thank you so much Dee for your time. It's been a true honor to talk to you and discuss this iconic franchise and a very different take on the film that we hadn't seen before.

Dee Wallace: I truly thank you for asking me to be on. The funny thing is, as mentioned in emails to set this interview up, I am in hair and makeup for a movie as I was needed on set last minute and didn't want to cancel on you as we had this planned already, so I found a way to get both jobs done (laughs).

Scotty McCoy: I truly appreciate that too. It really was amazing of you to keep your commitment to me, and it's awesome that I can interview while you are on set and getting ready to film a movie. An absolute honor. I thank you, Dee. You have an amazing and wonderful rest of your day and break a leg on set!

Dee Wallace: Thank you, Scotty, and best wishes on your book. I am a fan of yours already!

Ken Foree

"Joe Grizzly," Halloween (2007)

Scotty McCoy: Wow! A legend for sure. Ken Foree, you have been in *Leatherface: The Texas Chainsaw Massacre 3* (1990), *The Devil's Rejects* (2005), and, of course, *Halloween* (2007). How are you doing, Ken?
Ken Foree: I am doing good, Scotty. Thank you so much for having me and interviewing me to discuss some interesting and classic films.

Scotty McCoy: Of course! The pleasure is all mine. You have one legendary career; can you tell us how it all started?
Ken Foree: I sure can! I got my start off Broadway in New York City. Strange story, I was involved with politics and community work. As a matter of fact, I started at the Walter Reed Organization. I was the assistant manager there for a theater in New York and we opened with *The Exorcist* (1973). I then went over to the Fine Arts side of things and I was part of a film festival with the producers of a film starring Gene Wilder. I later went to a few premieres, at one of which I got to meet Mel Brooks, Paul Newman, John Woodward, Eli Wallach, and a string of others. It was such a great time.

Scotty McCoy: That is really interesting. I always ask the celebrities on how they got their start because everyone had a different way on getting into the industry. But not everyone can say that they were in a *Halloween* (1978) film and killed by Michael Myers. How did you happen to get involved with Rob Zombie's *Halloween* (2007) film?
Ken Foree: I knew Rob from working with him previously in *The Devil's Rejects* (2005) and he asked me if I wanted a small cameo

role and have a gruesome death scene. Want to hear a funny story about that?

Scotty McCoy: Yeah, absolutely!

Ken Foree: So, I was drinking cheap liquor with a few buddies, and I ended up throwing snowballs at the security of the hotel I was staying at. We ran away and a big security guard was banging on our door an hour or so later. He threatened to throw me out and put me in jail and I ended up hurting my knee. Rob called me asking me to do this big stunt scene with Tyler and I told him I can't do that and told him the story of what happened, and he was like, "You hurt your knee, didn't you?" (Laughs)

Scotty McCoy: That is wild! So, did you still do your own stunt scene?

Ken Foree: Yes, I did. But it was not as big as it was meant to be.

Scotty McCoy: Was that a real bathroom you were filming the scene in?

Ken Foree: Yes and no. It was a real bathroom. However, it was built on a sound stage. It was built specifically for that scene. The walls that I got banged against was hard as a rock and I was limping for about a week after we filmed. Hell, I was limping before we filmed due to hurting my knee. I did try to hide it on screen, but I do not know how well it came off.

Scotty McCoy: The last question I do have for you, Ken, is your infamous line "I'm Joe Grizzly bitch!" How did that come about?

Ken Foree: (Laughs) I used to make insurance calls before I became an actor and someone answered the phone and said, "I'm (their name) bitch!" and hung up. So, I used that as inspiration for the scene and I believe it came out quite well for the scene!

Scotty McCoy: Thank you, Ken, for the interesting stories.

Ken Foree: Pleasure is all mine. Best of luck in all you do, brother!

Photo Gallery

All photographs by Kim Gottlieb Walker

Author, *On the Set with John Carpenter* (Titan Books, 2014)

H2: a bigger burn than expected

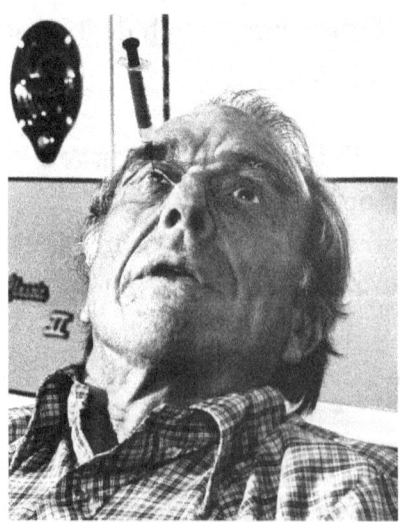

Needle in eye projection

Associate Producer Barry Bernardi, Debra Hill, and Rick Rosenthal

H2: Sound man Tommy Causey w Nancy Stephens and Donald Pleasance

H2: Joking shape on set

H2: Camera Crew: Dean Cundey, Ray Stella, and gaffer Mark Walthour with Rick Rosenthal

Trivia Section

Halloween (1978)

1. Who was the killer of *Halloween* (1978)?
    - a. Jason Voorhees
    - c. Freddy Krueger
    - b. Michael Myers
    - d. Mrs. Voorhees
2. Who directed *Halloween* (1978)?
    - a. Debra Hill
    - c. Sean S. Cunningham
    - b. Wes Craven
    - d. John Carpenter
3. What year did Michael kill Judith?
    - a. 1963
    - c. 1965
    - b. 1964
    - d. 1962
4. Who played Michael Myers?
    - a. Nick Castle
    - c. Dick Warlock
    - b. Christopher Durand
    - d. George P. Wilbur
5. Who was the final girl of *Halloween* (1978)?
    - a. Annie Brackett
    - c. Laurie Strode
    - b. Lynda Van Der Klok
    - d. Jamie Lloyd
6. Who played Dr. Sam Loomis?
    - a. Charles Cyphers
    - c. Donald Pleasence
    - b. John Saxon
    - d. Peter Boyle
7. What was the budget for *Halloween* (1978)?
    - a. $550,000
    - c. $300,000
    - b. $275,000
    - d. $425,000

8. How much did *Halloween* (1978) gross at the box office?
    a. $75 million
    c. $50 million
    b. $70 million
    d. $25 million
9. How old was Michael when he killed Judith?
    a. Five
    c. Seven
    b. Twelve
    d. Six
10. When was *Halloween* (1978) released theatrically?
    a. October 31, 1978
    c. October 25, 1978
    b. October 30, 1978
    d. October 28, 1978
11. What was the body count in *Halloween* (1978)?
    a. Six
    c. Three
    b. Five
    d. Four
12. What is the address of the Myers house?
    a. 45 Lampkin Lane
    c. 43 Lampkin Lane
    b. 50 Lampkin Lane
    d. 47 Lampkin Lane
13. What was the tagline for *Halloween* (1978)?
    a. The Night HE Came Home
    b. The Night HE Returned Home
    c. The Night When HE Came Home
    d. The Night HE Came Home to Kill
14. What does Lynda say when she reveals her breasts to Michael Myers, thinking he was Bob?
    a. See anything you like
    b. See anything you would like to touch
    c. See anything you want
    d. See anything you need

15. What was the story of Michael Myers?

a. Yeah, you know every town has something like this happen . . . I remember over in Russellville, old Charlie Bowles, about fifteen years ago . . . One night, he finished dinner, and he excused himself from the table. He went out to the garage and got himself a hacksaw. Then he went back into the house, kissed his wife and his two children goodbye, and then he proceeded to . . . .

b. I- I- I watched him for fifteen years, sitting in a room, staring at a wall, not seeing the wall, looking past the wall – looking at this night, inhumanly patient, waiting for some secret, silent alarm to trigger him off. Death has come to your little town, Sheriff. Now you can either ignore it, or you can help me to stop it.

c. I met him, fifteen years ago; I was told there was nothing left; no reason, no conscience, no understanding; and even the most rudimentary sense of life or death, of good or evil, right or wrong. I met this six-year-old child, with this blank, pale, emotionless face, and the blackest eyes . . . the devil's eyes. I spent eight years trying to reach him, and then another seven trying to keep him locked up because I realized that what was living behind that boy's eyes was purely and simply . . . evil.

d. He was my patient for fifteen years. He became an obsession with me until I realized that there was nothing within him, neither conscious nor reason that was . . . even remotely human. An hour ago, I stood up and fired six shots into him and then he just got up and walked away. I am talking about the real possibility that he is STILL OUT THERE!

16. Who was Annie babysitting?

a. Tommy Doyle
b. Jamie Lloyd
c. Lindsay Wallace
d. Lonnie Elam

17. Jamie Lee Curtis is the daughter of Janet Leigh. Janet is known for her role in what horror film?
    a. *Psycho* (1960)
    b. *The Birds* (1963)
    c. *Rosemary's Baby* (1968)
    d. *Night of the Living Dead* (1968)
18. What does Lynda do as an extracurricular activity in school?
    a. Softball
    b. Basketball
    c. Cheerleading
    d. Volleyball
19. What is the name of the mental hospital where Michael Myers was locked up?
    a. Samson's Grove Sanitarium
    b. Scott's Grove Sanitarium
    c. Smith's Grove Sanitarium
    d. Simpson's Grove Sanitarium
20. What was the setting of *Halloween* (1978)?
    a. Chicago, Illinois
    b. Bloomington, Illinois
    c. Springfield, Illinois
    d. Haddonfield, Illinois
21. What Halloween costume did Michael Myers wear when he killed his sister?
    a. Vampire
    b. Clown
    c. Magician
    d. Police Officer
22. When Sheriff Brackett scared Laurie, what did he say?
    a. It's Halloween, everyone is entitled to one good jump
    b. It's Halloween, everyone is entitled to one good scare
    c. It's Halloween, everyone is entitled to one good scream
    d. It's Halloween, everyone is entitled to one good fright
23. Which book did Laurie forget at school?
    a. Math
    b. English
    c. Chemistry
    d. History

24. What was Annie and Laurie smoking in the car?
    a. Cigarette
    b. Pipe
    c. Marijuana
    d. Cigar

25. What character name is Michael Myers credited as?
    a. The Figure
    b. The Illusion
    c. The Shape
    d. The Evil

26. What is the name of the nurse who works with Dr. Loomis?
    a. Marion Kaufman
    b. Marion Billings
    c. Marion Klingerman
    d. Marion Chambers

27. How many times did Dr. Loomis shoot Michael?
    a. Six
    b. Three
    c. Five
    d. Four

28. What name was on the matchbox?
    a. Red Rooster Lounge
    b. Red Rabbit Lounge
    c. Red Robin Lounge
    d. Red Roadrunner Lounge

29. Who created the famous theme song of *Halloween* (1978)?
    a. Debra Hill
    b. Harry Manfredini
    c. John Carpenter
    d. Moustapha Akkad

30. Who played the arm of Michael Myers when he killed his sister?
    a. Ari Lehman
    b. Debra Hill
    c. Will Sandin
    d. Malek Akkad

31. Every time Tommy sees Michael Myers; what does he say he saw?
    a. Michael Myers
    b. The Boogeyman
    c. A Monster
    d. A Stalker

32. Who did Laurie say she'd rather go to the prom with?
    a. Ben Tramer
    b. Paul Freedman
    c. Ted Hollister
    d. Bob Simms

33. Who wrote the *Halloween* (1978) screenplay?
    a. John Carpenter and Moustapha Akkad
    b. John Carpenter and Donald Pleasence
    c. John Carpenter and Debra Hill
    d. John Carpenter and Nick Castle

34. Who did Annie say was staring at Laurie?
    a. Mr. Riddle
    b. Ben Tramer
    c. Michael Myers
    d. Mr. Strode

35. Who was the doctor that Dr. Loomis was speaking to about Michael's escape?
    a. Dr. Wynn
    b. Dr. Hoffman
    c. Dr. Mixter
    d. Dr. Whale

36. How many dogs did Michael Myers kill?
    a. Three
    b. Two
    c. One
    d. None

37. What four textbooks did Lynda say she always forgets?
    a. Chemistry, Math, English, and Spanish
    b. Chemistry, Math, English, and German
    c. Chemistry, Math, English, and French
    d. Chemistry, Math, English, and Latin

38. Who played the voice of Paul?
    a. John Carpenter
    b. Nick Castle
    c. Tony Moran
    d. David Kyle

39. Who was Laurie babysitting?

    a. Tommy Doyle   c. Lindsay Wallace

    b. Jamie Lloyd   d. Lonnie Elam

40. What does Laurie's father do for a living?

    a. Realtor   c. Banker

    b. Insurance Agent   d. Businessman

41. What three comic books did Tommy have that Laurie looked at?

    a. Laser Man, Neutron Man, and Arachnid Man

    b. Laser Man, Neutron Man, and Tarantula Man

    c. Laser Man, Neutron Man, and Anaconda Man

    d. Laser Man, Neutron Man, and Cobra Man

42. Who did Annie say Ben Tramer went out drinking with?

    a. Paul Freedman   c. Bob Simms

    b. Mike Godfrey   d. Bud Scarlotti

43. How old is Mr. Riddle?

    a. 88   c. 85

    b. 89   d. 87

44. Who did Lynda think was driving the car that Michael Myers was driving?

    a. Ben Tramer   c. Devon Graham

    b. Paul Freedman   d. Mike Godfrey

45. What does Dr. Loomis always call Michael Myers?

    a. Satan   c. Evil

    b. Devil   d. Demon

46. What did Annie spill on her clothes?

    a. Wine   c. Beer

    b. Butter   d. Juice

47. What was the name of Lindsay's dog?

   a. Lester

   b. Sundae

   c. Max

   d. Muffin

48. What does Annie hate in a guy that drives?

   a. No Sense of Humor

   b. No Style

   c. No Personality

   d. No Intelligence

49. What horror film was Lindsay watching while Annie was babysitting her?

   a. *Psycho* (1960)

   b. *The Texas Chainsaw Massacre* (1974)

   c. *The Thing from Another World* (1951)

   d. *Young Frankenstein* (1974)

50. What did Annie say kills, when she yelled at the car Michael Myers was driving?

   a. Acid

   b. Ecstasy

   c. Speed

   d. Crack

51. Who did Annie say Laurie should ask to the dance?

   a. Ben Tramer

   b. Devon Graham

   c. Dick Baxter

   d. Mike Godfrey

52. What two things did Annie say she plans on doing with Lindsay Wallace?

   a. Eating Popcorn and Watching *The Thing from Another World* (1951)

   b. Eating Popcorn and Watching *Psycho* (1960)

   c. Eating Popcorn and Watching *Dracula* (1931)

   d. Eating Popcorn and Watching *Dr. Dementia* (1951)

53. Annie said Laurie would always make a fabulous what?

   a. Babysitter
   c. Cheerleader
   b. Girl Scout
   d. Housewife

54. Who was Michael Myers' sister that he killed as a child?

   a. Judith Myers
   c. Joan Myers
   b. Jenny Myers
   d. Jillian Myers

55. What was taken from the cemetery by Michael Myers that showed he is back to finish what he started?

   a. Judith's Tombstone
   c. Judith's Flowers
   b. Judith's Corpse
   d. Judith's Casket

56. What did Lynda tell Bob to get her after they finished making love?

   a. Beer
   c. Soda
   b. Juice
   d. Water

57. What was stolen from the store?

   a. Halloween Masks, Knives, and Guns
   b. Halloween Masks, Knives, and Rope
   c. Halloween Masks, Knives, and Newspapers
   d. Halloween Masks, Knives, and Candy

58. What was the name of Judith's boyfriend who was seen at the beginning of *Halloween* (1978)?

   a. Donald Hodges
   c. Daniel Hodges
   b. Derek Hodges
   d. Dillon Hodges

59. What were the names of Michael's parents?

   a. Derrick and Ellen Myers
   c. Donald and Edith Myers
   b. Darren and Edna Myers
   d. Dennis and Eleanor Myers

60. Who did Michael kill on his way to Haddonfield?
    a. Train Conductor   c. Truck Driver
    b. Mechanic   d. Hitchhiker
61. What was Tommy holding in his arms when he was being bullied at school?
    a. Textbooks   c. Candy
    b. Halloween Mask   d. Pumpkin
62. What was the name of the store that was robbed?
    a. Noonan's Hardware Store   c. Nicholson's Hardware Store
    b. Nightingale's Hardware Store d. Nichol's Hardware Store
63. How does Michael kill Lester?
    a. Kicks Him   c. Stabs Him
    b. Breaks His Neck   d. Strangles Him
64. What was the first name of the kid that Dr. Loomis whispered to get away from the Myers house?
    a. Lance   c. Lenny
    b. Larry   d. Lonnie
65. When Lynda calls Laurie and Michael begins choking her, Laurie thinks it is Annie calling her. Laurie said to her "alright Annie, first I get your famous chewing, now I get your famous…" what?
    a. Screeching   c. Squealing
    b. Screaming   d. Squeaking
66. Who did Sheriff Brackett blame on robbing the store?
    a. Michael Myers   c. Kids
    b. Thieves   d. Lynda and Bob
67. *Halloween* (1978) is classified as what kind of horror film?
    a. Psychological Thriller   c. Sociological Suspense
    b. Mentally Emotional Mystery d. Sophisticated Slasher

68. What state has a Haddonfield in it that was the inspiration for the naming of the fictitious town?
    a. Pennsylvania
    c. New Jersey
    b. California
    d. New York
69. Who played the role of Lynda Van Der Klok?
    a. Nancy Loomis
    c. Jamie Lee Curtis
    b. P.J. Soles
    d. Kyle Richards
70. After Michael Myers was shot by Dr. Loomis, what happened to him to end the film?
    a. He was gone
    c. He sat up
    b. He died
    d. He walked away
71. Whose corpse did Michael have on the bed with his sister's tombstone above the corpse?
    a. Lynda Van Der Klok
    c. Annie Brackett
    b. Bob Simms
    d. Judith's Corpse
72. Whose house did Laurie tell Tommy and Lindsay to go to and call for help?
    a. McKenzie's
    c. McCoy's
    b. McCormick's
    d. McDonald's
73. Who played the role of Sheriff Brackett?
    a. Donald Pleasence
    c. Charles Cyphers
    b. Brian Andrews
    d. John Michael Graham
74. What did Laurie say she was going to do with Tommy?
    a. Watch Horror Movies
    c. Go Trick-or-Treating
    b. Play Pranks
    d. Carve Jack-o'-Lanterns

75. What did Laurie say to herself when she saw Tommy trick-or-treating?

   a. I thought you outgrew Halloween

   b. I thought you outgrew superstition

   c. I thought you outgrew tradition

   d. I thought you outgrew trick-or-treating

76. What were the names of the actor and actress to play the roles of Tommy Doyle and Lindsay Wallace?

   a. Brian Andrews and Kyle Richards

   b. John Michael Graham and P.J. Soles

   c. Donald Pleasence and Jamie Lee Curtis

   d. Charles Cyphers and Nancy Loomis

77. Who played the role of Annie Brackett?

   a. Sandy Johnson   c. P.J. Soles

   b. Nancy Kyes   d. Jamie Lee Curtis

78. What word did Lynda always say?

   a. Radical   c. Dude

   b. Totally   d. Definitely

79. Why did Lynda tell Bob to not rip her blouse?

   a. It was a rare piece of clothing   c. It was expensive

   b. It was her grandmother's   d. It was her favorite blouse

80. What time did Lynda say to Laurie that the dance started?

   a. 9 p.m.   c. 8 p.m.

   b. 7 p.m.   d. 10 p.m.

81. Where did Paul drag Annie into to tell her he has been grounded?

   a. Janitor's Closet c. Locker Room

   b. His Van   d. Boy's Bathroom

82. Where did Annie get stuck when she was washing her clothes?
    a. In the laundry room's window
    b. Underneath the door when it fell on her
    c. In between the washer and dryer
    d. She didn't get stuck

83. What did Annie say Lester found when he stopped barking?
    a. Someone else to hate   c. A dog bone
    b. A way into the house   d. A hot date

84. Who played the role of Bob Simms?
    a. John Michael Graham   c. Brian Andrews
    b. Nick Castle   d. Donald Pleasence

85. What did Michael kill Judith with?
    a. A pair of scissors   c. A fork
    b. A glass shard   d. A kitchen knife

86. What did Sheriff Brackett say could've eaten the dog in the Myers house?
    a. Skunk   c. Rat
    b. Opossum   d. Birds

87. In the living room, what did Laurie stab Michael in the neck with?
    a. Knife   c. Clothes Hanger
    b. Knitting Needle d. Fork

88. What did Laurie call Annie and Lynda in the following sentence: Alright _____ joke's over?
    a. Pranksters   c. Morons
    b. Meatheads   d. Idiots

89. What was the song lyric that Laurie sang when she dropped the key off at the Myers house?

   a. We all live in the yellow submarine

   b. Hello, is it me you're looking for

   c. I wish I had you all alone, just the two of us

   d. Who you gonna call, ghostbusters

90. How many miles away did Dr. Wynn tell Dr. Loomis Haddonfield was from Smith's Grove?

   a. 100 Miles
   c. 150 Miles

   b. 200 Miles
   d. 250 Miles

91. What grade did Laurie tell Tommy that Lonnie Elam probably won't get out of?

   a. 4th Grade
   c. 5th Grade

   b. 6th Grade
   d. 7th Grade

92. What did Laurie tell the teacher that Samuel thought fate was like?

   a. Religion
   c. Politics

   b. Historical
   d. Natural Element

93. Who played Michael Myers as a child in the beginning of the film?

   a. Erik Preston
   c. Billy Warlock

   b. Adam Gunn
   d. Will Sandin

94. When is Michael Myers' birthday?

   a. October 31, 1957
   c. October 30, 1957

   b. October 19, 1957
   d. October 2, 1957

95. After Dr. Loomis shot Michael, Michael fell off of what?

   a. Porch
   c. Balcony

   b. Steps
   d. Roof

96. As the movie ended, what could be heard from Michael that signified that he was still alive?

    a. Michael's deep breathing

    b. Michael humming the *Halloween* (1978) theme song

    c. Michael laughing

    d. Michael groaning and moaning

97. How did Laurie free herself from being strangled by Michael?

    a. Stabbing him in the neck with his knife

    b. Dr. Loomis showed up and distracted him

    c. Unmasking him

    d. Stabbed him in the eye

98. Who played Michael Myers during the closet scene?

    a. Nick Castle   c. John Carpenter

    b. Tony Moran   d. Tommy Lee Wallace

99. What is Michael's middle name?

    a. Audrey   c. Allan

    b. Andrew   d. Albert

100. Who played the role of Laurie Strode?

    a. P.J. Soles   c. Jamie Lee Curtis

    b. Sandy Johnson   d. Nancy Loomis

Halloween II (1981)

1. What is the story of Samhain as told by Dr. Loomis?

   a. He was my patient for fifteen years. He became an obsession with me until I realized that there was nothing within him, neither conscious nor reason that was . . . even remotely human. An hour ago, I stood up and fired six shots into him and then he just got up and walked away. I am talking about the real possibility that he is STILL OUT THERE!

   b. I- I- I watched him for fifteen years, sitting in a room, staring at a wall, not seeing the wall, looking past the wall – looking at this night, inhumanly patient, waiting for some secret, silent alarm to trigger him off. Death has come to your little town, Sheriff. Now you can either ignore it, or you can help me to stop it.

   c. In order to appease the gods, the Druid priests held fire rituals. Prisoners of war, criminals, the insane, animals . . . were . . . burned alive in baskets. By observing the way they died, the Druids believed they could see omens of the future. Two thousand years later, we've come no further. Samhain isn't evil spirits. It isn't goblins, ghosts or witches. It's the unconscious mind. We're all afraid of the dark inside ourselves.

   d. I met him, fifteen years ago; I was told there was nothing left; no reason, no conscience, no understanding; and even the most rudimentary sense of life or death, of good or evil, right or wrong. I met this six-year-old child, with this blank, pale, emotionless face, and the blackest eyes . . . the devil's eyes. I spent eight years trying to reach him, and then another seven trying to keep him locked up because I realized that what was living behind that boy's eyes was purely and simply . . . evil.

2. Who was the final girl of *Halloween II* (1981)?

   a. Jill Franco   c. Laurie Strode

   b. Janet Marshall   d. Karen Bailey

3. What was the name of the hospital?

   a. Haddonfield General   c. Haddonfield Memorial Hospital

   b. Haddonfield Clinic   d. Haddonfield University Hospital

4. What was the budget of *Halloween II* (1981)?

   a. $2.3 million   c. $2.5 million

   b. $2.7 million   d. $2.9 million

5. Who directed *Halloween II* (1981)?

   a. Debra Hill   c. Rick Rosenthal

   b. John Carpenter   d. Tommy Lee Wallace

6. When was *Halloween II* (1981) released theatrically?

   a. October 30, 1981   c. October 31, 1981

   b. October 29, 1981   d. October 25, 1981

7. What was the name of Laurie's father?

   a. Michael Strode   c. Matthew Strode

   b. Morgan Strode   d. Mason Strode

8. Which actress portrayed Nurse Jill Franco?

   a. Pamela Susan Shoop   c. Ana Alicia

   b. Gloria Gifford   d. Tawny Moyer

9. What are the names of the two EMTs that took Laurie to the hospital?

   a. Gary Hunt and Leigh Brackett

   b. Jimmy Lloyd and Budd Scarlotti

   c. Frederick Mixter and Ben Tramer

   d. Sam Loomis and Mr. Garrett

10. Which character on *Days of our Lives* (1965) did the young boy that was holding the boom box portray years after the release of *Halloween II* (1981)?

    a. Max Brady   c. Frankie Brady

    b. Shawn Douglas Brady d. Rex Brady

11. How old is Michael Myers?

    a. Twenty   c. Twenty-Two

    b. Twenty-One   d. Twenty-Three

12. What is the name of the dentist who checked the teeth and gums of the charred corpse?

    a. Gabriel   c. Gerry

    b. Graham   d. Garrison

13. In the beginning of the film, which character from the first film's neighbor went to check what the commotion was after Dr. Loomis shot Michael Myers?

    a. Lindsay Wallace   c. Annie Brackett

    b. Laurie Strode   d. Tommy Doyle

14. When Jimmy brought Laurie to the hospital, where did Nurse Jill say Dr. Mixter was at?

    a. Country Club   c. His Office

    b. Halloween Party   d. Staff Meeting

15. In the television version of the film, the Marshall wasn't killed with his throat slit like in the theatrical version of the film. How was he killed?

    a. Stabbed in the back c. Stabbed in the stomach

    b. Stabbed in the eye   d. Stabbed in the chest

16. What did Jimmy slip on when he was looking for help in finding Laurie?
    a. Water
    b. Juice
    c. Blood
    d. Floor Wax
17. Who does Karen give a ride home to before she goes to work at the hospital?
    a. Debra
    b. Dora
    c. Dina
    d. Darcy
18. According to Karen, where is Eddie Lee at?
    a. Chicago
    b. Springfield
    c. Russellville
    d. Smith's Grove
19. Who did the governor send with the Marshall to find Dr. Loomis just in case he found Michael Myers?
    a. Dr. Wynn
    b. Dr. Hoffman
    c. Dr. Mixter
    d. Marion Chambers
20. Which doctor from Smith's Grove Sanitarium is afraid the melee caused by Michael Myers will jeopardize the whole rehabilitation program?
    a. Dr. Mixter
    b. Dr. Rogers
    c. Dr. Wynn
    d. Dr. Hoffman
21. Of the characters killed in the first film, which character's corpse is shown in *Halloween II* (1981)?
    a. Lynda Van Der Klok
    b. Judith Myers
    c. Annie Brackett
    d. Bob Simms
22. Nurse Janet said who saw Michael Myers when coming to work?
    a. Jenna
    b. Joanie
    c. Julie
    d. Jessica

23. Which actress portrayed Nurse Karen Bailey?

   a. Gloria Gifford
   c. Tawny Moyer
   b. Pamela Susan Shoop
   d. Ana Alicia

24. Who was mistaken for Michael Myers, got killed, and was later revealed to not have been Michael?

   a. Eddie Lee
   c. Ben Tramer
   b. Mike Godfrey
   d. Paul Freedman

25. What did Bud tell Jimmy the first rule about being a paramedic is?

   a. Never get involved with nurses
   b. Never get involved with killers
   c. Never get involved with coworkers
   d. Never get involved with patients

26. How much did *Halloween II* (1981) gross at the box office?

   a. $25.5 million
   c. $25.1 million
   b. $25.2 million
   d. $25.8 million

27. Whose body did Jimmy find when he slipped?

   a. Mrs. Alves
   c. Mr. Garrett
   b. Nurse Jill Franco
   d. Dr. Mixter

28. Where did Nurse Janet say Julie saw Michael Myers at?

   a. Behind the Haddonfield Drive In
   b. Behind the Lost River Drive In
   c. Behind the Halloween Memorial Drive In
   d. Behind the Haddonfield Outskirts Drive In

29. Which actress portrayed the head nurse of the hospital, Mrs. Alves?

   a. Tawny Moyer
   c. Gloria Gifford
   b. Ana Alicia
   d. Pamela Susan Shoop

30. In this television version of the film, who is revealed to be alive and okay in the hospital with Laurie Strode?
   a. Sam Loomis
   c. Jimmy Lloyd
   b. Mrs. Alves
   d. Dr. Mixter

31. What was the last name of the elderly couple in the beginning of the film?
   a. Englewood
   c. Emery
   b. Everett
   d. Elrod

32. What did Dr. Loomis say "Samhain" translated to?
   a. Lord of the Sacrifices
   c. Lord of the Rituals
   b. Lord of the Dead
   d. Lord of the Night

33. What is the name of Jimmy's brother?
   a. Zachary
   c. Ziggy
   b. Zeke
   d. Zorro

34. Before blowing up the room, what two substances does Dr. Loomis fill the room with as a distraction to allow Laurie to escape right?
   a. Ether and Oxygen Gas
   b. Ether and Carbon Monoxide
   c. Ether and Helium
   d. Ether and Carbon Dioxide

35. Who did Michael first kill in *Halloween II* (1981)?
   a. Alice Martin
   c. Mr. Garrett
   b. Nurse Karen Bailey
   d. Nurse Janet Marshall

36. What major twist was introduced in this film?

   a. Michael Myers is controlled by the curse of the thorn

   b. Michael Myers can only be stopped, but never killed

   c. Michael Myers is the brother of Laurie Strode

   d. Michael Myers is only able to kill on Halloween night

37. Which of the following actors portrayed Michael Myers in *Halloween II* (1981)?

   a. Nick Castle   c. Tom Morga

   b. Dick Warlock   d. Christopher Durand

38. Years after the release of *Halloween II* (1981), the actor who portrayed Dr. Mixter had a recurring role in which television sitcom?

   a. *Seinfeld* (1989)   c. *Everybody Loves Raymond* (1996)

   b. *The King of Queens* (1998)   d. *Friends* (1994)

39. What is the date that the film is set in?

   a. October 31, 1981   c. October 31, 1978

   b. October 31, 1980   d. October 31, 1979

40. What did Dr. Mixter have in his eye that described the way Michael killed him?

   a. Scalpel   c. Syringe

   b. Pen   d. Nail

41. Which actress portrayed Nurse Janet Marshall?

   a. Ana Alicia   c. Pamela Susan Shoop

   b. Tawny Moyer   d. Gloria Gifford

42. After Sheriff Brackett is given time to grieve after the death of his daughter, who is put in charge of finding Michael Myers?

   a. Gary Hunt   c. Dr. Loomis

   b. The Governor   d. The Marshall

43. When Sheriff Brackett said to Dr. Loomis that he let Michael Myers out, Dr. Loomis responded by saying he didn't let him out but gave orders for him to be what?

   a. Committed   c. Evaluated
   b. Confined   d. Restrained

44. The first patrolman told Gary Hunt that the Myers House is empty and that he also covered all of what part of town?

   a. North   c. South
   b. East   d. West

45. Upon seeing Karen, Budd sang his version of what song?

   a. "Amazing Grace"   c. "Purple Rain"
   b. "Call Me Maybe"   d. "Jailhouse Rock"

46. Dr. Mixter asks Nurse Janet Marshall to get him some more what?

   a. Bandages   c. Donuts
   b. Coffee   d. Syringes

47. Karen told Darcy to go ask for a ride from whom?

   a. Ben Tramer   c. Alice Martin
   b. Eddie Lee   d. Janet Marshall

48. When Michael Myers killed Nurse Janet Marshall, what did it cause in her brain by injecting her with a syringe of air?

   a. Aneurysm   c. Embolism
   b. Catheter   d. Immobilization

49. What did Michael Myers burn and eventually drown Karen in?

   a. Swimming Pool   c. Shower
   b. Therapy Tub   d. Jacuzzi

50. How did Michael Myers kill Mrs. Alves?

   a. He slit her throat with a scalpel

   b. He strapped her to a surgical table and drained her blood with a catheter

   c. He filled her head with air from a syringe

   d. He hit her in the head with the claw of a hammer

51. Whose corpse did Laurie Strode find?

   a. Dr. Mixter   c. Mrs. Alves

   b. Mr. Garrett   d. Nurse Karen Bailey

52. What jumped out of the dumpster when Mr. Garrett was looking for a trespasser?

   a. Rabbit   c. Cat

   b. Dog   d. Rat

53. Who or what was responsible for sealing the records of Laurie Strode?

   a. Her parent's   c. The court

   b. The Governor   d. The state

54. When Nurse Jill Franco went to get help, why couldn't she leave the hospital?

   a. The cars' tires were slashed and wouldn't start up

   b. The cars in the parking lot were damaged upon repair

   c. The cars' gas was completely drained

   d. The cars in the parking lot were vandalized and thus scared her back into the hospital

55. What did the dentist say the charred corpse had nothing of?

   a. Gum Disease   c. Cavities

   b. Damaged Nerves   d. Fillings

56. What was Laurie going into that alerted Nurse Janet to go and find Dr. Mixter?

   a. Seizure
   c. Coma
   b. Shock
   d. Hypertension

57. What did Michael steal from the elderly couple?

   a. Sandwich
   c. Radio
   b. Kitchen Knife
   d. Halloween Mask

58. The actor who played Michael Myers in *Halloween II* (1981) also played what other minor role in the film?

   a. Medic
   c. Patrolman #3
   b. Announcer
   d. Producer

59. What was the name of the kid with the boom box?

   a. Randy
   c. Tommy
   b. Craig
   d. Billy

60. What was the tagline for *Halloween II* (1981)?

   a. The Continuation of the Night HE Came Home
   b. The Second Part of the Night HE Came Home
   c. More of the Night HE Came Home
   d. The Aftermath of the Night HE Came Home

61. Who were the two producers of *Halloween II* (1981)?

   a. John Carpenter and Debra Hill
   b. Moustapha and Malek Akkad
   c. Rick Rosenthal and Tommy Lee Wallace
   d. Dean Cundey and Mark Goldblatt

62. What time did Ben Tramer leave the Halloween party when his friends came to Gary Hunt with concern of his whereabouts?

   a. 11 p.m.
   c. 10 p.m.
   b. 9 p.m.
   d. 12 a.m.

63. How many years had it been since the anniversary of Michael Myers killing his sister?

   a. Thirteen Years
   c. Fifteen Years

   b. Ten Years
   d. Sixteen Years

64. How old did Gary Hunt say he was the night Michael Myers killed his sister?

   a. Fifteen
   c. Thirteen

   b. Fourteen
   d. Sixteen

65. As Laurie is in the ambulance and being taken away, what was she having flashbacks of?

   a. Michael Myers attacking her
   c. The bodies of her friends

   b. Michael Myers' burning body
   d. Dr. Loomis shooting Michael

66. When Gary Hunt asks the patrolman what the count is so far, what number does he respond with?

   a. Eleven
   c. Nine

   b. Ten
   d. Thirteen

67. Which child actor played Michael Myers as a young boy in *Halloween II* (1981)?

   a. Brian Andrews
   c. Will Sandin

   b. Adam Gunn
   d. Billy Warlock

68. Where does the film start off?

   a. Laurie Strode being rushed to the hospital

   b. Michael Myers escaping into a dark alley

   c. Directly after the end of the first film

   d. Dr. Loomis calling the police

69. What is similar about the death of Mr. Garrett in *Halloween II* (1981) compared to the death of Deputy Winslow in *Friday the 13th Part II* (1981)?

   a. Both are officers of the law that were killed with a hammer claw to the head

   b. Both are officers of the law that were driving cop cars before their death

   c. Both are officers of the law that found their killers' homes before they died

   d. Both are officers of the law that were killed and had their bodies part of the memorial for deceased family members

70. How late was Nurse Karen Bailey to work at the hospital?

   a. Ten Minutes   c. One Hour

   b. Fifteen Minutes   d. Thirty Minutes

71. Why did Mrs. Elrod scream?

   a. From the horror movie her husband was watching

   b. She saw blood on her cutting board

   c. Her husband was found dead

   d. There was a dead dog on her porch

72. What part of the hospital does Nurse Karen work in?

   a. Intensive Care Unit   c. Burn Center

   b. Coronary Care Unit   d. Maternity Ward

73. Where did Michael Myers leave clues that Dr. Loomis ended up finding?

   a. Myers House   c. Elementary School

   b. Haddonfield Memorial Hospital   d. Police Station

74. How many times did Dr. Loomis shoot Michael in the hospital?
    a. Six   c. Five
    b. Four   d. Three
75. Where did Laurie shoot Michael when he wounded Dr. Loomis?
    a. In the head   c. In his eyes
    b. In the stomach   d. In the groin
76. What room in the hospital did Dr. Loomis and Laurie Strode lure Michael into for the official "kill"?
    a. Operating Room   c. Waiting Room
    b. Basement   d. Physical Therapy Room
77. Where did Laurie Strode run from Michael to narrowly escape him before heading to the parking lot?
    a. Boiler Room   c. Break Room
    b. Recovery Room   d. Cardiology Room
78. Who was wheeling Laurie Strode in the wheelchair towards the ambulance at the end of the film?
    a. Dr. Loomis   c. Gary Hunt
    b. Jimmy Lloyd   d. Marion Chambers
79. What did Michael Myers stab Nurse Jill Franco in the back with to kill her?
    a. Syringe   c. Scalpel
    b. Knife   d. Spear
80. What type of officer was Mr. Garrett?
    a. Police Officer   c. Security Guard
    b. Sheriff   d. Deputy

81. What made Dr. Loomis think that Ben Tramer was Michael Myers?

   a. He was walking like he was injured

   b. He had blood on his clothes

   c. He was wearing Michael's mask

   d. He was holding a knife

82. What does Michael do when he first arrives at the hospital?

   a. Kill Mr. Garrett   c. Shut off the lights

   b. Cut the phone lines d. Attack Laurie Strode

83. *Halloween II* (1981) was supposed to be the last film to be about what?

   a. The last film of the *Halloween* (1978) franchise

   b. The last film based on Michael Myers and the town of Haddonfield

   c. The last film to feature Dr. Loomis

   d. The last film in the franchise to feature John Carpenter behind-the-scenes

84. Who ordered Dr. Loomis to be sent back to Smith's Grove?

   a. Marion Chambers   c. The Marshall

   b. The Governor   d. Dr. Wynn

85. What did Marion Chambers use to call for help to the hospital?

   a. The Marshall's Walkie Talkie   c. The Marshall's Two-Way Radio

   b. The Marshall's Phone   d. The Marshall's PDA

86. How does Dr. Loomis get the Marshall to turn around and drive to the hospital?

   a. Threatens to kill him   c. Fires a warning shot

   b. Blackmails him   d. Pleads him to help save Laurie

87. What are the last words that Dr. Loomis says to Michael before blowing them both up?

    a. Time to burn, Michael   c. It's time, Michael

    b. Go to Hell, Michael   d. Hell awaits, Michael

88. What type of gun does Dr. Loomis have on him during his hunt for Michael?

    a. Pistol   c. Revolver

    b. Rifle   d. Shotgun

89. What three curse words does Nurse Janet Marshall say Bud always says?

    a. Hell, shit, and damn   c. Ass, bitch, and bastard

    b. Fuck, Christ, and cunt   d. Slut, whore, and ho

90. What store by the mall did Janet say Julie saw Michael at when she stopped by the light?

    a. Shop and Bag   c. Shop and Leave

    b. Shop and Pay   d. Shop and Stop

91. What does Dr. Loomis say to Gary Hunt about Michael being like some kind of animal?

    a. In order to appease the gods, the Druid priests held fire rituals. Prisoners of war, criminals, the insane, animals… were… burned alive in baskets. By observing the way they died, the Druids believed they could see omens of the future. Two thousand years later, we've come no further. Samhain isn't evil spirits. It isn't goblins, ghosts or witches. It's the unconscious mind. We're all afraid of the dark inside ourselves.

    b. He was my patient for fifteen years. He became an obsession with me until I realized that there was nothing within him, neither conscious nor reason that was… even remotely human. An hour ago, I stood up and fired six shots into him and then he just got up and walked away. I am talking about the real possibility that he is STILL OUT THERE!

   c. I ought to handcuff you to the wheel, but I have a feeling I'm gonna need you in there. Can I trust you?

   d. I shot him 6 times! I shot him in the heart – but... HE'S NOT HUMAN!

92. What were the lyrics of "Amazing Grace" that Budd sang about Nurse Karen Bailey?

    a. Amazing Grace, give me no space / Don't make me cry / I tell no lie....

    b. Amazing Grace, wear leather and lace / Don't make me cry / I would die....

    c. Amazing Grace, I sense your trace / Don't make me cry / I'm a typical guy....

    d. Amazing Grace, come sit on my face / Don't make me cry / I need your pie....

93. What is Gary Hunt's rank with the Haddonfield Police Department?

    a. Sheriff   c. Officer

    b. Homicide Detective   d. Deputy

94. Why does Sheriff Brackett go off duty and put Gary Hunt in charge of finding Michael Myers with Dr. Loomis?

    a. To grieve the loss of his daughter, Annie

    b. To tell his wife of Annie's death

    c. To plan for Annie's funeral

    d. To find out why Michael killed Annie

95. What does Dr. Loomis tell Gary Hunt the gun does for him?

    a. It raises his guard   c. It heightens his security

    b. It better prepares him d. It increased his protection

96. When Dr. Loomis asks if he can trust the Marshal, the Marshal responds by saying "What have I got to lose, except my _____." What does he say is the only thing he can lose?

   a. Life
   b. License
   c. Job
   d. Dignity

97. How long does Karen tell Darcy it takes to get to her house and then back to the hospital?

   a. Five minutes
   b. Fifteen Minutes
   c. Ten Minutes
   d. Thirty Minutes

98. How much time does Mrs. Alves give Jimmy to visit Laurie?

   a. Three Minutes
   b. Two Minutes
   c. Five Minutes
   d. Four Minutes

99. Where does Mr. Garrett think someone broke into?

   a. The Hospital
   b. The Ambulance
   c. The Storage Room
   d. The Myers House

100. Dr. Rogers doesn't want anyone from which department anywhere near Haddonfield?

   a. Psychiatric Department
   b. Therapeutic Department
   c. Health Department
   d. Rehabilitation Department

Halloween III: Season of the Witch (1982)

1. Who directed *Halloween III: Season of the Witch* (1982)?
    a. John Carpenter
    b. Dwight H. Little
    c. Debra Hill
    d. Tommy Lee Wallace
2. What was the name of the company that made the Halloween masks?
    a. Silver Shamrock Novelties
    b. Clever n' Evil Novelties
    c. Spooky Halloween Novelties
    d. All Hallows' Eve Novelties
3. What were the businessmen that were created by Conal Cochran?
    a. Cyborgs
    b. Androids
    c. Robots
    d. Zombies
4. What was the budget of *Halloween III: Season of the Witch* (1982)?
    a. $2.2 million
    b. $2.7 million
    c. $2.5 million
    d. $2.9 million
5. What children's song does the commercial play its version of?
    a. "Ring Around the Rosie"
    b. "Patty Cake"
    c. "London Bridges"
    d. "Mary Had a Little Lamb"
6. When was *Halloween III: Season of the Witch* (1982) released theatrically?
    a. October 30, 1982
    b. October 31, 1982
    c. October 22, 1982
    d. October 24, 1982

7. Who were the two producers of *Halloween III: Season of the Witch* (1982)?

    a. John Carpenter and Debra Hill

    b. Debra Hill and Tommy Lee Wallace

    c. John Carpenter and Tommy Lee Wallace

    d. Moustapha and Malek Akkad

8. What do each of the masks have on it that will activate when a child wears the mask and watches the commercial?

    a. Microchip   c. Battery

    b. Antenna   d. Radio

9. What is the date in the beginning of the film?

    a. Friday, October 31, 1982

    b. Sunday, October 30, 1982

    c. Thursday, October 29, 1982

    d. Saturday, October 23, 1982

10. Harry Grimbridge is holding which of the Silver Shamrock masks in his hands?

    a. Witch   c. Jack-o'-Lantern

    b. Ghost   d. Skeleton

11. What is the city and state that is home to the Silver Shamrock Novelties?

    a. San Diego, California   c. Haddonfield, Illinois

    b. Santa Mira, California   d. Los Angeles, California

12. With what does Marge Guttman recklessly poke the microchip?

    a. Pen   c. Safety Pin

    b. Paperclip   d. Bobby Pin

13. Where does Harry Grimbridge collapse before being taken to the hospital?

    a. Gas Station
    c. Highway
    b. Car Garage
    d. Convenience Store

14. What is the first name of Harry's daughter?

    a. Ellen
    c. Emily
    b. Ellie
    d. Ella

15. What is the name of Dr. Daniel Challis' friend that does a lot of research for him?

    a. Teddy
    c. Terri
    b. Tanya
    d. Trish

16. What did Conal Cochran reveal about the way the children die when watching the commercial wearing the Halloween masks?

    a. The children will die as sacrifices to the Old Gods, bringing about a ritual to appease them.

    b. The children will die as sacrifices to the Old Gods, bringing about a return of ancient Celtic rituals in celebration of Samhain.

    c. The children will die as sacrifices to the Old Gods, bringing about a resurrection of the ancient age of witchcraft.

    d. The children will die as sacrifices to the Old Gods, bringing about a rapture of all lost souls and spirits during the ancient times of Samhain custom practices.

17. Who from the original *Halloween* (1978) film returned in this film as the ex-wife of Dr. Daniel Challis?

    a. Laurie Strode
    c. Annie Brackett
    b. Lynda Van Der Klok
    d. Marion Chambers

18. When Dr. Daniel Challis found the kidnapped Ellie Grimbridge, she turned out to be what?

    a. A Brainwashed Killer   c. A Hypnotized Zombie

    b. A Cloned Human   d. A Duplicated Android

19. What were the first names of Dr. Daniel Challis' children?

    a. Wally and Brenda   c. Wilbur and Billie

    b. Willie and Bella   d. Wallace and Betsy

20. Which behind-the-scenes crew member played the role of the Silver Shamrock announcer on the commercials?

    a. John Carpenter   c. Debra Hill

    b. Tommy Lee Wallace   d. Dean Cundey

21. How much did *Halloween III: Season of the Witch* (1982) gross at the box office?

    a. $14.4 million   c. $14 million

    b. $14.6 million   d. $14.8 million

22. What were the three types of masks sold by Silver Shamrock Novelties?

    a. Vampire, Mummy, and Zombie

    b. Clown, Frankenstein, and Ghost

    c. Jack-o'-Lantern, Witch, and Skeleton

    d. Michael Myers, Wolf, and Devil

23. What do the microchips contain that causes the signal in the commercial to activate the microchip?

    a. Subliminal Messages   c. Glass Fragments

    b. Radio Waves   d. Stonehenge

24. What is the name of the gas station attendant who drove Harry Grimbridge to the hospital?

   a. William James c. Warner Jonas

   b. Walter Jones d. Wayne Johnson

25. What are the first names of the Kupfer family?

   a. Buddy, Betty, and Little Buddy

   b. Bernie, Beatrice, and Little Bernie

   c. Barry, Blanche, and Little Barry

   d. Barney, Bertha, and Little Barney

26. What is the name of Dr. Dan Challis' ex-wife?

   a. Lori c. Lisa

   b. Lorraine d. Linda

27. Who from the original *Halloween* (1978) film played an uncredited double role as both the curfew announcer and the telephone operator?

   a. Marion Chambers c. Lynda Van Der Klok

   b. Laurie Strode d. Annie Brackett

28. Which character from *Halloween II* was the actor who played the Android Assassin in *Halloween III: Season of the Witch* (1982)?

   a. Gary Hunt c. Michael Myers

   b. Jimmy Lloyd d. Ben Tramer

29. What room number did Dr. Daniel Challis put Harry Grimbridge in?

   a. Thirty-One c. Thirteen

   b. Eighteen d. Twenty-One

30. What time does the "big giveaway" take place according to the commercial?

    a. 9 p.m.
    b. 10 p.m.
    c. 11 p.m.
    d. 12 a.m.

31. Harry Grimbridge's closed-down toy store was located where?

    a. Sierra Madre
    b. Death Valley
    c. Inglewood
    d. Claremont

32. Who is the owner of the motel in Santa Mira, California where Dr. Challis and Ellie Grimbridge rent a room?

    a. Ralphy
    b. Rourke
    c. Rory
    d. Rafferty

33. Why is Marge Guttman upset when she is first seen in the film?

    a. The factory overcharged her on her orders
    b. The factory lost her orders and has to reorder them for her
    c. The factory already mailed her the orders she had and she stayed in the motel for no reason
    d. The factory screwed up her orders and she has to stay in the motel again

34. What time is the town's curfew?

    a. 5 p.m.
    b. 6 p.m.
    c. 7 p.m.
    d. 8 p.m.

35. What did Starker say he would do to make sure that this would be the last Halloween for Conal Cochran and his factory?

    a. Blow it up with homemade bombs
    b. Burn it down with Molotov cocktails
    c. Demolish it with construction equipment
    d. Close them down by speaking with the Better Business Bureau

36. What did Teddy say was in the car that blew up when the android committed suicide?

   a. Plastic and Metal Shavings   c. Teeth and Bone Fragments

   b. Gasoline and Human Flesh   d. Blood and DNA

37. According to his daughter, Ellie, what color and type of car did Harry Grimbridge drive?

   a. Blue Station Wagon   c. Red Station Wagon

   b. Orange Station Wagon   d. Green Station Wagon

38. What did Conal Cochran steal from Stonehenge and bring to the factory?

   a. Five-Ton Redstone   c. Five-Ton Bluestone

   b. Five-Ton Greenstone   d. Five-Ton Brimstone

39. What color was the blood in the androids when they became "deactivated"?

   a. Blue   c. Red

   b. Yellow   d. Orang

40. What type of mask was Little Buddy wearing when he and his family were killed?

   a. Skeleton   c. Frankenstein

   b. Jack-o'-Lantern   d. Witch

41. What venomous creature were Little Buddy's parents swarmed and killed by right after they witnessed the death of their son?

   a. Spiders   c. Snakes

   b. Scorpions   d. Bees

42. Which body part of Teddy's did the Silver Shamrock android drive the power drill through to kill her?

   a. Eye   c. Ear

   b. Mouth   d. Throat

43. What mask did Conal Cochran place over Dr. Challis' head when he kidnapped him?

   a. Witch

   b. Michael Myers

   c. Jack-o'-Lantern

   d. Skeleton

44. Conal Cochran said the last festival of Samhain took place how long ago?

   a. 2000 years ago

   b. 1000 years ago

   c. 5000 years ago

   d. 3000 years ago

45. What is the name of the marathon that the commercial will air to kill all the children watching while wearing their Silver Shamrock masks?

   a. Fear-a-Thon

   b. Scare-a-Thon

   c. Horror-a-Thon

   d. Scream-a-Thon

46. What are the last words of the film said by Dr. Challis?

   a. STOP IT!

   b. END IT!

   c. QUIT IT!

   d. RESET IT!

47. What did Harry Grimbridge say when he was brought to the hospital?

   a. They're going to find us. All of us.

   b. They're going to kill us. All of us.

   c. They're going to scare us. All of us.

   d. They're going to control us. All of us.

48. What horror movie on the television in a commercial when Dr. Challis was at the bar?

   a. *The Thing From Another World* (1951)

   b. *The Texas Chainsaw Massacre* (1974)

   c. *Halloween* (1978)

   d. *Psycho* (1960)

49. What was Harry Grimbridge given a dosage of to calm him down?

   a. Thorazine

   b. Olanzapine

   c. Risperidone

   d. Quetiapine

50. What did the announcer say after the commercial sang eight more days till Halloween?

   a. Yes, kids, you, too can own one of the big Halloween three. That's right, three horrific masks to choose from. They're scary, they're terrifying, and they glow in the dark.

   b. Yes, kids, you, too can own one of the big Halloween three. That's right, three horrific masks to choose from. They're unique, they're iconic, and they glow in the dark.

   c. Yes, kids, you, too can own one of the big Halloween three. That's right, three horrific masks to choose from. They're fun, they're frightening, and they glow in the dark.

   d. Yes, kids, you, too can own one of the big Halloween three. That's right, three horrific masks to choose from. They're horrifying, they're monsterific, and they glow in the dark.

51. When driving to Santa Mira, Dr. Challis says you have to go how many miles after the next exit before turning right onto 33?

   a. Five

   b. Fifteen

   c. Ten

   d. Twenty

52. How many days till Halloween does the commercial say first?

   a. Eight

   b. Four

   c. Nine

   d. Seven

53. In the beginning of the film, where does it say they are currently located?

   a. Northern California

   b. Eastern California

   c. Southern California

   d. Western California

54. In the opening credits, what Halloween-related object is being drawn?
    a. Ghost
    b. Witch
    c. Jack-o'-Lantern
    d. Black Cat

55. Where does Marge Guttman say her shop is located?
    a. Union Square in San Diego
    b. Union Square in San Bernardino
    c. Union Square in San Jose
    d. Union Square in San Francisco

56. When did the receptionist at the Silver Shamrock Novelties headquarters say Harry Grimbridge picked up his order?
    a. October 20th
    b. October 22nd
    c. October 18th
    d. October 21st

57. After Ellie Grimbridge saw her father's car, what did Dr. Challis say it was time for?
    a. The Marines
    b. The Airforce
    c. The National Guard
    d. The S.W.A.T. Team

8. Who was Harry Grimbridge supposed to have dinner with on October 21st (who was involved with Michael Myers in a later sequel)?
    a. Dr. Terrence Wynn
    b. Kara Strode
    c. Minnie Blankenship
    d. Jamie Lloyd

59. According to his records, where was Harry Grimbridge on October 19th?
    a. Football Game
    b. Merchant's Council Meeting
    c. Picking up Halloween Masks
    d. Dinner with Minnie Blankenship

60. According to Conal Cochran, who sold more Silver Shamrock masks than anyone else in the country?

   a. Marge Guttman   c. Buddy Kupfer

   b. Harry Grimbridge   d. Starker

61. What did Buddy Kupfer tell Dr. Challis that Conal Cochran invented as the ultimate practical joker?

   a. Sticky Toilet Paper   c. Whoopie Cushion

   b. Hand Buzzer   d. Fart Spray

62. What last name did Ellie Grimbridge say was hers and Dr. Challis'?

   a. Doe   c. Smith

   b. Jones   d. Anderson

63. The mask that Little Buddy wanted was turned down by Conal Cochran for what reason?

   a. It hasn't been through final processing

   b. It is another customer's order

   c. It hasn't been tested out yet

   d. It hasn't been logged for completion

64. According to what Betty told Ellie, how did Conal Cochran become one of the richest men in the country?

   a. By selling cheap gags and Halloween masks

   b. By selling practical jokes and toys

   c. By selling books he wrote

   d. By selling food and drinks

65. When visiting the factory, what made Dr. Challis suspicious?

   a. Seeing Harry Grimbridge's car

   b. Seeing two businessmen wearing suits in the parking lot

   c. Seeing Marge Guttman's corpse

   d. Seeing people being turned into androids

66. What are the cities on the commercial of children getting ready for the giveaway?

   a. St. Louis, Dallas, Philadelphia, Miami, Detroit, and Atlanta

   b. Boston, Phoenix, Sacramento, Pittsburgh, Baltimore, and Oklahoma City

   c. Dayton, New York City, Omaha, Baton Rouge, Los Angeles, and Seattle

   d. Chicago, Richmond, Houston, San Francisco, Las Vegas, and Minneapolis

67. What is the date when Dr. Challis asks Teddy to look into the businessman that killed Harry Grimbridge and then himself?

   a. Wednesday the 27th   c. Friday the 29th

   b. Saturday the 23rd   d. Saturday the 30th

68. Why does the sheriff think that the businessman killed Harry?

   a. Because he was on drugs   c. Because he was owed money

   b. Because he was a serial killer d. Because he held a grudge

69. What is the name of the gas station in Santa Mira?

   a. Rafferty's Convenience Shop   c. Rafferty's Deluxe

   b. Rafferty's Gas Station   d. Rafferty's Pump

70. What does Rafferty tell Dr. Challis and Ellie are the reasons why the motel is a good one to stay at?

   a. It's comfy, it's peaceful, and it's affordable

   b. It's cozy, it's quiet, and the price is right

   c. It's nice, it's warm, and the price is cheap

   d. It's beautiful, it's private, and it's free

71. What did Conal Cochran say happened to Marge Guttman?

   a. Misfire   c. Heart Attack

   b. Accidental Overdose   d. Stroke

72. What is Teddy's job title?

   a. Assistant Coroner   c. Coroner

   b. Forensic Expert   d. Tech Expert

73. In the beginning of the film, what is the date?

   a. October, Friday the 23rd

   b. October, Saturday the 23rd

   c. October, Sunday the 23rd

   d. October, Monday the 23rd

74. According to his records, where was Harry Grimbridge on October 18th?

   a. Picking up Halloween Masks

   b. Football Game

   c. Dinner with Minnie Blankenship

   d. Merchant's Council Meeting

75. What was seen recording Dr. Challis' conversation on the phone with Teddy?

   a. Tape Recorder   c. Bug

   b. Surveillance Camera d. Camcorder

76. What did Dr. Challis' wife ask him when he called her from the factory?

   a. Is he stoned
   b. Is he joking
   c. Is he high
   d. Is he drunk

77. Who was the cinematographer of *Halloween III: Season of the Witch* (1982)?

   a. Alan Howarth
   b. Millie Moore
   c. Dean Cundey
   d. Nigel Kneale

78. What nationality is Conal Cochran?

   a. Scottish
   b. Irish
   c. English
   d. American

79. When Dr. Challis was kidnapped, how did he escape?

   a. Through a ventilation shaft
   b. Killing an android and escaping through the door
   c. Pickpocketing a key from a visiting android and escaping through the door when the coast was clear
   d. Ellie came to his rescue

80. What did Dr. Challis decapitate Ellie with when he found out she was cloned into an android?

   a. Tire Iron
   b. Axe
   c. Machete
   d. Sickle

81. How many hours later did Harry Grimbridge arrive at the gas station where he collapsed?

   a. One Hour Later
   b. Two Hours Later
   c. Three Hours Later
   d. Four Hours Later

82. What documentary was Walter Jones watching in the gas station before Harry Grimbridge showed up?

   a. *Stonehenge* (1982)   c. *Blood Moons* (1981)

   b. *Samhain* (1979)   d. *History of Haddonfield* (1980)

83. What was Teddy researching that had her call the authorities right before she was murdered?

   a. Android parts from the car explosion

   b. Silver Shamrocks Halloween Mask

   c. Conal Cochran's plan for the commercial giveaway

   d. The history of the Silver Shamrocks factory

84. What was the name of the motel that Dr. Challis and Ellie stayed at?

   a. Silver Shamrocks Motel

   b. Irish n' Celtic Historical Motel

   c. Rose of Shannon Motel

   d. Samhain Monumental Motel

85. What did Conal Cochran say the hills ran red from at the last Samhain festival?

   a. From the blood of celebrants

   b. From the blood of sacrifices

   c. From the blood of criminals and the insane

   d. From the blood of children and animals

86. What is Stonehenge according to Conal Cochran?

   a. An ancient, ritualistic circle

   b. An ancient, historical circle

   c. An ancient, monumental circle

   d. An ancient, sacrificial circle

87. Who is the joke on, according to Conal Cochran, when speaking about the giveaway?
   a. The Children
   b. The Country
   c. The Halloween Celebrants
   d. The World

88. According to his records, what was Harry Grimbridge supposed to do on October 20th?
   a. File for bankruptcy
   b. Pick up more Halloween masks
   c. Go to the bank to receive his loan
   d. Order more inventory

89. What was the date that Harry Grimbridge checked into the motel?
   a. October 21st
   b. October 18th
   c. October 20th
   d. October 19th

90. What does Teddy say she's always good at?
   a. Romancing
   b. Researching
   c. Moonlighting
   d. Investigating

91. How many women are in the room clapping when Conal Cochran says Buddy Kupfer sold more Silver Shamrock masks than anyone else in the country?
   a. Five
   b. Six
   c. Four
   d. Eight

92. When Buddy wanted to see the final processing, what did Conal Cochran say that it involves that is very dangerous?
   a. Poisonous Chemicals
   b. Acidic Chemicals
   c. Radioactive Chemicals
   d. Volatile Chemicals

93. Where does Ellie say she lives?

    a. Sacramento   c. Los Angeles

    b. Oakland   d. Santa Monica

94. When arriving in Santa Mira, what small animal did Ellie say she felt like with Dr. Challis responding, "company town"?

    a. Squirrel   c. Bug

    b. Goldfish   d. Spider

95. What kind of technology did Conal Cochran tell Dr. Challis he had in his underground laboratory?

    a. Ancient   c. Magical

    b. Dangerous   d. Advanced

96. How much money does Starker ask Dr. Challis if he could spare?

    a. $1.00   c. $5.00

    b. $10.00   d. $20.00

97. When Dr. Challis asks Teddy to look into Conal Cochran, what does Teddy say this'll cost Dr. Challis?

    a. Some serious vacation time

    b. Some serious overtime hours

    c. Some serious dinners

    d. Some serious raise discussions

98. What does the commercial announcer say to watch on the TV screen during the big giveaway?

    a. Magic Witch   c. Magic Pumpkin

    b. Magic Skeleton   d. Magic Cloverleaf

99. What kind of inspection did Conal Cochran say the final processing entails?

   a. Advanced

   b. Chemical

   c. Quality

   d. Security

100. When and where did Conal Cochran say the android of his grandmother was made?

   a. Munich, Germany in 1750

   b. Munich, Germany in 1880

   c. Munich, Germany in 1785

   d. Munich, Germany in 1825

Halloween 4: The Return of Michael Myers (1988)

1. Who was the final girl of *Halloween 4: The Return of Michael Myers* (1988)?
   - a. Rachel Carruthers
   - c. Lindsay Wallace
   - b. Jamie Lloyd
   - d. Kelly Meeker

2. What was the budget of *Halloween 4: The Return of Michael Myers* (1988)?
   - a. $5 million
   - c. $10 million
   - b. $7 million
   - d. $3 million

3. Who played Michael Myers?
   - a. Dick Warlock
   - c. George P. Wilbur
   - b. Don Shanks
   - d. Christopher Durand

4. When was *Halloween 4: The Return of Michael Myers* (1988) released theatrically?
   - a. October 31, 1988
   - c. October 21, 1988
   - b. October 25, 1988
   - d. October 28, 1988

5. How much did *Halloween 4: The Return of Michael Myers* (1988) gross at the box office?
   - a. $17.5 million
   - c. $17.9 million
   - b. $17.2 million
   - d. $17.7 million

6. Who directed *Halloween 4: The Return of Michael Myers* (1988)?
   - a. John Carpenter
   - c. Tommy Lee Wallace
   - b. Joe Chappelle
   - d. Dwight H. Little

7. Where did Sheriff Brackett move to after he retired from the Haddonfield police force?
    a. California
    b. Florida
    c. Hawaii
    d. North Carolina
8. How long has Michael Myers been in a coma for?
    a. Five Years
    b. Ten Years
    c. Eleven Years
    d. Seven Years
9. Who is Jamie Lloyd's mother?
    a. Darlene Carruthers
    b. Lindsay Wallace
    c. Laurie Strode
    d. Annie Brackett
10. What character from the first film has a small role in this film, but played by a different actor/actress?
    a. Tommy Doyle
    b. Laurie Strode
    c. Lindsay Wallace
    d. Sheriff Brackett
11. Who is the new sheriff of Haddonfield?
    a. Sheriff Ben Meeker
    b. Sheriff Miguel Acosta
    c. Sheriff Gary Hunt
    d. Sheriff Clark Hudson
12. Where did Reverend Jackson Sayer say he was going to?
    a. The Promise Land
    b. Smith's Grove
    c. Haddonfield
    d. Hollywood
13. Dr. Hoffman said that if Dr. Loomis read _____ he'd be at Ridgemont?
    a. Notes
    b. Letters
    c. Emails
    d. Memos
14. Dr. Loomis saw six bodies between Haddonfield and what other town?
    a. Smith's Grove
    b. Russellville
    c. Ridgemont
    d. Blairstown

15. Which deputy was guarding the door at Sheriff Ben Meeker's house?
    a. Deputy Winslow   c. Deputy Logan
    b. Deputy Gary Hunt d. Deputy Rick Cologne
16. When arguing with Brady, what nickname did Rachel give Kelly Meeker?
    a. Little Miss Hot Panties   c. Little Miss Hot Ass
    b. Little Miss Hot Breasts   d. Little Miss Hot Bra
17. What is the name of the power worker killed by Michael?
    a. Braun   c. Barry
    b. Branson   d. Bucky
18. Who is the owner of the bar that leads the mob to find and kill Michael Myers?
    a. Unger   c. Big Al
    b. Earl   d. Orrin Gateway
19. Who went to ask Kelly out at the convenient store as a bet with Brady?
    a. Walter   c. Will
    b. Wade   d. Warren
20. What child actor was married to the lady who played the dead waitress?
    a. Corey Feldman   c. Shavar Ross
    b. Mike Lookinland   d. Gary Coleman
21. What was the name of the gas station where Michael Myers killed the mechanic and waitress?
    a. Penney's Gas Station   c. Pauley's Gas Station
    b. Polly's Gas Station   d. Perrey's Gas Station

22. Who are Jamie's foster parents?
    a. Richard and Darlene Carruthers
    c. Ben and Kelly Meeker
    b. Brady and Rachel
    d. Tommy and Lindsay

23. Who did Earl and his friends kill when they thought it was Michael Myers?
    a. Ted Hollister
    c. Kyle
    b. Wade
    d. Jackson Sayer

24. What town in Florida did Sheriff Brackett move to upon retirement?
    a. Orlando
    c. St. Petersburg
    b. Miami
    d. Fort Lauderdale

25. Where were Rachel's parents going to be?
    a. The Waldorfs
    c. The Fallbrooks
    b. The Shmenkmans
    d. The Polygraphs

26. Where did Darlene say that Rachel's grandmother lives?
    a. Columbus
    c. Cincinnati
    b. Cleveland
    d. Parma

27. When is Jamie's bedtime?
    a. 9 p.m.
    c. 10 p.m.
    b. 8 p.m.
    d. 9 p.m.

28. What is the name of the convenient store that Brady works at?
    a. Discount Mart
    c. Sale Mart
    b. BOGO Mart
    d. Coupon Mart

29. What does Jamie stab her foster mother with, in a similar fashion to the way Michael stabbed his sister when he was a child?
    a. Butcher Knife
    c. Glass Shard
    b. Knitting Needle
    d. Scissors

30. What did Jamie dress up as for Halloween?
    a. Fairy
    b. Clown
    c. Witch
    d. Princess

31. How long has Jackson Sayer been searching for Armageddon?
    a. Twenty-Five Years
    b. Fifty Years
    c. Twenty Years
    d. Thirty Years

32. Who played Jamie Lloyd?
    a. Leslie L. Rohland
    b. Kyle Richards
    c. Danielle Harris
    d. Stephanie Dees

33. What year did Sheriff Brackett retire?
    a. 1978
    b. 1979
    c. 1980
    d. 1981

34. Who did the special effects for Earl's death scene?
    a. Tom Savini
    b. Sean S. Cunningham
    c. John Carpenter
    d. John Carl Buechler

35. Where does Dr. Loomis take Jamie Lloyd to hide from Michael Myers?
    a. Jamie's House
    b. The Schoolhouse
    c. The Myers' House
    d. The Police Station

36. What did Dr. Hoffman say Dr. Loomis' position was?
    a. More Practical than Medical
    b. More Political than Medical
    c. More Ceremonial than Medical
    d. More Spiritual than Medical

37. What is the name of Rachel and Jamie's dog?
    a. Lester
    b. Max
    c. Sundae
    d. Mario

38. Who played Kelly Meeker?

   a. Ellie Cornell
   c. Danielle Harris
   b. Kathleen Kinmont
   d. Melody Gold

39. Who were the four men in the mob trying to find and kill Michael Myers?

   a. Earl, Big Al, Wade, and Orrin Gateway
   b. Earl, Big Al, Unger, and Orrin Gateway
   c. Earl, Big Al, Kyle, and Orrin Gateway
   d. Earl, Big Al, Brady, and Orrin Gateway

40. Who did the security guard at Ridgemont say has nothing to do with this place?

   a. God
   c. Jesus
   b. Satan
   d. Lucifer

41. Who was Brady and Wade hanging out with at the convenient store?

   a. Kyle
   c. Tommy
   b. Earl
   d. Bucky

42. Who played Brady?

   a. Beau Starr
   c. Sasha Jenson
   b. Jeff Olson
   d. Richard Stay

43. What achievement did Rachel ask Jamie if she was going for because she couldn't sleep?

   a. Eight-Year-Old Insomniacs Hall of Fame
   b. Nine-Year-Old Insomniacs Hall of Fame
   c. Six-Year-Old Insomniacs Hall of Fame
   d. Seven-Year-Old Insomniacs Hall of Fame

44. How many nights hadn't Jamie slept for?

    a. Five

    b. Three

    c. Six

    d. Four

45. What is the first name of Jamie's babysitter?

    a. Sharon

    b. Shannon

    c. Susie

    d. Stacy

46. Finish the quote that Rachel said to her mom: "Do you want a/an _____ for a daughter?"

    a. Mooer

    b. Woofer

    c. Oinker

    d. Meower

47. Since Jamie is too young to be Michael's legal guardian, who was then said to have been the owner of Michael's lifeless body?

    a. The State

    b. The Federal Prison

    c. Smith's Grove Sanitarium

    d. Dr. Loomis

48. How did Laurie Strode die?

    a. Michael Myers found and killed her

    b. She had cancer

    c. She was in a car accident

    d. She committed suicide

49. Who played Rachael Carruthers?

    a. Kathleen Kinmont

    b. Ellie Cornell

    c. Karen Alston

    d. Nancy Borgenicht

50. Who played the young Michael Myers when Jamie saw him in the convenience store's mirror?

    a. Will Sandin

    b. Erik Preston

    c. Adam Gunn

    d. Daeg Faerch

51. The character of Jamie Lloyd was named in homage to Jamie Lee Curtis. What was the original working first name of Jamie Lloyd in the script?

    a. Brittany
    b. Billie
    c. Barbie
    d. Bethany

52. Including the dog, what was the body count of the film?

    a. Eighteen
    b. Twenty
    c. Nineteen
    d. Sixteen

53. Which actress auditioned for the role of Jamie, but lost to Danielle Harris?

    a. Sara Gilbert
    b. Melissa Joan Hart
    c. Kyle Richards
    d. Jennifer Banko

54. Who was Jamie originally supposed to stab at the end of the film?

    a. Lindsay Wallace
    b. Richard Carruthers
    c. Rachel Carruthers
    d. Sheriff Ben Meeker

55. With the death of Sundae in the movie, how many dogs died in the *Halloween* franchise?

    a. Four
    b. Three
    c. Two
    d. One

56. Which main cast member was supposed to die in a battle with Michael Myers?

    a. Dr. Sam Loomis
    b. Rachel Carruthers
    c. Jamie Lloyd
    d. Sheriff Ben Meeker

57. Due to budgetary constraints, which of the following scenes was eliminated from the film?

   a. The gas station explosion when Michael Myers sped off in the truck

   b. The ambulance accident that Michael Myers caused by killing the paramedics

   c. The house was supposed to catch fire when Rachel and Jamie ran from Michael Myers by climbing up the roof of the house

   d. Michael Myers being shot at by the firing squad and then blown up by a dynamite

58. This is the first film in the *Halloween* (1978) franchise wherein which individual was not creatively involved?

   a. John Carpenter   c. Alan Howarth

   b. Moustapha Akkad   d. Alan B. McElroy

59. Which of the following films was the reason behind having Michael Myers return?

   a. *Halloween* (1978)

   b. *Halloween II* (1981)

   c. *Halloween III: Season of the Witch* (1982)

   d. *Friday the 13th Part 6: Jason Lives* (1986)

60. What is the tagline for *Halloween 4: The Return of Michael Myers* (1988)?

   a. Five Years Ago HE Changed the Face of Halloween. Tonight HE'S BACK!

   b. Seven Years Ago HE Changed the Face of Halloween. Tonight HE'S BACK!

   c. Ten Years Ago HE Changed the Face of Halloween. Tonight HE'S BACK!

   d. Twenty Years Ago HE Changed the Face of Halloween. Tonight HE'S BACK!

61. What did Reverend Jackson Sayer say you cannot kill?

   a. Evil

   b. The Devil

   c. Damnation

   d. End of the World

62. What did Earl say could land on Sheriff Ben Meeker's doorstep and all he'd do is spit once and get himself a shotgun?

   a. Aliens

   b. Demons

   c. Martians

   d. Giants

63. Dr. Hoffman said he hoped Dr. Loomis would do what with Michael Myers now gone?

   a. Transfer, Retire, or Move

   b. Transfer, Retire, or Die

   c. Transfer, Retire, or Quit

   d. Transfer, Retire, or Leave

64. How far is Haddonfield from the location the ambulance containing Michael Myers crashed?

   a. Two Hour Drive

   b. Four Hour Drive

   c. Three Hour Drive

   d. Five Hour Drive

65. What Caribbean Island did Darlene tell Rachel would be a place they could go on vacation if Richard gets the promotion?

   a. The Bahamas

   b. Cuba

   c. St. Lucia

   d. Bermuda

66. What alarmed Earl and some of his loyal customers that something was wrong when they called the police station?

   a. The phone just kept ringing

   b. The phone went straight to an operator

   c. The phone was answered with no one talking on the other end

   d. The phone didn't ring

67. What kind of gun does Sheriff Meeker give to Brady to use for protection?

   a. Pistol
   c. Rifle
   b. Shotgun
   d. Assault Rifle

68. In the beginning of the film, what was the date shown?

   a. October 31, 1988
   c. October 30, 1988
   b. October 27, 1988
   d. October 29, 1988

69. What does the text say on Kelly Meeker's nightgown?

   a. Cops Do It By Their Own Rules
   b. Cops Do It By The Book
   c. Cops Do It By The Law
   d. Cops Do It By The Way They Were Trained

70. When Rachel goes with the kids to Sheriff Meeker's house, what Halloween monster was shown on the front door hanging as a decoration?

   a. Jack-o'-Lantern
   c. Skeleton
   b. Witch
   d. Vampire

71. How does Dr. Loomis know that Michael Myers was in Jamie's room at the Carruthers' house?

   a. Found a picture of Laurie Strode
   b. Found a message written in blood
   c. Found Jamie's dog dead
   d. Found the mask Michael wears

72. What two colors was the truck that Michael stole from the gas station?

   a. Orange and White
   c. Orange and Black
   b. Orange and Blue
   d. Orange and Red

73. What did Richard Carruthers dip his tie in by accident that he needed a new one?
    a. Orange Juice
    c. Apple Juice
    b. Tea
    d. Coffee

74. What was Darlene making for breakfast?
    a. Eggs
    c. Pancakes
    b. French Toast
    d. Cereal

75. Where did Darlene tell Richard another tie was at?
    a. Their Bedroom
    c. The Living Room
    b. The Laundry Room
    d. His Closet

76. Why can't Jamie's babysitter babysit?
    a. She broke her leg
    c. She broke her ankle
    b. She broke her arm
    d. She broke her foot

77. The kids who were teasing Jamie said her mommy is a what?
    a. Ghost
    c. Devil
    b. Mummy
    d. Demon

78. Who is Michael Myers to Jamie?
    a. Father
    c. Brother
    b. Cousin
    d. Uncle

79. What was Darlene doing for Jamie before she was stabbed by Jamie?
    a. Running Jamie a bath
    c. Making Jamie's bed
    b. Cooking Jamie dinner
    d. Doing Jamie's laundry

80. How did Michael get to Sheriff Meeker's house?

   a. Followed Sheriff Meeker by walking there

   b. Hiding in the back of Deputy Logan's police car

   c. Drove there by following the state police cars

   d. Walked there after hearing about their whereabouts on the police scanner

81. How does Michael kill Brady?

   a. Impaled with a gun   c. Shot with a gun

   b. Neck crushed   d. Stabbed in the stomach

82. Why does Jamie attack and stab Darlene?

   a. Because of her relation to Michael Myers

   b. Because she hates her foster mom

   c. Because she misses her mom

   d. Because she witnessed murders

83. Who led the state police in the shooting of Michael Myers that supposedly killed him?

   a. Dr. Sam Loomis   c. Deputy Logan

   b. Sheriff Ben Meeker   d. The Lynch Mob

84. What branch of the military did Rachel say her parents most likely have the numbers for in case of an emergency?

   a. Army   c. National Guard

   b. Airforce   d. Marines

85. What did all the kids teasing Jamie keep repeating to her?

   a. Jamie's a killer   c. Jamie's a Boogeyman

   b. Jamie's an orphan   d. Jamie's unwanted

86. What did Kelly Meeker make for Deputy Logan before her death?

   a. Tea
   c. Cider
   b. Coffee
   d. Hot Cocoa

87. What was Wade wearing in the convenience store?

   a. Halloween Mask
   c. Hat
   b. Sunglasses
   d. Headphones

88. How was Kelly Meeker killed by Michael?

   a. Throat was slit
   c. Impaled with a gun
   b. Strangled by Michael's bare hands
   d. Stabbed in the back

89. Where did Jamie's babysitter hurt herself at?

   a. School
   c. Cheerleading Practice
   b. Ice Rink
   d. Halloween Party

90. What did Darlene fall into when Jamie stabbed her?

   a. Closet
   c. Bathtub
   b. Sink
   d. Washing Machine

91. Finish the quote from Brady: _____ talks and _____ walks.

   a. Money talks and rejection walks
   b. Money talks and Kelly walks
   c. Money talks and bullshit walks
   d. Money talks and bravery walks

92. When the convertible of cheerleaders pulled over for Dr. Loomis, how many miles did the sign say to Haddonfield?

   a. 100 Miles
   c. 110 Miles
   b. 128 Miles
   d. 119 Miles

93. What were the lyrics of the song Reverend Jackson Sayer was singing in the truck with Dr. Loomis?

   a. Yes, we'll gather at the river, the gorgeous, gorgeous river, gather with the saints at the river

   b. Yes, we'll gather at the river, the holy, holy river, gather with the saints at the river

   c. Yes, we'll gather at the river, the beautiful, beautiful river, gather with the saints at the n river

   d. Yes, we'll gather at the river, the marvelous, marvelous river, gather with the saints at the river

94. What time did Rachel say she'll be home from Trick or Treating with Jamie so Brady could stop by?

   a. 8 p.m.   c. 9 p.m.
   b. 7 p.m.   d. 10 p.m.

95. Who was the person in the first picture that Michael picked up in Jamie's room?

   a. Laurie Strode   c. Jamie Lloyd
   b. Himself as a child   d. Dr. Sam Loomis

96. Rachel found Brady cheating on her with whom?

   a. Lindsay Wallace   c. Her Neighbor
   b. Kelly Meeker   d. Her Mother

97. What did Michael Myers throw Dr. Loomis through when he was going after Jamie?

   a. The Schoolhouse Window   c. The Car Windshield
   b. The Sheriff's Front Door   d. The Police Car Windshield

98. Which lynch mob members were killed and then had their corpses thrown off of the moving truck by Michael?

   a. Orrin Gateway, Unger, and Earl

   b. Orrin Gateway, Big Al, and Earl

   c. Big Al, Earl, and Unger

   d. Orrin Gateway, Big Al, and Unger

99. What was the mechanic asking for before he was killed by Michael?

   a. ¼ socket

   b. $1/3$ socket

   c. ½ socket

   d. $9/16$ socket

100. When the convertible of cheerleaders pulls over for Dr. Loomis, what are the names of the three towns/cities that are on the sign?

   a. Eaton, Haddonfield, and Smith's Grove

   b. Eaton, Haddonfield, and Russellville

   c. Eaton, Haddonfield, and Chicago

   d. Eaton, Haddonfield, and Ridgemont

Halloween 5: The Revenge of Michael Myers (1989)

1. Who played Michael Myers in *Halloween 5: The Revenge of Michael Myers* (1989)?
    a. Brad Loree
    b. Christopher Durand
    c. Tyler Mane
    d. Don Shanks

2. When was *Halloween 5: The Revenge of Michael Myers* (1989) released theatrically?
    a. October 31, 1989
    b. October 11, 1989
    c. October 29, 1989
    d. October 13, 1989

3. Who was the final girl of *Halloween 5: The Revenge of Michael Myers* (1989)?
    a. Rachel Carruthers
    b. Jamie Lloyd
    c. Tina Williams
    d. Samantha Thomas

4. What was revealed about the ending of *Halloween 4: The Return of Michael Myers* (1989) in this film?
    a. That Jamie Lloyd is the new Michael Myers
    b. That Darlene Carruthers has survived her attack from Jamie
    c. That Jamie Lloyd has been committed to Smith's Grove Sanitarium
    d. That Michael Myers is the father of Jamie Lloyd biologically

5. What is the body count of *Halloween 5: The Revenge of Michael Myers* (1989), including Max and the opossum Dr. Loomis finds in the laundry chute?
   a. Nineteen
   c. Twenty
   b. Twenty-One
   d. Seventeen

6. What was the name of Rachel's dog?
   a. Sundae
   c. Max
   b. Lester
   d. Gordon

7. How many police officers were killed in the shootout at the police station by the Man in Black?
   a. Eight
   c. Nine
   b. Ten
   d. Five

8. What did Michael use to slice Samantha's stomach open?
   a. Sickle
   c. Scythe
   b. Hatchet
   d. Butcher Knife

9. How many years have passed between Michael's supposed death and his alleged resurrection?
   a. Two Years
   c. One Year
   b. Three Years
   d. Five Years

10. What was the budget of *Halloween 5: The Revenge of Michael Myers* (1989)?
    a. $3 million
    c. $4 million
    b. $2 million
    d. $5 million

11. What pet did the Mountain Man have?
    a. Spider
    c. Snake
    b. Mouse
    d. Parrot

12. How did Michael survive the TNT blast after being shot by a firing squad?
    a. He shielded himself with a huge boulder
    b. He wasn't near the TNT blast
    c. He disappeared from the area and his body wasn't in the hole
    d. He escaped through a hole in the ground and floated down the river

13. What weapon does Michael kill Rachel with?
    a. Butcher Knife
    b. Scissors
    c. Glass Shard
    d. Hunting Knife

14. What animal does Spitz and Samantha see in the barn?
    a. Puppy
    b. Kitten
    c. Rabbit
    d. Mouse

15. What was the name of Jamie's doctor at the clinic?
    a. Dr. Miguel Hart
    b. Dr. Max Hart
    c. Dr. Mickey Hart
    d. Dr. Mark Hart

16. Who directed *Halloween 5: The Revenge of Michael Myers* (1989)?
    a. Rick Rosenthal
    b. Dominique Othenin-Girard
    c. Steve Miner
    d. Dwight H. Little

17. How much did *Halloween 5: The Revenge of Michael Myers* (1989) gross at the box office?
    a. $11.6 million
    b. $11.9 million
    c. $11.5 million
    d. $11.1 million

18. Which of the following characters from *Halloween 4: The Return of Michael Myers* (1988) doesn't return in this film?
    a. Sheriff Ben Meeker
    b. Rachel Carruthers
    c. Lindsay Wallace
    d. Jamie Lloyd

19. What was the hole that Michael Myers fell down after being shot by a firing squad?
    a. Fox Hole
    c. Mine Shaft
    b. Grave
    d. Sand Trap

20. How does Jamie know when Michael will kill someone?
    a. She has some type of telepathic link to Michael
    b. She has the heart of a killer
    c. She heard the voice Michael did when he was a kid
    d. She has genetic connections to him and his killer instincts

21. What is Jamie's condition at the clinic?
    a. She has been rendered mentally and psychologically insane
    b. She has been rendered physical and emotionally unstable
    c. She has been rendered a mute due to psychological trauma
    d. She has been rendered verbally, visually, and mentally crazy

22. What is the name of Tina's boyfriend?
    a. Mikey
    c. Jason
    b. Freddy
    d. Chucky

23. What did Billy dress up as for Halloween?
    a. Vampire
    c. Pirate
    b. Clown
    d. Mummy

24. After Dr. Loomis attacked Michael and trapped him, why did he collapse?
    a. He has a heart attack
    b. He is suffering from exhaustion
    c. He has a stroke
    d. He is relieved on Michael's capture

25. Whose corpses does Jamie see in the attic of the Myers house?

   a. Rachel Carruthers, Spitz, and Max

   b. Rachel Carruthers, Samantha Thomas, and Max

   c. Rachel Carruthers, Mikey, and Max

   d. Rachel Carruthers, Tina Williams, and Max

26. What was the name of the gas station that Tina was at when Jamie felt the presence of Michael Myers?

   a. Dick's Gas Station   c. Darren's Gas Station

   b. Denny's Gas Station   d. Dale's Gas Station

27. What was the name of the Mountain Man's parrot?

   a. Cookie   c. Snookie

   b. Pookie   d. Rookie

28. What was the name of Jamie's nurse at the clinic?

   a. Nurse Peggy   c. Nurse Penny

   b. Nurse Patsey   d. Nurse Perrey

29. What did Jamie dress up as for Halloween?

   a. Clown   c. Witch

   b. Fairy   d. Princess

30. What was the name of the store that Rachel and Tina went to?

   a. Quick Food Mart   c. Discount Mart

   b. Convenient Service Mart   d. Cheap Item Mart

31. What did the note say that was thrown through the window?

   a. The Evil Child Is The Boogeyman

   b. The Evil Child Must Die

   c. The Evil Child Must Be Sacrificed

   d. The Evil Child Is What He Wants

32. What was the location of the big Halloween party that Tina was going to?
    a. Cornmaze Farm   c. Tower Farm
    b. Pumpkin Farm   d. Raver Farm

33. What did Jamie write on her chalkboard?
    a. He's Still Alive   c. He's Coming For Me
    b. He's In Haddonfield   d. He's Gonna Sacrifice Me

34. Where did the officer say the location of the gas station was?
    a. 5th and Main   c. 1st and Main
    b. 2nd and Main   d. 3rd and Main

35. Where was Jamie Lloyd stabbed originally, but it was cut from the film due to the MPAA deeming it as "too disturbing"?
    a. Leg   c. Arm
    b. Foot   d. Hand

36. When Rachel visits Jamie, as she is leaving, she tells Jamie she'll be back when?
    a. One Day   c. Three Days
    b. Two Days   d. One Week

37. When Jamie couldn't breathe, what did Dr. Max Hart say he had to open for Jamie so she won't die?
    a. Esophagus   c. Trachea
    b. Heart   d. Lungs

38. How many cases of alcohol can Spitz get for Mikey from the store he works at?
    a. Two Cases   c. Four Cases
    b. Three Cases   d. Five Cases

39. What is the name of Spitz's boss?
    a. Mr. Casy   c. Mr. Cosick
    b. Mr. Collins   d. Mr. Cruz

40. How old is Jamie Lloyd?

   a. Ten Years Old   c. Eight Years Old

   b. Nine Years Old   d. Seven Years Old

41. At the Halloween party, who dressed up as Michael Myers as a prank?

   a. Mikey   c. Tina Williams

   b. Samantha Thomas   d. Spitz

42. What does Tina want to get at the gas station?

   a. Lottery Tickets   c. Case of Beer

   b. Change for a $20   d. Pack of Cigarettes

43. While waiting for Michael Myers in the Myers house, what is Jamie doing in the bedroom?

   a. Setting traps   c. Pacing back and forth

   b. Brushing her hair d. Crying

44. *Halloween 5: The Revenge of Michael Myers* (1989) is the only movie in the *Halloween* (1978) franchise to never be released in which European country?

   a. United Kingdom   c. Italy

   b. France   d. Germany

45. How many dogs have been killed in the *Halloween* (1978) franchise, including Max?

   a. Three   c. Four

   b. Five   d. Six

46. What popped out dead in the laundry chute when Dr. Loomis was snooping around the Myers house?

   a. Opossum   c. Skunk

   b. Cat   d. Rat

47. What unique weapon does Michael use on Mikey?
   a. Garden Claw
   b. Rake
   c. Hoe
   d. Shovel

48. Whose bodies fall on Tina Williams when she is in the barn?
   a. Spitz and Rachel Carruthers
   b. Spitz and Mikey
   c. Spitz and Samantha Thomas
   d. Deputy Nick Ross and Deputy Tom Farrah

49. Who was the officer that was watching Jamie at the end of the film after Michael was taken to the station?
   a. Sheriff Ben Meeker
   b. Deputy Charlie Bloch
   c. Deputy Tony
   d. Deputy Eddy Grey

50. How did Michael Myers kill the Mountain Man?
   a. Slit his throat
   b. Strangled with Michael's bare hands
   c. Knifed in the back
   d. Head bashed on a rock wall

51. When was Spitz killed by Michael with a pitchfork?
   a. When looking for Samantha in the barn
   b. When yelling for help after finding a dead body
   c. When having sex with Samantha in the barn
   d. When he found a cat with blood on its fur

52. What does Rachel's death scene resemble?
   a. The time that Michael killed his sister when he was a boy
   b. The time that Jamie Lloyd stabbed her foster mother
   c. The time that Dr. Loomis put Michael in a coma for ten years
   d. The time that Rachel stopped Michael exactly one-year prior

53. Who played the role of Samantha Thomas?
    a. Ellie Cornell
    c. Danielle Harris
    b. Tamara Glynn
    d. Wendi Kaplan

54. How many different sections of the laundry chute were filmed during the laundry chute scene?
    a. Ten
    c. Thirty
    b. Twenty
    d. Fifty

55. Which musician was the Man in Black's wardrobe made to resemble?
    a. Tommy Lee Jones
    c. Alice Cooper
    b. Elvis Presley
    d. Johnny Cash

56. When Michael was wearing a different mask while pretending to be Tina's boyfriend, Mikey, it was originally scripted that he wore a mask of a United States President's face until it was changed due to not involving the film with politics? Which President was it?
    a. Abraham Lincoln
    c. George H.W. Bush
    b. Ronald Reagan
    d. Jimmy Carter

57. What is the tagline of *Halloween 5: The Revenge of Michael Myers* (1989)?
    a. Michael Lives. And This Time They're Prepared
    b. Michael Lives. And This Time They're Aware
    c. Michael Lives. And This Time They're Ready
    d. Michael Lives. And This Time They're Ending It

58. Who created the music for *Halloween 5: The Revenge of Michael Myers* (1989)?
    a. John Carpenter
    c. Alan Howarth
    b. Harry Manfredini
    d. Malek Akkad

59. Who oversaw cinematography on set for *Halloween 5: The Revenge of Michael Myers* (1989)?

    a. Robert Draper   c. Dean Cundey

    b. Peter Lyons Collister d. David Geddes

60. Who played the role of Spitz?

    a. Matthew Walker   c. Troy Evans

    b. Jeffrey Landman   d. Beau Starr

61. How is Tina classified as the hero of the film?

    a. She killed Michael Myers

    b. She found out how Michael Myers can be stopped

    c. She sacrificed herself to save Jamie's life

    d. She knows why Michael kills on Halloween nights

62. Where did Sheriff Ben Meeker take Michael at the end of the film so he can spend the rest of his days there until he was broken out by the Man in Black?

    a. Police Station Holding Cell   c. Maximum Security Prison

    b. Solitary Confinement   d. Psychiatric Ward

63. What type of explosive do the state troopers throw down the mine shaft to kill Michael once and for all at the beginning of the film?

    a. Grenade   c. TNT

    b. Dynamite   d. Bomb

64. Who played the role of Mikey?

    a. Frank Como   c. David Ursin

    b. Matthew Walker   d. Jonathan Chapin

65. Who does Michael Myers kill at the clinic?

    a. Billy   c. Dr. Max Hart

    b. Nurse Patsey d. Both B and C

66. Where does Michael kill Tina's boyfriend, Mikey?
    a. At the Halloween party
    b. In his car
    c. In a car garage
    d. In a barn

67. How does the film begin?
    a. With Michael floating down the river
    b. With the ending of the previous film
    c. With Michael being found by a Mountain Man
    d. With Rachel visiting Jamie at the clinic

68. The script included a "clown theme" of the bumbling cops, Deputies Nick Ross and Tom Farrah, to pay homage to which classic film?
    a. *IT* (1990)
    b. *The Funhouse* (1981)
    c. *The Last House on the Left* (1972)
    d. *Friday the 13th* (1980)

69. Who played the role of Tina Williams?
    a. Tamara Glynn
    b. Danielle Harris
    c. Wendi Kaplan
    d. Ellie Cornell

70. The Mountain Man in the beginning of the film was originally going to be what?
    a. A young man by the name of Dr. Evil
    b. A young man by the name of Dr. Shape
    c. A young man by the name of Dr. Death
    d. A young man by the name of Dr. Blood

71. How was Rachel originally going to be killed?
    a. Being stabbed in the eye with a pair of scissors
    b. Having her head chopped off with a butcher knife
    c. Having her body chopped into pieces with a butcher knife
    d. Having a pair of scissors shoved down her throat

72. What plot point of the film did Donald Pleasence have disagreements about with Moustapha Akkad and the director?

   a. Donald thought that Jamie should be "all-evil"

   b. Donald thought that Rachel should not have been killed

   c. Donald thought that there should've been more blood and gore

   d. Donald thought that Dr. Sam Loomis should've been killed off

73. What state was *Halloween 5: The Revenge of Michael Myers* (1989) filmed in?

   a. California

   b. Louisiana

   c. Arizona

   d. Utah

74. Who played the role of Billy?

   a. Corey Feldman

   b. Harper Roisman

   c. Troy Evans

   d. Jeffrey Landman

75. What did Michael Myers use to kill Deputies Nick Ross and Tom Farrah?

   a. Scythe

   b. Butcher Knife

   c. Machete

   d. Pitchfork

76. When Michael lifted his mask, what did Jamie do that made him go psycho?

   a. She went to give him a hug

   b. She went to wipe his tears from his eyes

   c. She went to give him a kiss

   d. She went to take the knife off of him

77. Originally, what was going to be in the young man's shack that he would've used to bring Michael back to life, but was cut in favor of the Mountain Man?

   a. Ancient Runes and Crystals

   b. Ancient Runes and Potions

   c. Ancient Runes and Tablets

   d. Ancient Runes and Spells

78. What was the address of where the Myers house was filmed?

   a. 1005 1st Avenue   c. 1007 1st Avenue

   b. 1009 1st Avenue   d. 1134 1st Avenue

79. How did Dr. Loomis weaken Michael?

   a. Shot him six times with his gun

   b. Beat him with a wooden plank

   c. Shot him with a tranquilizer gun

   d. He strapped him into a straitjacket

80. How did Dr. Loomis lure Michael into his trap to drop the net onto him?

   a. He kept baiting Michael with insulting words

   b. He had Michael chase him

   c. He used Jamie as bait to lure Michael

   d. He recreated the scene of the night he killed his sister

81. What disability does Billy have?

   a. Autism   c. Tourette's Syndrome

   b. Bipolar   d. Stuttering

82. What happens to Jamie during the pageant?

   a. She falls off the stage when getting another telekinetic vision of Michael

   b. She starts talking and warning everyone of Michael

   c. She runs off the stage to look for Rachel and Tina

   d. She starts hyperventilating when reliving what she did to her foster mother

83. When Spitz and Samantha are making love, what "goof" happens during the sex scene?

   a. The condom Spitz has is opened

   b. Samantha takes her gloves off twice

   c. Spitz and Samantha are obviously wearing clothes while making love

   d. You can see the shadow of the director

84. What happens to Sheriff Ben Meeker at the end of the film?

   a. He dies in the shootout of the police station

   b. He takes Jamie to protection from the police station shootout

   c. He, along with Jamie, find Michael gone after the police station shootout

   d. He takes Dr. Loomis to visit Michael in the jail cell only to find out he escaped

85. What kind of dog is Max?

   a. Labrador Retriever   c. German Shepherd

   b. Doberman   d. Rottweiler

86. Where did Dr. Loomis pray Michael would go, but realized it would not have him?

   a. Smith's Grove Sanitarium   c. Hell

   b. Death's Door   d. The Afterlife

87. What is the name of the store where Spitz works?

    a. Victor Drug Store   c. Val Drug Store

    b. Vincent Drug Store d. Vito Drug Store

88. Which character from the *Friday the 13th* (1980) franchise does Jamie Lloyd have a striking parallel with?

    a. Reggie the Reckless c. Tina Shepard

    b. Tommy Jarvis   d. Rennie Wickham

89. What was Samantha dressed up as at the Halloween party?

    a. Angel   c. Witch

    b. Devil   d. French Maid

90. What personality trait does Tina have?

    a. Outgoing   c. Mischievous

    b. Prankster   d. Obnoxious

91. What does Jamie hide in when running from Michael, after she finds the bodies in his attic?

    a. Casket   c. Bathtub

    b. Closet   d. Laundry Chute

92. All the other actors who played Michael Myers were 6'2" except for Don Shanks. How tall was he?

    a. 6'1"   c. 6'0"

    b. 5'10"   d. 6'3"

93. What was the working title of *Halloween 5: The Revenge of Michael Myers*?

    a. *Halloween 5: The Wrath of Michael Myers* (1989)

    b. *Halloween 5: Season of Evil* (1989)

    c. *Halloween 5: And Things Go Pump in the Night* (1989)

    d. *Halloween 5: Day of the Dead* (1989)

94. How many minutes does Rachel appear in *Halloween 5: The Revenge of Michael Myers* (1989)?

   a. 30 Minutes

   b. 25 Minutes

   c. 15 Minutes

   d. 20 Minutes

95. What did Dr. Loomis repeatedly hit Michael with?

   a. Lead Pipe

   b. Hammer

   c. 2x4

   d. His fists

96. Why was Rachel's death scene changed from the original death written in the script?

   a. Because the actress who played Rachel wanted a more gruesome death scene

   b. Because the actress who played Rachel thought the death was too gruesome

   c. Because the actress who played Rachel originally wanted to survive the film

   d. Because the actress who played Rachel didn't want a child actress to see such a death

97. What did Moustapha Akkad say one of his biggest regrets was in this movie?

   a. That he killed off Rachel Carruthers

   b. That Dr. Sam Loomis wasn't killed off

   c. That the ending wasn't originally written

   d. That the Man in Black wasn't revealed

98. In which magazine was the director quoted as saying that the ending of the film wasn't scripted?

   a. *Fangoria*

   b. *Rue Morgue*

   c. *Apex*

   d. *Nightmare*

99. Which scene with Billy was originally cut from the film to avoid an X rating from the MPAA?

   a. Being killed by Michael Myers

   b. Being attacked by Michael Myers

   c. Being chased by Michael Myers

   d. Being hit in the leg with the car Michael Myers was driving

100. This is the last film of the series to feature what in the opening credits?

   a. The *Halloween* (1978) theme song

   b. Having the names of the cast

   c. Having a pumpkin graphic

   d. Having the title of the film featured

Halloween 6: The Curse of Michael Myers (1995)

1. When was *Halloween 6: The Curse of Michael Myers* (1995) released into theaters?
   a. September 29, 1995   c. September 25, 1995
   b. September 30, 1995   d. September 18, 1995

2. What was the budget of *Halloween 6: The Curse of Michael Myers* (1995)?
   a. $3 million   c. $5 million
   b. $7 million   d. $9 million

3. Danielle Harris refused to return as Jamie Lloyd. Who took over the role of Jamie Lloyd?
   a. Jennifer Banko   c. J.C. Brandy
   b. Kyle Richards   d. Amber Pawlick

4. Who directed *Halloween 6: The Curse of Michael Myers* (1995)?
   a. Dwight H. Little   c. John Carpenter
   b. Joe Chappelle   d. Tommy Lee Wallace

5. Which character from the original *Halloween* (1978) film returned as a main character?
   a. Laurie Strode   c. Tommy Doyle
   b. Lindsay Wallace   d. Sheriff Brackett

6. What is the curse that keeps driving Michael Myers to kill?
   a. Bonfire   c. Thorn
   b. Skull   d. Hellfire

7. Who was the final girl of *Halloween 6: The Curse of Michael Myers* (1995)?

    a. Debra Strode   c. Kara Strode

    b. Jamie Lloyd   d. Beth

8. Who played Michael Myers?

    a. Nick Castle   c. Dick Warlock

    b. George P. Wilbur   d. Don Shanks

9. What happened to Dr. Loomis?

    a. He died   c. He moved to Russellville

    b. He is institutionalized   d. He is retired

10. What movie was Mrs. Blankenship watching in her home?

    a. *The Phantom of the Opera* (1925)

    b. *Citizen Kane* (1941)

    c. *The Wizard of Oz* (1939)

    d. *Casablanca* (1943)

11. What was the body count of *Halloween 6: The Curse of Michael Myers* (1995)?

    a. Twenty   c. Twenty-Two

    b. Twenty-One   d. Twenty-Three

12. How much did *Halloween 6: The Curse of Michael Myers* (1995) gross in the box office?

    a. $15.5 million   c. $15.3 million

    b. $15.7 million   d. $15.1 million

13. Which actress was considered for and later turned down for the role of Beth?

    a. Leah Remini   c. Candace Cameron-Bure

    b. Denise Richards   d. Julia Roberts

14. What was the original working title of *Halloween 6: The Curse of Michael Myers* (1995)?

    a. *Halloween 666: The Curse of Michael Myers* (1995)

    b. *Halloween 666: The History of Michael Myers* (1995)

    c. *Halloween 666: The Origin of Michael Myers* (1995)

    d. *Halloween 666: The Lore of Michael Myers* (1995)

15. When Danielle Harris turned down the film, it was because Dimension Films refused to pay her how much money for the role?

    a. $10,000
    c. $7,000

    b. $5,000
    d. $3,000

16. What name did Tommy give to Jamie's baby?

    a. Stephen
    c. Scott

    b. Sean
    d. Stanley

17. Which character hears the voice that Michael once heard as a child?

    a. Danny Strode
    c. Tommy Doyle

    b. Tim Strode
    d. Jamie Lloyd

18. Who was revealed as being the Man in Black from *Halloween 5: The Revenge of Michael Myers* (1989) who ultimately helped Michael escape from the maximum-security prison?

    a. Dr. Sam Loomis
    c. Tommy Doyle

    b. John Strode
    d. Dr. Terrence Wynn

19. What room number in Smith's Grove Sanitarium is Kara being locked in?

    a. 233
    c. 235

    b. 237
    d. 239

20. What character from *Halloween 6: The Curse of Michael Myers* (1995) was named after Bob Simms from *Halloween* (1978)?

   a. Barry Simms
   c. Bobby Simms
   b. Billy Simms
   d. Barney Simms

21. What type of truck was Jamie driving in the beginning of the film?

   a. Chevrolet Colorado
   c. Chevrolet Silverado
   b. Chevrolet Tahoe
   d. Chevrolet Blazer

22. What did it say on Tim's t-shirt?

   a. Barry Kicks Ass
   c. Barry Kisses Ass
   b. Barry Slaps Ass
   d. Barry Kills Ass

23. What was Beth dressed up as for the Halloween party?

   a. Witch
   c. Bride of Frankenstein
   b. Queen
   d. Princess

24. According to Mrs. Blankenship, what did the voice tell Michael to do when he was a child?

   a. To hate his family
   c. To become evil
   b. To kill his family
   d. To leave his family

25. Besides Tommy and Dr. Loomis, who else knew of Jamie's baby?

   a. Mrs. Blankenship
   c. John Strode
   b. Dr. Terrence Wynn
   d. Debra Strode

26. What was the phone number to Barry Simms' station?

   a. 1-800-968-7836 (YOU SUCK)
   b. 1-800-968-7814 (YOU SUCK)
   c. 1-800-968-7825 (YOU SUCK)
   d. 1-800-968-7837 (YOU SUCK)

27. What did Danny dress up as for Halloween?
    a. The identical twin brother of Tim Strode
    b. The identical twin brother of Tommy Doyle
    c. The identical twin brother of Michael Myers
    d. The identical twin brother of Barry Simms
28. How did Mrs. Blankenship know Michael Myers?
    a. She adopted him after he killed his sister
    b. She visited him during her volunteer work at Smith's Grove Sanitarium
    c. She helped him plot his revenge on Haddonfield in 1978
    d. She babysat him the night he killed his sister
29. What does it say on the sign that was posted on the Strode's front lawn?
    a. He's Back
    b. He's Alive
    c. He's Here
    d. He's Coming
30. What was the name of Barry Simms' radio show?
    a. *Smacktalk with Barry Simms* (1995)
    b. *Haddonfield Gossip with Barry Simms* (1995)
    c. *Sex Therapy with Barry Simms* (1995)
    d. *Backtalk with Barry Simms* (1995)
31. What color and make vehicle did Tommy have?
    a. Red Blazer
    b. Red Mercedes
    c. Red Ferrari
    d. Red Jeep
32. What was the name of the nurse who helped Jamie escape?
    a. Marcia
    b. Mary
    c. Megan
    d. Margaret

33. What was Mrs. Blankenship's first name, as told in *Halloween III: Season of the Witch* (1982)?
    a. Mary Ann   c. Mary Ellen
    b. Maxine   d. Minnie

34. What colors was the truck that Jamie was driving in the beginning of the film?
    a. Blue and White   c. Blue and Red
    b. Black and White   d. Black and Blue

35. Who played the role of Tommy Doyle?
    a. Paul Rudd   c. Brian Andrews
    b. Thom Mathews   d. John Shepherd

36. Whose house did Beth tell Barry Simms on his show that Tim's family lives in?
    a. The Doyle House   c. The Myers House
    b. The Wallace House d. The Meeker House

37. What was Tim dressed up as for the Halloween party?
    a. Dracula   c. Wolfman
    b. Frankenstein   d. Mad Scientist

38. What did Barry Simms ask Tim if Beth does in bed?
    a. If Beth wears crotch less panties and fakes her orgasms
    b. If Beth wears crotch less panties and curses uncontrollably
    c. If Beth wears crotch less panties and barks like a dog
    d. If Beth wears crotch less panties and roleplays

39. Who is John and Debra's niece?
    a. Jamie Lloyd   c. Kara Strode
    b. Laurie Strode   d. Rachel Carruthers

40. Which subject was Kara studying at her college?

   a. Sociology
   c. Biology

   b. Psychology
   d. Physiology

41. Which of the following is one of the differences in the Producer's Cut that was excluded from the theatrical release of the film?

   a. Danny hears the voice Michael heard as a child

   b. The ending of the film

   c. Jamie's death scene

   d. All of the Above

42. What did the little girl say when she was under the tree where Barry Simms' corpse was located?

   a. Mommy it's a man   c. Mommy it's raining red

   b. Mommy it's warm raindrops   d. Mommy it's a climber

43. Who played the role of Kara Strode?

   a. J.C. Brandy
   c. Marianne Hagan

   b. Kim Darby
   d. Mariah O'Brien

44. Why does Dr. Wynn visit Dr. Loomis?

   a. Because he wants Dr. Loomis to find Michael Myers

   b. Because he wants Dr. Loomis to come out of retirement and return to Smith's Grove

   c. Because he wants Dr. Loomis to study the reason Michael kills on Halloween

   d. Because he wants Dr. Loomis to join his cult

45. When does Michael Myers know to kill on Halloween?

   a. When the constellations form the symbol of the jack-o'-lantern

   b. When the constellations form the symbol of the devil

   c. When the constellations form the symbol of the thorn

   d. When the constellations form the symbol of the Celtics

46. According to the Producer's Cut of *Halloween 6: The Curse of Michael Myers* (1995), who is the father of Jamie's baby?

   a. Tommy Doyle   c. Michael Myers

   b. Tim Strode   d. Dr. Terrence Wynn

47. Who played the role of Danny Strode?

   a. Paul Rudd   c. Devin Gardner

   b. Keith Bogart   d. Leo Geter

48. Who were the characters of John and Debra Strode named after?

   a. John Wayne and Debra Jo Rupp

   b. John Carpenter and Debra Hill

   c. John Lennon and Debra Messing

   d. John Travolta and Debra Marshall

49. Who turned down the role of Barry Simms when he was offered the role?

   a. Alice Cooper   c. Bubba the Love Sponge

   b. Marilyn Manson   d. Howard Stern

50. How many different drafts did the film go through?

   a. Ten   c. Twelve

   b. Eleven   d. Thirteen

51. Why did Marianne Hagan almost not get the role of Kara Strode?

   a. Because Miramax Films thought she was too thin, and her chin was too pointy

   b. Because Miramax Films thought she was too old and too boring

   c. Because Miramax Films thought she was too ugly and too feminine

   d. Because Miramax Films thought she was too unbelievable and too bad of an actress

52. In January 1995, *Entertainment Tonight* (1981) had a special on the making of this movie stating that it was going to be called what title in its early stages of development?

   a. *Halloween 6: Michael's Return* (1995)

   b. *Halloween 6: Michael's Curse* (1995)

   c. *Halloween 6: Michael's Back* (1995)

   d. *Halloween 6: Michael's Revenge* (1995)

53. According to the Curse of Thorn, what would happen after Michael killed his entire family in his bloodline?

   a. The curse would allow Michael to be killed

   b. The curse would be passed onto another young child

   c. The curse would cease to exist

   d. The curse would make Michael Myers disappear from existence

54. Where does the Curse of Thorn come from?

   a. Ancient Celtic Rituals   c. Ancient Irish Rituals

   b. Ancient Samhain Rituals   d. Ancient Wiccan Rituals

55. In *Halloween* (1978), Dr. Wynn makes a brief appearance saying Michael cannot drive a car. What does Dr. Wynn say in *Halloween 6: The Curse of Michael Myers* (1995) as to how Michael learned to drive a car?

   a. He allowed him to take driving lessons at a local DMV

   b. He taught him how to drive a car

   c. He blackmailed Marion Chambers into teaching him how to drive a car

   d. He allowed Michael to teach himself how to drive a car around the parking lot of Smith's Grove Sanitarium

56. What is Dr. Wynn's position at Smith's Grove Sanitarium?

   a. Chief Psychiatrist   c. Chief Executive Officer

   b. Chief Administrator   d. Chief Operating Officer

57. What did Beth say Tommy rates on a weirdness scale of 1 to 10?

   a. Eleven   c. Thirteen

   b. Twelve   d. Twenty

58. Who played the role of Dr. Terrence Wynn?

   a. Mitchell Ryan   c. Donald Pleasence

   b. Bradford English   d. Keith Bogart

59. Which of the following was the opening narration of the film?

   a. After my stroke six years ago they practically had to hold a pistol to my head to get me to retire. But things are different now – I'm different. I've buried the ghosts; I've buried them in this manuscript. I don't want to practice medicine anymore.

   b. I've wanted to believe it. But I've felt Michael's presence, behind these walls, just like all those years ago. Plotting, staring, and staring. Waiting for some signal. I can't go through this again, not alone. Please, as my colleague, as my friend. Help me.

   c. After Jamie escaped last night, I knew she would come to you. And I knew you would lead us to her baby, her very special baby. I needed her, just as I need you now. It's your destiny Sam, it lives inside you. It always has, you know that don't you?

   d. When Michael Myers was six years old, he stabbed his sister to death. He was locked up for years in Smith's Grove Sanitarium, but he escaped. Soon after, Halloween became another word for mayhem! One by one, he killed his entire family, until his nine-year-old niece, Jamie Lloyd, was the only one left alive. Six years ago – Halloween night – Michael and Jamie vanished. Most people believed them dead, but I believe someone hid them away. Someone who keeps Michael, protects him . . . tries to control him. If there's one thing I know, you can't control evil. You can lock it up, burn it, and bury it, and pray that it dies, but it never will. It just . . . rests awhile. You can lock your doors, and say your prayers, but the evil is out there . . . waiting. And maybe, just maybe . . . it's closer than you think!

60. What was the story Mrs. Blankenship told Danny?

   a. Spirits and powers of the flame, attend and witness this ritual. Bear our gifts to Thorn. Open us to the path of Darkness. By these runes transform us. Let the hammer descend upon the Chosen One to whom we offer this sacrifice of Innocent Blood. And then Danny, your journey begins. Kill for him!

   b. When Michael Myers was six years old, he stabbed his sister to death. He was locked up for years in Smith's Grove Sanitarium, but he escaped. Soon after, Halloween became another word for mayhem! One by one, he killed his entire family, until his nine-year-old niece, Jamie Lloyd, was the only one left alive. Six years ago – Halloween night – Michael and Jamie vanished. Most people believed them dead, but I believe someone hid them away. Someone who keeps Michael, protects him . . . tries to control him. If there's one thing I know, you can't control evil. You can lock it up, burn it, and bury it, and pray that it dies, but it never will. It just . . . rests awhile. You can lock your doors, and say your prayers, but the evil is out there . . . waiting. And maybe, just maybe . . . it's closer than you think!

   c. A long, long time ago, it was a night of great power. When the days grew short, the spirits of the dead returned to their homes to warm themselves by the fire's side. All across the land, huge bonfires were lit. Ohhh, there was a marvelous celebration. People danced, and they played games, and they dressed up in costumes, hoping to ward off the evil spirits. Especially the Boogeyman.

   d. In order to appease the gods, the Druid priests held fire rituals. Prisoners of war, criminals, the insane, animals . . . were . . . burned alive in baskets. By observing the way they died, the Druids believed they could see omens of the future. Two thousand years later, we've come no further. Samhain isn't evil spirits. It isn't goblins, ghosts, or witches. It's the unconscious mind. We're all afraid of the dark inside ourselves.

61. Which plastic surgery did Dr. Loomis tell Dr. Wynn he got due to his past encounters with Michael Myers?
    a. Skin Grafts
    c. Facial Rejuvenation
    b. Facial Contouring
    d. Body Contouring

62. Who does Dr. Wynn plan on using to replace Michael Myers with the Curse of Thorn?
    a. Danny Strode
    c. Tommy Doyle
    b. Jamie Lloyd
    d. Stephen

63. In the Producer's Cut of the film, who was under the mask of Michael Myers when Michael escaped?
    a. Dr. Terrence Wynn
    c. Dr. Sam Loomis
    b. Tommy Doyle
    d. Mrs. Blankenship

64. In the Producer's Cut of the film, who does Dr. Wynn tell Michael his final sacrifice is?
    a. Stephen
    c. Kara Strode
    b. Danny Strode
    d. Tommy Doyle

65. Whose bed did Tim and Beth make love in?
    a. Tim's nephew's bed
    c. Tim's parents' bed
    b. Tim's sister's bed
    d. Tim's bed

66. What type of help did Barry Simms tell Tommy there is for people like him over the phone?
    a. Electromagnetic Therapy
    c. Electroshock Therapy
    b. Electroconvulsive Therapy
    d. Electron Therapy

67. Besides Tommy, who was the other caller to Barry Simms' radio show that had a name?
    a. Duanne
    c. Darren
    b. David
    d. Dustin

68. How old did Tommy say he was when he saw Michael Myers?
    a. Seven Years Old   c. Nine Years Old
    b. Eight Years Old   d. Ten Years Old
69. Who played the role of Tim Strode?
    a. Bradford English   c. Paul Rudd
    b. Keith Bogart   d. Devin Gardner
70. What led Tommy into finding Jamie's baby?
    a. A trail of milk   c. A trail of crumbs
    b. A trail of blood   d. A trail of piss
71. How did Jamie get in touch with Dr. Loomis about Michael being alive and coming after her?
    a. She called him
    b. She called into the Barry Simms radio show
    c. She called 911
    d. She called Smith's Grove
72. At the end of the Producer's Cut of the film, what happens to Dr. Loomis?
    a. He is killed   c. He gets the Curse of Thorn tattoo
    b. He kills Dr. Wynn   d. He helps Michael escape
73. In the Producer's Cut of the film, how does Jamie die?
    a. Stabbed with a knife   c. Shot by Dr. Wynn
    b. Impaled on farming equipment   d. Throat slit
74. What was Debra Strode doing before she was killed?
    a. Dusting   c. Cooking
    b. Sweeping   d. Laundry

75. Where did Jamie go to hide from Michael Myers and call for help?
    a. Subway
    c. Bus Terminal
    b. Airport
    d. Factory

76. Before Jamie died, what were her last words to Michael?
    a. You will never get my baby, Michael
    b. You can't have the baby, Michael
    c. You will never be able to find the baby, Michael
    d. You will not kill my baby, Michael

77. Who played the role of Debra Strode?
    a. Marianne Hagan
    c. Susan Swift
    b. Janice Knickrehm
    d. Kim Darby

78. What did one of the signs say at the Halloween party?
    a. He will be back
    c. He will return
    b. He will kill again
    d. He will find us

79. Before Jamie called out to Dr. Loomis, what did Dr. Loomis think happened to her?
    a. She died in the explosion at the police station
    b. She was committed into a psychiatric institute
    c. She committed suicide
    d. She was in a car accident

80. What does Tommy use to look out his window and into the Myers house?
    a. Telescope
    c. Binoculars
    b. Magnifying Glass
    d. Night Vision Goggles

81. What county is Smith's Grove Sanitarium in?
    a. Warren County
    c. Schuylkill County
    b. Luzerne County
    d. Wessex County

82. In the Producer's Cut of the film, what Christian children's tune is the little girl singing "Mommy it's raining, it's raining red"?

   a. "Joy to the World"

   b. "Jesus Loves Me This I Know"

   c. "He's Got the Whole World in His Hands"

   d. "Away In A Manger"

83. What did Dr. Loomis tell Debra Strode that Michael has at their house that makes it sacred to him?

   a. Feelings   c. Fits of Rage

   b. Memories   d. Nightmares

84. What did Debra Strode notice was gone to be alarmed that Michael Myers is nearby?

   a. Butcher Knife   c. Axe

   b. Scythe   d. Scissors

85. Who played the role of Beth?

   a. Kim Darby   c. Mariah O'Brien

   b. Marianne Hagan d. J.C. Brandy

86. How many years have passed from the end of *Halloween 5: The Revenge of Michael Myers* (1989) to the current events in *Halloween 6: The Curse of Michael Myers* (1995)?

   a. Six Years   c. Five Years

   b. Seven Years   d. Ten Years

87. Who was revealed to be the one behind Michael's rage and final sacrifice with the Curse of Thorn?

   a. Dr. Sam Loomis c. Mrs. Blankenship

   b. Tommy Doyle   d. Dr. Terrence Wynn

88. Who did Dr. Terrence Wynn have tied up in a crucifix for a Satanic Samhain ritual?

   a. Tommy Doyle
   c. Danny Strode
   b. Stephen
   d. Kara Strode

89. What symbol did the Man in Black carve into Jamie's baby in the beginning of the film?

   a. Thorn
   c. Jack-o'-Lantern
   b. Ghost
   d. Devil Horns

90. What was Jamie trying to tell the Motorist to do before Michael killed him?

   a. To get into the truck with her
   c. To beware of Michael
   b. To run
   d. To call for help

91. What did John Strode find odd about the washing machine when he was in the basement?

   a. It is running when the power is out
   b. The clothes weren't getting cleaned
   c. It leaked water all over the floor
   d. It wouldn't turn on

92. What incident featuring Tommy Doyle from the original *Halloween* film happened to Danny Strode in *Halloween 6: The Curse of Michael Myers* (1995)?

   a. Danny Strode kept telling Kara that he saw the Boogeyman
   b. Danny Strode tripped and smashed his jack-o'-lantern
   c. Danny Strode was followed by Michael Myers when leaving school
   d. Danny Strode ran out of the house calling for help when Michael was in the house with Kara

93. What did Jamie Lloyd have wrapped in the blanket instead of her baby to trick Michael?

   a. A Shirt
   c. A Diaper
   b. A Pillow
   d. A Towel

94. Why did Mary help Jamie to escape?

   a. So Michael wouldn't kill Jamie
   b. To help her escape the rituals
   c. So she can save her baby
   d. To keep her secret about her baby's daddy

95. What did Tim Strode do to prove his father's point that kids have no respect?

   a. He farted
   c. He burped
   b. He snorted
   d. He sneezed

96. Who gave Tim his towel after he finished his shower?

   a. Danny Strode
   c. Michael Myers
   b. Beth
   d. Dr. Terrence Wynn

97. Who played the role of John Strode?

   a. Leo Geter
   c. Keith Bogart
   b. Mitchell Ryan
   d. Bradford English

98. What did the end of the theatrical release of the film symbolize?

   a. Dr. Loomis was finally killed by Michael Myers due to the actor dying after filming concluded
   b. Dr. Loomis became the new evil of Haddonfield
   c. Dr. Loomis killed Dr. Terrence Wynn to put a stop to Michael once and for all
   d. Dr. Loomis finally was able to kill Michael Myers to end his reign of terror for good

99. Who did Kara see get killed in her bed?
   - a. Beth
   - b. Debra Strode
   - c. Tim Strode
   - d. John Strode

100. How does Michael Myers kill Tim Strode?
   - a. Slits his throat with a hunting knife
   - b. Slits his throat with a butcher knife
   - c. Slits his throat with a glass shard
   - d. Slits his throat with a pair of scissors

Halloween H20: 20 Years Later (1998)

1. Which actor/actress made their ultimate return to the *Halloween* (1978) franchise in *Halloween H20: 20 Years Later* (1998)?

    a. Brian Andrews　　c. Jamie Lee Curtis

    b. Kyle Richards　　d. Charles Cyphers

2. What was the budget of *Halloween H20: 20 Years Later* (1998)?

    a. $18 million　　c. $17 million

    b. $15 million　　d. $16 million

3. When was *Halloween H20: 20 Years Later* (1998) released into theaters?

    a. August 1, 1998　　c. August 5, 1998

    b. August 3, 1998　　d. August 12, 1998

4. How much did *Halloween H20: 20 Years Later* (1998) gross at the box office?

    a. $50 million　　c. $55 million

    b. $60 million　　d. $65 million

5. Who directed *Halloween H20: 20 Years Later* (1998)?

    a. John Carpenter　　c. Steve Miner

    b. Tommy Lee Wallace　　d. Dwight H. Little

6. What name is Laurie Strode going by?

    a. Keri Tate　　c. Kimmy Tate

    b. Kathy Tate　　d. Karen Tate

7. Who scares Laurie Strode, saying "It's Halloween, everyone is entitled to one good scare" just like Sheriff Brackett said in the original *Halloween* (1978) film?

   a. Will Brennan   c. John Tate

   b. Norma Watson   d. Molly Cartwell

8. What is the name of the school where Laurie Strode works?

   a. Hightop Academy   c. Honorwood Academy

   b. Hampton Academy   d. Hillcrest Academy

9. In the beginning of the film, she is now divorced, and Michael finally kills her. She is the last of the original night in 1978 he needed to kill who was associated with Dr. Loomis. Who is she?

   a. Lindsay Wallace   c. Marion Chambers

   b. Laurie Strode   d. Darlene Carruthers

10. Where did everyone go for the class field trip?

    a. Zion National Park   c. Yosemite National Park

    b. Yellowstone National Park   d. Redwood National Park

11. At the end of the film, what did Ronny tell his wife he wanted to write?

    a. Romantic Comedy   c. Docudrama

    b. Horror Comedy   d. Romantic Thriller

12. What was written on the chalkboard as Laurie taught the class?

    a. The Purgatory of C.S. Lewis, Where Does It Begin?

    b. The Purgatory of W.B. Yeats, Where Does It Begin?

    c. The Sinking of the Titanic, Where Does It Begin?

    d. The Diary of Anne Frank, Where Does It Begin?

13. What was the name of the town that Marion lived in?

    a. Langdon, Illinois   c. Russellville, Illinois

    b. Ridgemont, Illinois   d. Haddonfield, Illinois

14. What was Molly's advice to Laurie about fate, based on her answer in class?

   a. If it was fate, it must be conquered

   b. If it was fate, it must be faced

   c. If it was fate, it must be meant to happen

   d. If it was fate, it must be destined

15. What unusual object did Laurie stab Michael with?

   a. American Flag   c. Boy Scouts Flag

   b. California State Flag d. Hillcrest Academy Flag

16. What was the number of the highway that Michael was driving on and where was it precisely located?

   a. Highway 140, Northern California

   b. Highway 135, Northern California

   c. Highway 139, Northern California

   d. Highway 141, Northern California

17. What was Marion's street address?

   a. 4238 Cypress Pond Road   c. 4946 Cypress Pond Road

   b. 4752 Cypress Pond Road   d. 4118 Cypress Pond Road

18. What was the name of the town where the school is located?

   a. Big Bear, California   c. Summer Glen, California

   b. Claremont, California   d. Inglewood, California

19. What rapper played the role of Ronny Jones?

   a. Will Smith   c. LL Cool J

   b. Usher   d. Snoop Dogg

20. Who voiced the role of Dr. Sam Loomis in the beginning of the film?

   a. Donald Pleasence
   c. Malcolm McDowell
   b. Tom Kane
   d. Steve Miner

21. What was Will Brennan's job title at Hillcrest Academy?

   a. Physics Teacher
   c. Dean of Students
   b. Guidance Counselor
   d. Assistant Principal

22. What was the body count in *Halloween H20: 20 Years Later* (1998)?

   a. Seven
   c. Eight
   b. Six
   d. Nine

23. In *Halloween* (1978), Laurie Strode tells Tommy and Lindsay to go down the street to the McKenzie's house. In *Halloween H20: 20 Years Later* (1998), Laurie Strode tells John and Molly to go down the street to whose house, in reference to *Scream* (1996)?

   a. Becker's
   c. Campbell's
   b. Weathers'
   d. Riley's

24. Who played Michael Myers in *Halloween H20: 20 Years Later* (1998)?

   a. Christopher Durand
   c. Brad Loree
   b. George P. Wilbur
   d. Don Shanks

25. P.J. Soles, who played Lynda in *Halloween* (1978), was approached to play which character in *Halloween H20: 20 Years Later* (1998)?

   a. Molly Cartwell
   c. Sarah Wainthrope
   b. Keri Tate
   d. Norma Watson

26. What is the first name of Ronny's wife?

   a. Shirley
   c. Sharon
   b. Shannon
   d. Sherry

27. What is Laurie Strode's job title at Hillcrest Academy, under the name of Keri Tate?

   a. Psychology Teacher   c. Principal

   b. Headmistress   d. Superintendent

28. In which film directed by Steve Miner did Jamie Lee Curtis first work with him?

   a. *Friday the 13th Part II* (1981)   c. *Forever Young* (1992)

   b. *Night of the Creeps* (1986)   d. *Warlock* (1989)

29. What was the original working title for *Halloween H20: 20 Years Later* (1998)?

   a. *Halloween 7: The Return of Laurie Strode* (1998)

   b. *Halloween 7: Laurie vs. Michael* (1998)

   c. *Halloween 7: The Life of Laurie Strode* (1998)

   d. *Halloween 7: The Revenge of Laurie Strode* (1998)

30. How did Laurie "kill" Michael Myers at the end of the film?

   a. She beheaded Michael with an axe

   b. She had him blown up in an exploding ambulance

   c. She stabbed him repeatedly in the face

   d. She gave him a lethal injection

31. What happened to Jamie Lee Curtis one month after the film's release?

   a. She was stalked by a man in a Michael Myers costume

   b. She got a star on the Hollywood Walk of Fame

   c. She got labeled as a true horror "Scream Queen"

   d. She was inducted into the Horror Hall of Fame

32. Who played the role of Will Brennan?

   a. Adam Arkin   c. LL Cool J

   b. Josh Hartnett   d. Joseph Gordon-Levitt

33. John Tate turned the same age that Laurie's sister was when she was killed by Michael. She now knows that Michael will be coming after him due to that age. How old did John turn?

   a. Fifteen
   b. Seventeen
   c. Sixteen
   d. Eighteen

34. Who did Laurie Strode shoot thinking it was her brother?

   a. Ronny Jones
   b. Norma Watson
   c. Will Brennan
   d. Charlie Deveraux

35. How many times did Jimmy say he was suspended for getting a little crazy with a hockey stick?

   a. Three
   b. Four
   c. Five
   d. Six

36. What children's song was the little girl humming in the bathroom?

   a. "Itsy Bitsy Spider"
   b. "Humpty Dumpty"
   c. "Mary Had a Little Lamb"
   d. "Patty Cake"

37. What famous slasher film is Janet Leigh, who plays Norma, most noticeable for starring in?

   a. *Friday the 13th* (1980)
   b. *Psycho* (1960)
   c. *A Nightmare on Elm Street* (1984)
   d. *The Texas Chainsaw Massacre* (1974)

38. Why isn't Charlie going to Yosemite?

    a. He flunked his Algebra midterm exam

    b. He was turned down for his scholarship

    c. He didn't hand in his History report

    d. He never got his permission slip signed

39. What time do the buses leave for Yosemite?

    a. 4:30 Sharp   c. 4:15 Sharp

    b. 4:45 Sharp   d. 4:00 Sharp

40. Why did Will Brennan say he cannot join the girls for a night of fun?

    a. It isn't professional   c. He is having his nipples pierced

    b. He has a date   d. He must make his rounds

41. What did Molly hit Michael with when she was just about to kill John?

    a. Log   c. Rock

    b. Cinder Block   d. Brick

42. What did Ronny's wife say is not working out for him?

    a. His job as a security guard   c. His career as a writer

    b. His marriage with her   d. His moves during sex

43. When Will asked Laurie why she didn't want to go camping, what did she say was her reason?

    a. It sounds like a blast   c. It sounds like a great time

    b. It sounds like fun   d. It sounds like a hoot

44. What kind of addict is John's father?

    a. Heroin   c. Cocaine

    b. Pill Popping   d. Methadone

45. How many months late is the birthday card that John got from his father?

    a. One Month   c. Three Months

    b. Five Months   d. Two Months

46. Who played the role of Jimmy Howell?

    a. Adam Hann-Byrd   c. Joseph Gordon-Levitt

    b. Josh Hartnett   d. Adam Arkin

47. What is Norma Watson's job title at Hillcrest Academy?

    a. Secretary   c. Vice Principal

    b. Calculus Teacher   d. Lunch Monitor

48. Why did the little girl scream in the bathroom?

    a. She saw Michael Myers   c. She saw a spider

    b. She fell in the toilet   d. She heard someone walk in

49. How did Sarah get out of going to Yosemite?

    a. She has a fever of 102 and has to stay in bed all weekend long

    b. She has a death in the family and has to go back to her hometown

    c. She got a job and cannot get the weekend off of work

    d. She promised to take her little brother Trick-or-Treating

50. What kind of white wine was Laurie drinking while on lunch with Will?

    a. Semillon   c. Chardonnay

    b. Sauvignon Blanc   d. Pinot Grigio

51. What were the five things that Laurie told Will she tried to recover from her past?

    a. 12-Steps, Self Help, Group Therapy, Shrinks, and Yoga

    b. 12-Steps, Self Help, Group Therapy, Shrinks, and Meditation

    c. 12-Steps, Self Help, Group Therapy, Shrinks, and Kickboxing

    d. 12-Steps, Self Help, Group Therapy, Shrinks, and Fear Counseling

52. What book did the class read as a homework assignment, assigned by Laurie?

    a. *Bram Stoker's Dracula* (1897)   c. *Of Mice and Men* (1937)

    b. *Mary Shelley's Frankenstein* (1818)   d. *Beowulf* (1815)

53. When Laurie got into her car, what song played on the radio?

    a. "Monster Mash"   c. "The Addams Family"

    b. "Mr. Sandman"   d. "I Will Survive"

54. Which actress from *Scream 2* is seen on the television in Molly and Sarah's bedroom?

    a. Neve Campbell   c. Sarah Michelle Gellar

    b. Courtney Cox-Arquette   d. Laurie Metcalf

55. LL Cool J wasn't just playing a security guard who is also a writer. What did LL Cool J do a month after the film was released?

    a. He had a fiction novel published

    b. He had a romantic thriller novel published

    c. He had a biographical novel published

    d. He had an autobiography published

56. What word was Michael originally supposed to speak at the end of the film before it was cut from the final script?

    a. Sister   c. Sis

    b. Laurie   d. Help

57. In the original script, who was Ronny going to be?

   a. A female named Hattie
   c. A female named Hillary
   b. A female named Haley
   d. A female named Heidi

58. What did Will tell Laurie he is great at that may be helpful for her recovery?

   a. Listening
   c. Giving Advice
   b. Giving Motivational Speeches
   d. Giving Encouragement

59. Who played the role of Charlie Deveraux?

   a. Joseph Gordon-Levitt
   c. Josh Hartnett
   b. Adam Hann-Byrd
   d. LL Cool J

60. Which main character was supposed to be killed off but survived in the final script?

   a. John Tate
   c. Laurie Strode
   b. Norma Watson
   d. Molly Cartwell

61. What movie was playing on the television when Marion found Jimmy's corpse?

   a. *Plan 9 from Outer Space* (1959)
   b. *The Thing from Another World* (1951)
   c. *ET: The Extra-Terrestrial* (1982)
   d. *Alien* (1979)

62. What is Marion's surname now that she is divorced?

   a. Williamson
   c. Wallace
   b. Whittington
   d. Washington

63. In the original script, Marion was not going to be in the film. In her place, a new character would be introduced as Dr. Loomis' daughter. What was his daughter's name going to be when written in the original script?

   a. Rochelle Loomis   c. Rosie Loomis

   b. Rachel Loomis   d. Renata Loomis

64. P.J. Soles was originally supposed to portray Norma Watson because she played a character named "Norma Watson" in which classic horror film?

   a. *April Fool's Day* (1986)   c. *Carrie* (1976)

   b. *Final Exam* (1981)   d. *Sleepaway Camp* (1983)

65. Who played the role of Molly Cartwell?

   a. Nancy Stephens   c. Jodi Lyn O'Keefe

   b. Janet Leigh   d. Michelle Williams

66. In an original draft of the film written by Daniel Farrands, there was going to be a student who did a book report on the book that would tie in all of the films of the franchise? What would that title have been?

   a. The Curse of Haddonfield   c. The Halloween Murders

   b. The Michael Myers Legend   d. Evil Never Dies

67. In the beginning of the film, what is the date?

   a. October 25, 1998   c. October 30, 1998

   b. October 29, 1998   d. October 31, 1998

68. Janet Leigh, as Norma Watson, is her first role in a major film in how many years?

   a. Fifteen Years   c. Twenty Years

   b. Ten Years   d. Eighteen Years

69. Which popular film did Josh Hartnett star in a few years after his success in *Halloween H20: 20 Years Later* (1998)?

   a. *Pearl Harbor* (2001)   c. *Shrek* (2001)

   b. *Black Hawk Down* (2001)   d. *Ocean's Eleven* (2001)

70. What type of school is Hillcrest Academy?

   a. Private University   c. Catholic High School

   b. Private Boarding School   d. Community College

71. Where does Sarah find Charlie's corpse?

   a. Stuffed in the refrigerator

   b. In the kitchen dumbwaiter

   c. On the kitchen floor

   d. Under the kitchen table

72. What did Michael use to kill Jimmy?

   a. Hockey Stick   c. Ice Skate

   b. Butcher Knife   d. Fireplace Poker

73. What did Michael steal from Marion's house?

   a. His diagnosis from Dr. Loomis

   b. His family history

   c. Information on Jamie Lloyd

   d. A file regarding Laurie Strode

74. What films of the *Halloween* franchise does this film ignore?

   a. *Halloween III* (1982) to *6* (1995)

   b. *Halloween 4* (1988) and *5* (1989)

   c. *Halloween 1* (1978) and *II* (1981)

   d. *Halloween III* (1982)

75. Who played the role of Sarah Wainthrope?
    a. Jodi Lyn O'Keefe   c. Michelle Williams
    b. Lisa Gay Hamilton   d. Jamie Lee Curtis
76. What was Ronny's job at the school?
    a. Security Guard   c. Custodian
    b. Groundskeeper   d. Hall Monitor
77. What does Laurie steal at the end of the film to make sure Michael is killed once and for all?
    a. Ambulance   c. Police Car
    b. Coroner's Van   d. School Bus
78. Where does Michael hang Sarah's corpse?
    a. School Parking Lot c. Hallway
    b. Basement   d. Pantry
79. What did Michael embed into Charlie's throat to kill him?
    a. Bottle Opener   c. Pocket Knife
    b. Pizza Cutter   d. Corkscrew
80. Where were John, Molly, Charlie, and Sarah hosting their intimate Halloween party?
    a. Cafeteria   c. Classroom
    b. Gymnasium   d. Basement
81. Early in the film, what is revealed about Laurie Strode?
    a. Laurie faked her death and went into hiding
    b. Laurie changed her name to avoid being found by Michael Myers
    c. Laurie never had a daughter named Jamie
    d. Laurie still has night terrors about her encounter with Michael 20 years ago

82. What is the official tagline of the film?

   a. This summer, terror won't be taking a vacation

   b. 20 years later, he comes home one last time

   c. He is back and this time, he finds who he wants

   d. Michael is back and he is thirsty for blood

83. Who produced *Halloween H20: 20 Years Later* (1998)?

   a. Daryn Okada   c. Paul Freeman

   b. Patrick Lussier   d. Robert Zappia

84. Molly and Sarah were watching *Scream 2* (1997) in their room. What were they watching in the original script before it was changed to *Scream 2* (1997) in post-production?

   a. *When A Stranger Calls* (1979)

   b. *The Texas Chainsaw Massacre* (1974)

   c. *A Nightmare on Elm Street* (1984)

   d. *So I Married an Axe Murderer* (1993)

85. Which actor/actress made his film debut in *Halloween H20: 20 Years Later* (1998)?

   a. Adam Hann-Byrd   c. Josh Hartnett

   b. Michelle Williams   d. Joseph Gordon-Levitt

86. Which line from the film was ad-libbed by LL Cool J due to Josh Hartnett's messy haircut?

   a. Comb your hair   c. Wash your hair

   b. Cut your hair   d. Do something to your hair

87. Why is the film titled *Halloween H20* (1998)?
    a. Because the film is a family feud and the old saying says "blood is thicker than water" with H20 being the chemical symbol for water
    b. Because the H stands for Halloween and the 20 stands for 20 years later
    c. Because H20 is the chemical symbol of water which has a pH balance of 7.0 and this is the seventh film in the franchise
    d. Because this film is classified as a direct sequel to the original film in 1978 and the H20 stands for Halloween 2.0
88. Who played the role of John Tate?
    a. Josh Hartnett
    b. Joseph Gordon-Levitt
    c. Adam Hann-Byrd
    d. Branden Williams
89. Which actor had a small role as a detective but was removed in the final draft of the script?
    a. Charles S. Dutton
    b. Jeff Goldblum
    c. Michael Clark Duncan
    d. Ed Harris
90. When Laurie catches Charlie and John outside and questions them, what is John's reply?
    a. Getting a little off campus lunch
    b. Getting an anniversary gift for Molly
    c. Getting some Halloween decorations for the party
    d. Getting some fresh air
91. Why did John and Charlie sneak off campus?
    a. They shoplifted some intimate items for their dates with Molly and Sarah
    b. They shoplifted some booze
    c. They shoplifted some Halloween decorations
    d. They shoplifted some jewelry for their girlfriends

92. Why was Laurie so pissed off and upset that John snuck off campus?

   a. Because California is a big state

   b. Because she can get in trouble with being the school's headmistress

   c. Because it is Halloween, and she is fearful of Michael's return

   d. Because he can get kicked out of Hillcrest Academy for breaking the code of conduct

93. How did John describe his mom to Charlie?

   a. A strict teacher
   c. A vulnerable mother

   b. A scared little girl
   d. A functioning alcoholic

94. How old was Laurie Strode when Michael came after her 20 years ago?

   a. Seventeen
   c. Sixteen

   b. Eighteen
   d. Nineteen

95. What did Norma tell Laurie is clogged again?

   a. The pipes in the boy's restroom

   b. The drains in the girl's shower room

   c. The toilets in the boy's locker room

   d. The sinks in the girl's restroom

96. What did John tell Ronny he wanted to get off campus?

   a. A gift for Molly for their date

   b. Condoms for his romantic night with Molly

   c. Candles and flowers for Molly

   d. Chocolates for Molly

97. What did Ronny say would happen to him at the hands of Laurie if he let John off campus again?

   a. He'd have his neck rung by her   c. He'd be suspended

   b. He'd lose his security license   d. He'd be fired

98. Who does Laurie keep visioning as Michael Myers?

   a. Will Brennan   c. Norma Watson

   b. John Tate   d. Ronny Jones

99. When Will asks Laurie "what do we do?" while running from Michael, what does Laurie respond with?

   a. Try to live   c. Try to kill him

   b. Try to escape   d. Try to run

100. Why can't Molly go to Yosemite?

   a. Because her dad flaked on her financial aid

   b. Because she never got her permission slip signed

   c. Because she plagiarized her book report

   d. Because she didn't maintain a B average

Halloween: Resurrection (2002)

1. What was the budget of *Halloween: Resurrection* (2002)?
    a. $10 million
    b. $11 million
    c. $15 million
    d. $13 million
2. Who played Michael Myers in *Halloween: Resurrection* (2002)?
    a. Christopher Durand
    b. Tyler Mane
    c. Brad Loree
    d. Nick Castle
3. When was *Halloween: Resurrection* (2002) released into theaters?
    a. July 12, 2002
    b. July 15, 2002
    c. July 19, 2002
    d. July 27, 2002
4. Who directed *Halloween: Resurrection* (2002)?
    a. Rick Rosenthal
    b. John Carpenter
    c. Moustapha Akkad
    d. Steve Miner
5. What was the body count of *Halloween: Resurrection* (2002)?
    a. Five
    b. Eight
    c. Seven
    d. Ten
6. What was Deckard's real name?
    a. Mikey Barton
    b. Mario Barton
    c. Myles Barton
    d. Max Barton

7. How did Michael escape his beheading at Hillcrest as explained by the nurses?

   a. He is immortal and thus never dies, even with a beheading

   b. He crushed a guard's larynx and switched uniforms with him

   c. He put a mechanical robot in his mask and attire and left unscathed

   d. He was resurrected by the Curse of Thorn

8. What is the name of the show that will star all six students?

   a. Dangertainment   c. Hallotainment

   b. Famoustainment   d. Riskytainment

9. Rudy pointed out that all the stuff they find is "too easy." Where did it come from?

   a. Most of the props were placed in the house by a delivering company

   b. Most of the props were placed in the house by intern students

   c. Most of the props were placed in the house by warehouse workers

   d. Most of the props were placed in the house by Freddie and his staff

10. What was Jen's motive for participating on the show?

    a. She hopes to find a boyfriend

    b. She hopes to get noticed by Hollywood through her performance

    c. She hopes to give a kick ass performance and entertain the audience

    d. She hopes to find Michael Myers

11. What became of Laurie after the incident at Hillcrest?

    a. She discovered she beheaded the wrong man and committed suicide

    b. She discovered she beheaded the wrong man and became a pill popper

    c. She discovered she beheaded the wrong man and was committed to a psychiatric sanitarium

    d. She discovered she beheaded the wrong man and began having night terrors

12. Who was Freddie's favorite Kung Fu actor?

    a. Bruce Lee
    c. Wai Chung Lee

    b. Jackie Chan
    d. Vincent Zhao

13. What was the name of the song and artist that Nora jammed to while Charley was killed?

    a. "Hot in Herre" by Nelly

    b. "If Tomorrow Never Comes" by Ronan Keating

    c. "All For You" by Janet Jackson

    d. "Still Waiting" by Sum 41

14. What was Donna's theory surrounding Michael Myers?

    a. That Michael Myers had an impulse control disorder, prompting his never-ending thirst to kill

    b. That Michael Myers had an obsessive-compulsive disorder, prompting his never-ending thirst to kill

    c. That Michael Myers had an attention deficit disorder, prompting his never-ending thirst to kill

    d. That Michael Myers had a post-traumatic stress disorder, prompting his never-ending thirst to kill

15. What was the name of the mental patient that cites the biography of serial killers?

    a. Willie   c. Harold

    b. Aron   d. Charley

16. What was the original working title of *Halloween: Resurrection* (2002)?

    a. *Halloween: The Homecoming* (2002)

    b. *Halloween: The Reunion* (2002)

    c. *Halloween: The Return* (2002)

    d. *Halloween: The Revival* (2002)

17. Which actor in this film with a small role was also in a much bigger role in *Freddy vs. Jason* (2003)?

    a. Jason Ritter   c. Brendan Fletcher

    b. Chris Gauthier   d. Kyle Labine

18. Who does Laurie Strode have a picture of hanging on the wall above her bed?

    a. Will Brennan   c. Jamie Lloyd

    b. John Tate   d. Jimmy

19. Laurie Strode is only in the film for 15 minutes. How many lines of dialogue does she speak within those 15 minutes?

    a. Ten   c. Twelve

    b. Eleven   d. Thirteen

20. Dr. Mixter, also the name of the doctor in *Halloween II* (1981), is a different character who is a professor of which field at Haddonfield University?

    a. Sociology   c. Anatomy and Physiology

    b. Psychology   d. Human Biology

21. Who did Dr. Mixter cite when he said, "We must face down our fears and face up to the figure"?

   a. Sigmund Freud
   c. Carl Jung
   b. Carl Rogers
   d. Albert Ellis

22. What was Rudy's major at Haddonfield University?

   a. Pastry Arts
   c. Culinary Arts
   b. Graphic Art
   d. Theatre

23. What was the last thing Laurie said to Michael Myers before plummeting to her death?

   a. You won't win, Michael
   b. You will die, Michael
   c. I'll see you in hell
   d. I still love you

24. What was the name of the cameraman?

   a. Charley Albans
   c. Bill Woodlake
   b. Jim Morgan
   d. Franklin Munroe

25. What rapper played the role of Freddie Harris?

   a. LL Cool J
   c. Busta Rhymes
   b. Will Smith
   d. Dr. Dre

26. Who was the final girl of *Halloween: Resurrection* (2002)?

   a. Donna Chang
   c. Sara Moyer
   b. Laurie Strode
   d. Jenna Danzig

27. What two directors turned down the opportunity to direct *Halloween: Resurrection* (2002)?

   a. John Carpenter and Dwight H. Little
   b. Whitney Ransick and Dwight H. Little
   c. Tommy Lee Wallace and Dwight H. Little
   d. Rob Zombie and Dwight H. Little

28. Freddie's last name was given to him in homage of which actress that previously starred in a film within the franchise?

   a. Ellie Cornell
   c. Jamie Lee Curtis
   b. Tamara Glynn
   d. Danielle Harris

29. Which actress in *Halloween: Resurrection* (2002) was originally supposed to play the role of Donna Chang, but was given a different character instead?

   a. Katee Sackhoff
   c. Tyra Banks
   b. Bianca Kajlich
   d. Lorena Gale

30. Which actress was scheduled to play Sara Moyer in *Halloween: Resurrection* (2002) but dropped out of the role shortly before production began?

   a. Jennifer Love Hewitt
   c. Sarah Michelle Gellar
   b. Drew Barrymore
   d. Jacinda Barrett

31. Nora's death was a reference to which nurse's death in *Halloween II* (1981)?

   a. Mrs. Alves
   c. Nurse Janet Marshall
   b. Nurse Jill Franco
   d. Nurse Karen Bailey

32. The ending was left open for another sequel, which would've featured which storyline according to Moustapha Akkad?

   a. John Tate would return to avenge his mother's death
   b. John Tate would return to find his mother that he believes faked her death again
   c. John Tate would return as the next intended target for Michael
   d. John Tate would return on a mission to kill Michael once and for all

33. Who played the role of Jim Morgan?

   a. Luke Kirby
   c. Thomas Ian Nicholas
   b. Ryan Merriman
   d. Brad Loree

34. Michael switching outfits with the paramedic (which explained how he survived the end of *Halloween H20: 20 Years Later* (1998)) is like the ending of which film in the franchise?

   a. *Halloween 4: The Return of Michael Myers* (1988)

   b. *Halloween III: Season of the Witch* (1982)

   c. *The Producer's Cut of Halloween 6: The Curse of Michael Myers* (1995)

   d. *Halloween 5: The Revenge of Michael Myers* (1989)

35. What happened in this film that happened in a previous film of the *Halloween* (1978) franchise to Michael Myers, both directed by the same director?

   a. Michael's eyes opened

   b. Michael is set on fire

   c. Michael is shown unmasked

   d. Michael is shown as a boy

36. Who is Freddie dressed as to scare his students?

   a. Jason Voorhees   c. Michael Myers

   b. Freddy Krueger   d. Pinhead

37. Who did Rudy say was a vegetarian when talking about having a poor diet?

   a. Joseph Stalin   c. Adolf Hitler

   b. Osama Bin Laden   d. Benedict Arnold

38. Who told the story of what happened at the end of *Halloween H20: 20 Years Later* (1998)?

   a. Nurse Wells   c. Nurse Phillips

   b. Professor Mixter d. Freddie Harris

39. What type of food did Rudy ask Michael if he liked when fighting him right before his death?

   a. Chicken Fried Rice   c. Pizza

   b. Tacos   d. Sushi

40. What did Freddie tell Sara is good to have when convincing her to not drop out of the contest at the Myers house?

   a. Panic   c. Danger

   b. Fear   d. Nervousness

41. What is the name of the guy that attends Haddonfield University who told the story of Michael as a kid when talking about the Myers house?

   a. Aron   c. Harold

   b. Willie   d. Franklin

42. What did Freddie tell Sara is the American dream?

   a. Being Rich   c. Being Famous

   b. Being Successful   d. Being Loved

43. When Jenna screamed, what did Jim say she must be going for?

   a. The first Internet Emmy   c. The first Webby

   b. The first Scream Award   d. The title of Scream Queen

44. What did Donna say interests her about Michael Myers?

   a. How Michael Myers embodies the politics of violence embedded in Greek mythology

   b. How Michael Myers embodies the politics of violence embedded in pop mythology

   c. How Michael Myers embodies the politics of violence embedded in folk mythology

   d. How Michael Myers embodies the politics of violence embedded in Norse mythology

45. Who played the role of Myles Barton?

   a. Ryan Merriman c. Billy Kay

   b. Sean Patrick Thomas d. Gus Lynch

46. How many endings were shot regarding the fate of Freddie Harris?

   a. One c. Three

   b. Two d. Four

47. Whose Halloween party did Myles go to?

   a. Mickey Stern c. Michael Shoffler

   b. Mario Sampson d. Max Steele

48. What grade is Myles in?

   a. Sophomore in High School c. Senior in High School

   b. Freshman in High School d. Junior in College

49. Why did Myles' friend's sister invite them to the Halloween party?

   a. So her mother doesn't find out she has a boyfriend

   b. So her mother doesn't find out she is pregnant

   c. So her mother doesn't find out about the party

   d. So her mother doesn't find out about her tattoo

50. Who played the role of Nora Winston?

   a. Lorena Gale c. Katee Sackhoff

   b. Daisy McCrackin d. Tyra Banks

51. Which actress in *Halloween: Resurrection* (2002) was originally supposed to play the role of Jenna Danzig but was given a different character instead?

   a. Daisy McCrackin c. Lorena Gale

   b. Tyra Banks d. Bianca Kajlich

52. When Nora asks Jenna what she hopes to find in the Myers house, what does she say?

   a. Michael Myers himself

   b. Her way into network broadcasting

   c. The truth behind the evil within Michael Myers

   d. A passing grade

53. What did Bill Woodlake say about Michael Myers during his audition with Dangertainment?

   a. He is the great white shark of our unconscious, he is the dark-eyed guy of our spirits, he's every murderous impulse we had, and he's the little voice that whispers to us to strangle the old lady trying to cross the street in busy traffic.

   b. He is the great white shark of our unconscious, he is the dark-eyed guy of our spirits, he's every murderous impulse we had, and he's the little voice that whispers to us to strangle the old lady that is being robbed for her purse by a street thug.

   c. He is the great white shark of our unconscious, he is the dark-eyed guy of our spirits, he's every murderous impulse we had, and he's the little voice that whispers to us to strangle the old lady that is taking too long at the checkout counter.

   d. He is the great white shark of our unconscious, he is the dark-eyed guy of our spirits, he's every murderous impulse we had, and he's the little voice that whispers to us to strangle the old lady that is a loving grandmother in the park with her grandchild.

54. What was Sara's answer to Nora's question as why ordinary people turn to murder?

   a. It has to do with upbringing and then the photographer knocked over a light and she screamed, not being able to finish answering the question

   b. It has to do with lack of discipline and then the photographer knocked over a light and she screamed, not being able to finish answering the question

   c. It has to do with family values and then the photographer knocked over a light and she screamed, not being able to finish answering the question

   d. It has to do with the environment surrounding him and then the photographer knocked over a light and she screamed, not being able to finish answering the question

55. Who played the role of Rudy Grimes?

   a. Dan Joffre
   b. Brent Chapman
   c. Sean Patrick Thomas
   d. Ryan Merriman

56. Which two on Dangertainment got high while in the Myers house?

   a. Rudy Grimes and Jenna Danzig

   b. Rudy Grimes and Sara Moyer

   c. Rudy Grimes and Donna Chang

   d. Rudy Grimes and Nora Winston

57. What did Freddie say Michael looked like when he was burnt on the stretcher?

   a. Chicken Leg
   b. Chicken Wing
   c. Chicken Breast
   d. Chicken Fried

58. Whose corpse did Sara find on the roof of the Myers house?

   a. Nora Winston   c. Bill Woodlake

   b. Charley Albans d. Laurie Strode

59. How many butcher knives did Michael stab Rudy with?

   a. One   c. Three

   b. Two   d. Four

60. What was the date in the film that Michael finally killed Laurie?

   a. October 31, 2002   c. October 31, 1999

   b. October 31, 2001   d. October 31, 2000

61. How did Sara, Jenna, Donna, Rudy, Jim, and Bill get to be on Dangertainment?

   a. They won a contest

   b. They were selected from a list of applicants

   c. They were recommended by the university committee

   d. They are all theater majors at the university

62. Laurie pretends to be what to prepare herself for the inevitable confrontation with Michael?

   a. Drunk   c. Insane

   b. Heavily Medicated   d. Comatose

63. When Jim and Donna are about to make love, the wall breaks with what falling on them?

   a. Fake Blood   c. Fake Corpses

   b. Fake Mice   d. Fake Spiders

64. What does Freddie say the audience will see when watching the internet reality show on Dangertainment?

   a. The person holding the camera

   b. A falsified set up of the Myers house

   c. Only what the person holding the camera sees

   d. The hologram of Michael Myers

65. In 2003, Tyra Banks, who played Nora Winston, created which successful show on The CW Network/UPN?

   a. *Project Runway* (2004)   c. *Shark Tank* (2009)

   b. *America's Next Top Model* (2003)   d. *The Real World* (1992)

66. What is the name of Myles' friend?

   a. Sean   c. Scott

   b. Saxon   d. Shane

67. Who played the role of Jenna Danzig?

   a. Katee Sackhoff   c. Daisy McCrackin

   b. Marisa Rudiak   d. Kelly Nielson

68. To whom did Michael give the butcher knife after he killed Laurie?

   a. Nurse Phillips   c. Harold

   b. Nurse Wells   d. Bob Green

69. The girl that was flirting with Scott at the Halloween party was dressed as what?

   a. Devil   c. Cat

   b. French Maid   d. Cheerleader

70. Which of the following horror films did Sean Patrick Thomas, who played Rudy Grimes, star in?

   a. *Dracula 2000* (2000)   c. *Final Destination* (2000)

   b. *Ginger Snaps* (2000)   d. *Scream 3* (2000)

71. Who were the two nurses on duty the night Laurie Strode was killed?

   a. Nurse Wells and Nurse McCarthy

   b. Nurse Wells and Nurse Hunter

   c. Nurse Wells and Nurse Williamson

   d. Nurse Wells and Nurse Phillips

72. What was Nora Winston making when Charley was killed?

   a. Cappuccino   c. Frappuccino

   b. Mocha Latte   d. Espresso

73. Who played the role of Aron, the creepy student at Haddonfield University?

   a. Gus Lynch   c. Haig Sutherland

   b. David Lewis   d. Billy Kay

74. What car was parked outside the Myers house that Nora had towed?

   a. Viper   c. Cadillac

   b. Firebird   d. Porsche

75. In 2006, Ryan Merriman, who played Myles Barton, starred in which horror film sequel?

   a. *The Texas Chainsaw Massacre: The Beginning* (2006)

   b. *The Grudge 2* (2006)

   c. *Final Destination 3* (2006)

   d. *I'll Always Know What You Did Last Summer* (2006)

76. Jamie Lee Curtis, who played Laurie Strode, stars in which of the following horror television shows as Cathy Munsch?

   a. *Scream: The TV Series* (2015)   c. *Scream Queens* (2015)

   b. *American Horror Story* (2011)   d. *The Walking Dead* (2010)

77. Who played the role of Donna Chang?

   a. Charisse Baker
   b. Daisy McCrackin
   c. Natassia Malthe
   d. Katee Sackhoff

78. Which two popular horror films did Jamie Lee Curtis star in, excluding any of the *Halloween* (1978) films?

   a. *Child's Play* (1988) and *A Nightmare on Elm Street* (1984)
   b. *The Fog* (1980) and *Prom Night* (1980)
   c. *The Texas Chainsaw Massacre* (1974) and *Scream* (1996)
   d. *Children of the Corn* (1984) and *Friday the 13th* (1996)

79. When Freddie is being interviewed by the media, what did he say they were going to enter in about the next 10 minutes?

   a. A mystery wrapped inside of a riddle inside of an enigma
   b. A mystery wrapped inside of a riddle inside of a myth
   c. A mystery wrapped inside of a riddle inside of a legend
   d. A mystery wrapped inside of a riddle inside of a killer

80. What weapon is used in the Dangertainment logo?

   a. Butcher Knife
   b. Axe
   c. Machete
   d. Meat Cleaver

81. Who played the role of Bill Woodlake?

   a. Sean Patrick Thomas
   b. Brad Sihvon
   c. Thomas Ian Nicholas
   d. Haig Sutherland

82. What type of film was *Halloween: Resurrection* (2002)?

   a. Thriller
   b. Mystery
   c. Suspense
   d. Found Footage

83. Who came up with the idea for Busta Rhymes to star in the film?

   a. Jamie Lee Curtis' Mother

   b. John Carpenter's Brother

   c. Rick Rosenthal's Wife

   d. Moustapha Akkad's Son

84. How does the film end?

   a. Michael is cremated

   b. Michael's eyes open in the morgue

   c. Michael kills the nurse

   d. Michael is gone from the morgue

85. What did Bill say could launch Jenna's career and light up a thousand computer screens?

   a. If she had sex with him   c. If he flashed the camera

   b. If she stripped   d. If she faked her death

86. What did Michael use to impale Charley in the throat?

   a. The leg of the tripod   c. A railroad spike

   b. A giant hook   d. A spear

87. In a deleted scene, what did Michael use to strangle Nora before impaling her to the ceiling with a butcher knife?

   a. Cable Noose   c. Camera Wire

   b. His bare hands   d. Rope

88. When did Sara, Rudy, and Jim realize that Jenna wasn't faking her screams?

   a. When Michael decapitated her

   b. When they found a dead body

   c. When they saw Jenna soaked in blood

   d. When they saw two Michael Myers

89. What did Donna see in the basement that she thought was a prop of Freddie's?

    a. A dead skunk
    c. A dead dog
    b. A dead cat
    d. A dead rat

90. What did Jim see on the arm of the corpse that fell on him and Donna that made him realize the entire show was a set up from the beginning?

    a. The text "Made in China"

    b. The text "Made in Japan"

    c. The text "Made in Taiwan"

    d. The text "Made in Hong Kong"

91. Myles and Scott went to the Halloween party dressed up as the characters of which film?

    a. *Scarface* (1983)
    c. *Pulp Fiction* (1994)
    b. *The Godfather* (1972)
    d. *Goodfellas* (1990)

92. When Myles was watching the internet show by Dangertainment at the Halloween party, he was interrupted by two people making out. When the guy noticed Myles at the desk, what did he call him?

    a. Big Freak
    c. Big Perv
    b. Big Daddy
    d. Big Loser

93. What caused the Myers house to catch on fire when Sara was battling Michael?

    a. Sara set Michael on fire gasoline and a match

    b. Sara was attacking Michael with a chainsaw and struck live wires

    c. Sara had Michael knocked out and used gasoline and a match to light the place on fire

    d. Sara blew the place up with propane when she escaped the house

94. Who played the role of Sara Moyer?
   a. Daisy McCrackin
   c. Bianca Kajlich
   b. Katee Sackhoff
   d. Tyra Banks

95. What caused Laurie to be tricked by Michael and ultimately killed?
   a. She was fearful that it wasn't the real Michael like the last time
   b. She was feeling remorse for everything her brother has been through
   c. She was feeling doubt on killing her flesh and blood
   d. She thought Michael wanted to start over with her

96. What mask did Harold wear?
   a. Jack-o'-Lantern
   c. Skeleton
   b. Clown
   d. Michael Myers

97. What did Laurie hide in the doll?
   a. Pictures of her son
   c. Her pills
   b. Memories of Michael's attacks on her
   d. A secret weapon

98. What did the nurse say Laurie Strode suffers from?
   a. Post-Traumatic Stress Disorder
   c. Extreme Dissociative Disorder
   d. Depression
   b. Bipolar Disorder

99. What does the doctor think Laurie is?
   a. A homicidal maniac
   c. A suicide threat
   b. A runaway patient
   d. A dangerous person

100. How much did *Halloween: Resurrection* (2002) gross at the box office?
   a. $37.5 million
   c. $37.7 million
   b. $37.3 million
   d. $37.6 million

Halloween (2007)

1. Who played Dr. Sam Loomis in *Halloween* (2007)?
    a. Brad Dourif
    b. John Hurt
    c. Malcolm McDowell
    d. Donald Pleasence
2. What was the budget for *Halloween* (2007)?
    a. $15 million
    b. $10 million
    c. $20 million
    d. $25 million
3. When was *Halloween* (2007) released into theaters?
    a. August 12, 2007
    b. August 1, 2007
    c. August 31, 2007
    d. August 16, 2007
4. Who was the final girl of *Halloween* (2007)?
    a. Annie Brackett
    b. Lynda Van Der Klok
    c. Laurie Strode
    d. Judith Myers
5. How much did *Halloween* (2007) gross at the box office?
    a. $80.7 million
    b. $80.5 million
    c. $80.2 million
    d. $80.8 million
6. Who played Michael Myers in *Halloween* (2007)?
    a. Nick Castle
    b. Tyler Mane
    c. Kane Hodder
    d. Dick Warlock
7. Who directed *Halloween* (2007)?
    a. John Carpenter
    b. Steve Miner
    c. Malek Akkad
    d. Rob Zombie

8. What was the body count of *Halloween* (2007)?

    a. Seventeen   c. Nineteen

    b. Eighteen   d. Twenty

9. What was Michael's hobby?

    a. Painting   c. Sculpturing

    b. Mask Making   d. Photography

10. What were the circumstances surrounding Laurie's adoption?

    a. Sheriff Brackett found Laurie at the scene of Deborah's suicide, and she was later adopted by the Strodes

    b. Sheriff Brackett found Laurie at the scene of Deborah's suicide, and she was then put into foster care

    c. Sheriff Brackett found Laurie at the scene of Deborah's suicide, and immediately called Children and Youth

    d. Sheriff Brackett found Laurie at the scene of Deborah's suicide, and adopted her himself

11. What was the name of Dr. Loomis' book?

    a. *The Eyes of Evil* (2007)   c. *The Devil's Eyes* (2007)

    b. *The Blackest Eyes* (2007)   d. *The Eyes of Pure Evil* (2007)

12. During the film's opening moments, Michael wore a t-shirt of what band?

    a. AC/DC   c. KISS

    b. Metallica   d. Limp Bizkit

13. What song did both Judith and Lynda listen to right before their deaths?

    a. "Bodies" by Drowning Pool

    b. "Don't Fear the Reaper" by Blue Oyster Cult

    c. "Feel So Numb" by Rob Zombie

    d. "St. Anger" by Metallic

14. What obscenity was written on Ronnie's cast when he flipped off Deborah?

    a. Dumb Cunt
    c. Suck It
    b. Stupid Bitch
    d. Cheap Whore

15. What type of gun did Dr. Loomis buy from Micky Dolenz?

    a. .32 Revolver
    c. .357 Magnum
    b. .303 British
    d. .45 Colt

16. What was the name of the cereal that Judith ate for breakfast?

    a. Fruity Pebbles
    c. Cinnamon Toast Crunch
    b. Fruit Loops
    d. Sugar Rice Pops

17. What type of costume did Laurie say she wore as a child?

    a. Witch
    c. Bride of Frankenstein
    b. Zombie
    d. Dead Little Red Riding Hood

18. Walking home from school, Lynda wore a t-shirt of what band?

    a. Avenge Sevenfold
    c. Black Sabbath
    b. Judas Priest
    d. Slayer

19. Who played the role of Annie Brackett?

    a. Kyle Richards
    c. Danielle Harris
    b. Nancy Kyes
    d. Jenny Gregg Stewart

20. Brad Dourif, who played Sheriff Brackett, starred as the villain of which horror franchise?

    a. *Leprechaun* (1993)
    c. *Child's Play* (1988)
    b. *Hellraiser* (1987)
    d. *Candyman* (1992)

21. Who played the role of Deborah Myers?

    a. Dee Wallace
    c. Sheri Moon Zombie
    b. Hanna R. Hall
    d. Patty Frost

22. At the start of the film, what was the quote shown on the screen by Dr. Sam Loomis?

   a. The evil souls are not those which choose to exist within the hell of the abyss, but those which choose to break free from the abyss and move silently among us

   b. The remorseful souls are not those which choose to exist within the hell of the abyss, but those which choose to break free from the abyss and move silently among us

   c. The darkest souls are not those which choose to exist within the hell of the abyss, but those which choose to break free from the abyss and move silently among us

   d. The deadly souls are not those which choose to exist within the hell of the abyss, but those which choose to break free from the abyss and move silently among us

23. Which actress auditioned for the role of Laurie Strode, but wasn't given the part?

   a. Emma Stone

   b. Billie Lourd

   c. Emma Roberts

   d. Abigail Breslin

24. Who played the role of Bob Simms?

   a. Travis Van Winkle

   b. John Michael Graham

   c. Glen Powell

   d. Nick Mennell

25. Skyler Gisondo auditioned for which role, but was instead cast as Tommy Doyle?

   a. Young Michael Myers

   b. Steve Haley

   c. Wesley Rhoades

   d. Paul

26. Where did Michael get his infamous mask that he hid the night he killed his family?

   a. Under Judith's mattress

   b. Under the floorboards

   c. Under the house

   d. Under the welcome mat

27. Skyler Gisondo, who played Tommy Doyle, was also in the hit television show *Once Upon a Time* (2011) as which character?

    a. Felix
    c. Devin
    b. Peter Pan
    d. Michael Darling

28. What job does Deborah Myers do for a living?

    a. Dancer at a local strip club
    c. Bartender
    b. Waitress
    d. Hooker

29. Who played the role of Lynda Van Der Klok?

    a. Kristina Klebe
    c. P.J. Soles
    b. Scout Taylor-Compton
    d. Danielle Harris

30. What Stephen King horror film did Dee Wallace, who played Cynthia Strode, star in?

    a. *IT* (1990)
    c. *Cujo* (1983)
    b. *Children of the Corn* (1984)
    d. *The Shining* (1980)

31. What were the names of Laurie's adoptive parents?

    a. Mason and Cynthia Strode
    c. Michael and Cynthia Strode
    b. Matthew and Cynthia Strode
    d. Maxwell and Cynthia Strode

32. Who played the role of Sheriff Brackett?

    a. Charles Cyphers
    c. Hunter Von Leer
    b. Beau Starr
    d. Brad Dourif

33. What was the name of the truck driver that Michael killed for his clothes?

    a. Ismael Cruz
    c. Morgan Walker
    b. Joe Grizzly
    d. Noel Kluggs

34. What did Michael put over the head of Paul after he killed him?

    a. Pumpkin
    c. Plastic Bag
    b. His Mask
    d. TV Set

35. As a child, Danielle Harris, who played Annie Brackett, also starred in two other *Halloween* (1978) films playing which character?

    a. Jamie Lloyd   c. Lindsay Wallace

    b. Samantha Thomas   d. Rachel Carruthers

36. What pet did Michael have as a kid?

    a. Rat   c. Dog

    b. Snake   d. Tarantula

37. What type of psychologist is Dr. Loomis?

    a. Human Psychologist c. Behavior Psychologist

    b. Child Psychologist d. Educational Psychologist

38. What does Michael use to make his masks?

    a. Clay   c. Papier-mâché

    b. Pottery   d. Putty

39. What did Michael say his favorite color is?

    a. White   c. Brown

    b. Gray   d. Black

40. What was the name of Deborah's boyfriend?

    a. Larry Redgrave   c. Zach Garrett

    b. Stan Payne   d. Ronnie White

41. What was the name of the principal who tried to stop the fight between Michael and Wesley?

    a. Principal Carson   c. Principal Cox

    b. Principal Chambers d. Principal Clinton

42. Who played the role of Judith Myers?

    a. Hanna R. Hall   c. Leslie Easterbrook

    b. Sybil Danning   d. Jenny Gregg Stewart

43. Before *Halloween* (2007) became a remake of the original film, it was originally going to be a prequel titled what?

   a. *Halloween: The Origin of Michael Myers* (2007)

   b. *Halloween: The Child Known As Michael Myers* (2007)

   c. *Halloween: The Missing Years* (2007)

   d. *Halloween: The Evil of Michael Myers* (2007)

44. Who played the young Michael Myers in *Halloween* (2007)?

   a. Will Sandin
   c. Daeg Faerch

   b. Skyler Gisondo
   d. Chase Wright Vanek

45. Which classic film was playing on television in an early scene of *Halloween* (2007)?

   a. *White Zombie* (1932)
   c. *Citizen Kane* (1941)

   b. *Casablanca* (1942)
   d. *The Wizard of Oz* (1939)

46. The hoodie Laurie Strode wore in *Halloween (2007)* was from Sheri Moon Zombie's personal clothing line. What is the name of that clothing line?

   a. The Walking Dead
   c. Undead Attire

   b. Total Skull
   d. Zombie Clothes

47. The sequel to this movie is *Halloween II* (2009), but the original plan for a sequel was titled what?

   a. *Halloween Returns* (2009)

   b. *Halloween: Retribution* (2009)

   c. *Halloween: Apocalypse* (2009)

   d. *Halloween: Emergence* (2009)

48. Which actress who starred in *Friday the 13th* (2009) auditioned for the role of Laurie Strode, but lost the role to Scout Taylor-Compton?

   a. Amanda Righetti
   c. Danielle Panabaker

   b. Julianna Guill
   d. Willa Ford

49. Scout Taylor-Compton, who played Laurie Strode, auditioned for which role in *Friday the 13ᵗʰ* (2009)?
    a. Jenna
    c. Whitney Miller
    b. Bree
    d. Chelsea
50. Who played the role of Paul?
    a. Nick Mennell
    c. Max Van Ville
    b. Daryl Sabara
    d. Adam Weisman
51. In the opening scene of the film, which song by KISS was heard playing?
    a. "Rock and Roll All Nite"
    c. "God of Thunder"
    b. "Heaven's on Fire"
    d. "Psycho Circus"
52. Which character is the only one to not be killed by Michael Myers?
    a. Ronnie White
    c. Wesley Rhoades
    b. Deborah Myers
    d. Ismael Cruz

53. What does Dr. Loomis say about the eyes of Michael Myers when giving a speech about his book?

   a. I met him, fifteen years ago; I was told there was nothing left; no reason, no conscience, no understanding; and even the most rudimentary sense of life or death, of good or evil, right or wrong. I met this six-year-old child, with this blank, pale, emotionless face, and the blackest eyes . . . the devil's eyes. I spent eight years trying to reach him, and then another seven trying to keep him locked up because I realized that what was living behind that boy's eyes was purely and simply . . . evil.

   b. These eyes will deceive you, they will destroy you. They will take from you, your innocence, your pride, and eventually your soul. These eyes do not see what you and I see. Behind these eyes one finds only blackness, the absence of light, these are of a psychopath.

   c. These eyes will deceive you, they will destroy you, and they will kill you. They will take from you, your innocence, your pride, and eventually your soul. These eyes do not see what you and I see. Behind these eyes one finds only blackness, the absence of light, these are of a psychopath. These are of a murderer. These are of someone who doesn't care if he lives or dies. These eyes are of someone that is purely and simply… evil.

   d. These eyes will deceive you, they will destroy you. They will take from you, your innocence, your pride, your life, your self-respect, and eventually your soul. These eyes do not see what you and I see. Behind these eyes one finds only blackness, the absence of light, the forthcoming of darkness, these are of a psychopath. Someone so sinister, so evil that he doesn't care who or what he destroys and even kills. Someone he will kill without a second thought. The eyes that only make someone that is evil become so enraged in life.

54. Michael asked Dr. Loomis if he liked his mask and stated that black was his favorite color. Dr. Loomis told Michael that black isn't a color. When explaining why black isn't a color, Dr. Loomis stated what?

   a. It's the misinterpretation of color. In the spectrum of colors, you go from black, which is no color, all the way through to white, which is every color. So, technically... not that it really matters, but black isn't a color.

   b. It's the disappearance of color. In the spectrum of colors, you go from black, which is no color, all the way through to white, which is every color. So, technically... not that it really matters, but black isn't a color.

   c. It's the absence of color. In the spectrum of colors, you go from black, which is no color, all the way through to white, which is every color. So, technically... not that it really matters, but black isn't a color.

   d. It's the blindness of color. In the spectrum of colors, you go from black, which is no color, all the way through to white, which is every color. So, technically... not that it really matters, but black isn't a color.

55. Where did Dr. Loomis speak about his book on Michael Myers?

   a. Westminster Hall   c. Webster Hall
   b. Wyomissing Hall   d. Warner Hall

56. What time was on the sign where Dr. Loomis was speaking about his book on Michael Myers?

   a. 11 a.m.   c. 12 p.m.
   b. 10 a.m.   d. 1 p.m.

57. What was the name of the bully that picked on Michael Myers at school?

   a. Derek Allen   c. Wesley Rhoades
   b. Chester Chesterfield   d. Taylor Madison

58. What was the name of Michael's rat?
    a. Elvis
    c. Erick
    b. Elias
    d. Emeril
59. What name does Ronnie call Michael to make fun of him?
    a. Minnie
    c. Mildred
    b. Michelle
    d. Mimi
60. Which character who was only mentioned in *Halloween* (1978) was an actual on-screen character in *Halloween* (2007)?
    a. Bob Simms
    c. Steve Haley
    b. Deborah Myers
    d. Paul
61. Sheriff Brackett told Dr. Loomis that it sounds like he is talking to whom when he talks to Michael?
    a. The Devil
    c. Satan
    b. The Antichrist
    d. A Demon
62. Michael Myers hasn't spoken in how many years when he is shown as an adult?
    a. Twenty Years
    c. Ten Years
    b. Fifteen Years
    d. Twenty-Five Years
63. Max Van Ville, who played the role of Paul, originally auditioned for the role of which character?
    a. Bob Simms
    c. Steve
    b. Wesley Rhoades
    d. Joe Grizzly
64. Who played the role of Ronnie White?
    a. William Forsythe
    c. Pat Skipper
    b. Ken Foree
    d. Daniel Roebuck

65. What Halloween song did Lindsay keep singing?

   a. Trick or Treat. Smell my feet. Give me something good to eat. If you don't, I don't care. I'll pull down Laurie's underwear!

   b. Trick or Treat. Smell my feet. Give me something good to eat. If you don't, I don't care. I'll pull down Lynda's underwear!

   c. Trick or Treat. Smell my feet. Give me something good to eat. If you don't, I don't care. I'll pull down Tommy's underwear!

   d. Trick or Treat. Smell my feet. Give me something good to eat. If you don't, I don't care. I'll pull down Annie's underwear!

66. What were the three reasons Tommy told Laurie why Lindsay can't come over?

   a. 1: She's a girl.
      2: She's not a boy.
      3: She smells like Annie

   b. 1: She's a girl.
      2: She's not a boy.
      3: She smells like Lynda.

   c. 1: She's a girl.
      2: She's not a boy.
      3: She smells like you.

   d. 1: She's a girl.
      2: She's not a boy.
      3: She smells like shit.

67. When speaking to Michael while taking a dump, what did Joe Grizzly say he ate?

   a. Burrito
   b. Quesadilla
   c. Taco Supreme
   d. Enchiladas

68. What name did Joe Grizzly call Michael right before he went to attack Michael?

   a. Danielle
   c. Daisy
   b. Demi
   d. Dory

69. Why did Dr. Loomis tell Michael he couldn't go home?

   a. Because he has done terrible things
   b. Because he has done illegal things
   c. Because he has done dangerous things
   d. Because he has done bad things

70. When Michael was holding Laurie hostage, what did he show her?

   a. A picture of them, trying to tell her that he is her brother
   b. A picture of them, trying to tell her she is adopted
   c. A picture of them, trying to tell her that he killed her family
   d. A picture of them, trying to tell her that their family is dead and he's alone

71. Whose body did Laurie find?

   a. Cynthia Strode
   c. Mason Strode
   b. Lynda Van Der Klok
   d. Bob Simms

72. Who did Laurie find lying in a pool of her own blood, but she didn't die, unlike the original film?

   a. Lynda Van Der Klok
   c. Annie Brackett
   b. Bob Simms
   d. Paul

73. Who played the role of Steve Haley?

   a. Adam Weisman
   c. Max Van Ville
   b. Nick Mennell
   d. Daryl Sabara

74. Nick Mennell, who played Bob Simms, was also in what other classic slasher/horror movie remake?

   a. *A Nightmare on Elm Street* (2010)

   b. *The Texas Chain Saw Massacre* (2003)

   c. *Friday the 13th* (2009)

   d. *Children of the Corn* (2009)

75. Who played the role of Joe Grizzly?

   a. Paul Kampf   c. Richmond Arquette

   b. Ken Foree   d. Sid Haig

76. When did Michael first come face to face with Laurie Strode?

   a. When Laurie discovered the corpses of Lynda and Bob

   b. When Laurie discovered the corpse of Paul and an injured Annie

   c. When Laurie found out she is really Michael Myers' sister through Dr. Loomis' book

   d. When Laurie dropped off the key to the Myers' House for her dad

77. Who played the role of Wesley Rhoades?

   a. Daeg Faerch   c. Daryl Sabara

   b. Richard Lynch   d. Max Van Ville

78. Where did Deborah Myers work?

   a. Rabbit in Red   c. The Rabbit Hole

   b. The Rabbit's Foot   d. Rabbit Ears

79. Which uncredited role did Ezra Buzzington play in *Halloween* (2007)?

   a. Graveyard Keeper   c. University Dean

   b. Drunk Patron   d. College Student

80. Deputy Charles was the same character in which previous *Halloween* film (but played by a different actor)?

   a. *Halloween II* (1981)

   b. *Halloween 4: The Return of Michael Myers* (1988)

   c. *Halloween 5: The Revenge of Michael Myers* (1989)

   d. *Halloween H20: 20 Years Later* (1998)

81. What was the name of the grave keeper that showed Dr. Loomis the missing tombstone of Judith Myers?

   a. Derek Allen   c. Jack Kendall

   b. Taylor Madison   d. Chester Chesterfield

82. What character did Rob Zombie's wife portray?

   a. Annie Brackett   c. Judith Myers

   b. Laurie Strode   d. Deborah Myers

83. When at Smith's Grove Sanitarium, what did Michael say his favorite color was?

   a. White   c. Black

   b. Red   d. Blue

84. When Michael's pet died, what did he say he had to do?

   a. Bury Him   c. Flush Him

   b. Resurrect Him   d. Eat Him

85. Who played the roles of Mason and Cynthia Strode?

   a. Richmond Arquette and Sybil Danning

   b. Pat Skipper and Dee Wallace

   c. William Forsythe and Sheri Moon Zombie

   d. Clint Howard and Linda Sypien

86. When Michael first came downstairs, what did Ronnie say to him?

    a. Hello Michelle my bell

    b. Hello Michael my cycle

    c. Hello Killer my miller

    d. Hello Mikey my Dikey

87. What did Judith ask Michael she did to his pet when he announced it died?

    a. Stroke it to death   c. Bore it to death

    b. Feed it to death   d. Stab it to death

88. When Wesley saw Michael come out of the bathroom stall, what did he call him?

    a. Shitpants   c. Shitface

    b. Shithead   d. Shitsticks

89. What is the principal's first name?

    a. John   c. Jason

    b. Jim   d. Jarod

90. In the original *Halloween* (1978) film, Michael strangled Lynda with a telephone cord. In this version of *Halloween* (2007), how does Michael strangle Lynda?

    a. Television Cable   c. Rope

    b. Electric Cord   d. His Bare Hands

91. What did the principal find in Michael's school bag?

    a. Pictures of him cutting himself

    b. Pictures of naked women

    c. Pictures of his weapons and masks

    d. Pictures of dead animals

92. What animal was also found dead in Michael's school bag wrapped in a plastic bag?
   a. A dead rat
   b. A dead dog
   c. A dead bird
   d. A dead cat

93. When Judith was eating cereal, what did Deborah say she was making for breakfast?
   a. Pancakes
   b. French Toast
   c. Eggs
   d. Toast

94. Ronnie said the waitress was giving him the "freaky eye." Where did she work?
   a. The Rabbit in Red
   b. The Haddonfield Diner
   c. The Bingo Lounge
   d. The Laugh Box

95. Lynda said her teacher was flirting with her? In which class was it?
   a. Biology
   b. French
   c. English
   d. Math

96. Who played the role of Laurie Strode?
   a. Danielle Harris
   b. Kristina Klebe
   c. Scout Taylor-Compton
   d. Hanna R. Hall

97. What did Judith say eggs are?
   a. Chicken Feces
   b. Chicken Embryos
   c. Chicken Abortions
   d. Chicken Fetes

98. Lynda asked Laurie if one of the following was flirting with her. Which one did she ask about?
   a. Dr. Loomis
   b. Paul Freedman
   c. Bob Simms
   d. Sheriff Brackett

99. Nick Mennell played Bob Simms in *Halloween* (2007). Who did he play in the other horror remake he starred in?

   a. Matt

   b. Maurice

   c. Manny

   d. Mike

100. Which two employees associated with Smith's Grove Sanitarium in the original *Halloween* (1978) film are absent from *Halloween* (2007)?

   a. Sam Loomis and Marion Chambers

   b. Sam Loomis and Terrence Wynn

   c. Marion Chambers and Terrence Wynn

   d. There was no absent employees in *Halloween* (2007)

Halloween II (2009)

1. Including Michael Myers, what was the body count of *Halloween II* (2009)?
   - a. Nineteen
   - b. Seventeen
   - c. Eighteen
   - d. Twenty

2. Who played Michael Myers in *Halloween II* (2009)?
   - a. Brad Loree
   - b. Christopher Durand
   - c. Dick Warlock
   - d. Tyler Mane

3. What was the budget of *Halloween II* (2009)?
   - a. $13 million
   - b. $11 million
   - c. $14 million
   - d. $15 million

4. Who directed *Halloween II* (2009)?
   - a. John Carpenter
   - b. Steve Miner
   - c. Dwight H. Little
   - d. Rob Zombie

5. When was *Halloween II* (2009) released into theaters?
   - a. August 12, 2009
   - b. August 24, 2009
   - c. August 1, 2009
   - d. August 28, 2009

6. What tattoo did Laurie have?
   - a. A star with the letters "FTW"
   - b. A moon with the letters "FTW"
   - c. A sun with the letters "FTW"
   - d. A jack-o'-lantern with the letters "FTW"

7. When Mya was calling 911, what did she say the address was of the Brackett household?
   - a. 15 Cherrywood Road
   - b. 31 Cherrywood Road
   - c. 13 Cherrywood Road
   - d. 7 Cherrywood Road

8. How much did *Halloween II* (2009) gross at the box office?

    a. $35.3 million   c. $33.3 million

    b. $39.3 million   d. $37.3 million

9. What type of car did Laurie have?

    a. Red Pontiac Firebird

    b. White Pontiac 3000 GT

    c. Blue Pontiac Grand Prix

    d. Orange Pontiac Sunfire

10. In the beginning, what music video was playing behind Laurie during her dream?

    a. "Nights in White Satin" by The Moody Blues

    b. "Feel So Numb" by Rob Zombie

    c. "Thriller" by Michael Jackson

    d. "Smoke on the Water" by Deep Purple

11. In the beginning of the film, what was the definition of a White Horse?

    a. Linked to instinct, purity, and the drive of the physical body to release powerful and emotional forces, like rage with ensuing damage and damnation.

    b. Linked to instinct, purity, and the drive of the physical body to release powerful and emotional forces, like rage with ensuing hellfire and brimstone.

    c. Linked to instinct, purity, and the drive of the physical body to release powerful and emotional forces, like rage with ensuing chaos and destruction.

    d. Linked to instinct, purity, and the drive of the physical body to release powerful and emotional forces, like rage with ensuing terror and fear.

12. What was the name of the talk show that Dr. Loomis appeared on?

    a. *The Power Hour* (2009)   c. *The Newman Hour* (2009)

    b. *The Culture Shock* (2009)   d. *The Pop Show* (2009)

13. Which rocker was featured on a poster in Laurie's bathroom?

    a. Rob Zombie   c. Ozzy Osbourne

    b. Metallica   d. Alice Cooper

14. What unusual inscription request did Chett have for Dr. Loomis at the book signing?

    a. To Chett, The Bringer of Death, Johns

    b. To Chett, The Bringer of Life, Johns

    c. To Chett, The Bringer of Evil, Johns

    d. To Chett, The Bringer of Murder, Johns

15. When Laurie woke up in the hospital, which movie was playing on her television?

    a. *Halloween II* (1981)

    b. *Night of the Living Dead* (1968)

    c. *Friday the 13th* (1980)

    d. *A Nightmare on Elm Street* (1984)

16. What was the name of the coffee shop where Laurie worked?

    a. Uncle Meat's Java Hole

    b. Uncle Meat's Java Hut

    c. Uncle Meat's Java Shoppe

    d. Uncle Meat's Java Club

17. According to a sign at the Rabbit in Red, what was Michael's nickname?

    a. The Legend of Haddonfield   c. The Butcher of Haddonfield

    b. The Myth of Haddonfield   d. The Psycho of Haddonfield

18. Which of the following is different from the original version of the film?

   a. In *Halloween II* (1981), Annie's corpse is discovered. In *Halloween II* (2009), Annie's corpse isn't found.

   b. In *Halloween II* (1981), Annie isn't in the film. In *Halloween II* (2009), Annie is in the film.

   c. In *Halloween II* (1981), Annie is already dead. In *Halloween II* (2009), Annie is killed by Michael Myers.

   d. In *Halloween II* (1981), Annie is Sheriff Brackett's daughter. In *Halloween II* (2009), Annie is Dr. Loomis' daughter.

19. What is the name of Dr. Loomis' new book?

   a. *The Evil Returned to Haddonfield* (2009)

   b. *The Legend of Michael Myers* (2009)

   c. *The Devil Walks Among Us* (2009)

   d. *The Curse Known As Michael Myers* (2009)

20. Who was also a guest on the talk show and embarrassed Dr. Loomis?

   a. Weird Al Yankovic   c. Howard Stern

   b. Bubba the Love Sponge   d. Regis Philbin

21. Who showed up to Dr. Loomis' book signing with a gun?

   a. The Father of Paul Freedman

   b. The Father of Lynda Van Der Klok

   c. The Father of Bob Simms

   d. The Father of Steve Haley

22. Who replaced Daeg Faerch as young Michael Myers?

   a. Chase Wright Vanek   c. Skyler Gisondo

   b. Angus T. Jones   d. Preston Bailey

23. One year after the events from *Halloween* (2007), who is Laurie living with?
    a. The Brackett's
    b. The Rockwell's
    c. The David's
    d. The Doyle's

24. This is the first film in the *Halloween* (1978) franchise that Michael does something as an adult that he didn't do before. What was it?
    a. Gets Naked
    b. Dies
    c. Speaks
    d. Both B and C

25. Whose picture does Laurie have over her bed?
    a. Drew Peterson
    b. Charles Manson
    c. Scott Peterson
    d. The Zodiac Killer

26. According to Annie, how many calories of sugar was in the pastry that Sheriff Brackett was going to have?
    a. 300 Calories
    b. 400 Calories
    c. 500 Calories
    d. 600 Calories

27. What was Annie making for breakfast?
    a. Egg Whites
    b. Turkey Bacon
    c. Jelly Toast
    d. Sausage

28. What did Sheriff Brackett say he was going to get on the way to the station?
    a. Marble Rye
    b. Bagel
    c. Boston Cream Donut
    d. Sticky Buns

29. Who played the role of Harley David?
    a. Angela Trimbur
    b. Scout Taylor-Compton
    c. Brea Grant
    d. Danielle Harris

30. What was Lou Martini dressed up as for Halloween?

    a. Dracula
    c. Wolfman
    b. Mummy
    d. Frankenstein

31. In the beginning of the film, when defining a White Horse, which book was that an excerpt from?

    a. *The Subconscious Nature of Nightmares* (2009)

    b. *The Subconscious Drive of Pattern Nightmares* (2009)

    c. *The Subconscious Psychosis of Dreams* (2009)

    d. *The Subconscious Psychological Understanding of Dreams* (2009)

32. What was the name of Laurie's psychiatrist?

    a. Dr. Benita McCoy
    c. Dr. Barbara Collier
    b. Dr. Billie McGinley
    d. Dr. Bea Canterbury

33. What was the name of the owner of the Rabbit in Red?

    a. Howard Boggs
    c. Misty Dawn
    b. Lou Martini
    d. Sherman Benny

34. What was the first name of Lynda's dad?

    a. Karl
    c. Kory
    b. Kyle
    d. Keith

35. What were the names of the three people Michael killed, along with their dog, that were driving in a pickup truck at night?

    a. Sherman Benny, Jazlean Benny, and Frank

    b. Sherman Benny, Jazlean Benny, and Freud

    c. Sherman Benny, Jazlean Benny, and Floyd

    d. Sherman Benny, Jazlean Benny, and Fred

36. What was the name of the talk show host who interviewed Dr. Loomis?

   a. David Newman
   c. Daniel Newman
   b. Derrien Newman
   d. Darryl Newman

37. What was the name of the night watchman at the hospital in Laurie's dream?

   a. Bobby
   c. Buddy
   b. Barry
   d. Billy

38. What is Laurie's actual first name?

   a. Angie
   c. Andi
   b. Angel
   d. Amy

39. What was the name of the driver who stopped to help Laurie but was ultimately killed by Michael Myers?

   a. Brett
   c. Becks
   b. Baron
   d. Bobby

40. Laurie's psychiatrist said that the print in the picture hanging on her wall prompted ambiguous stimuli in the brain to form a picture. What did Laurie see in the picture?

   a. One White Horse
   c. Three White Horses
   b. Two White Horses
   d. Four White Horses

41. What was the name of the news reporter who interviewed Dr. Loomis about his book outside of the Myers house?

   a. Jazlean Benny
   c. Wendy Snow
   b. Misty Dawn
   d. Jane Salvador

42. What animal caused a car accident for the ambulance Michael Myers was in?

   a. Deer
   c. Cow
   b. Horse
   d. Elephant

43. After the events of the first film, *Halloween* (2007), what did Laurie suffer from?

   a. Multiple Personality Disorder   c. Bipolar Disorder

   b. Post-Traumatic Stress Disorder   d. Attention Deficit Disorder

44. Who played the role of Wolfie?

   a. Chris Hardwick   c. Matt Bush

   b. Daniel Roebuck   d. Adam Boyer

45. What was the name of the deputy that Sheriff Brackett had watching over Annie?

   a. Deputy Andy Neale   c. Deputy Webb

   b. Deputy Lyons   d. Deputy Fred King

46. What literary character did the actor Justin Welborn dress up as for Halloween in *Halloween II (2009)*?

   a. Dr. Jekyll   c. Mr. Hyde

   b. Tom Sawyer   d. Huckleberry Finn

47. In her dream, who does Laurie kill?

   a. Sheriff Brackett   c. Annie Brackett

   b. Dr. Loomis   d. Mya Rockwell

48. When Laurie told her psychiatrist that she walked through a park and saw a farm, what did she say the lady let her hold?

   a. Goat   c. Chicken

   b. Pig   d. Rooster

49. What did Laurie's psychiatrist say she'd give her to hold her over?

   a. Concerta   c. Lexapro

   b. Ritalin   d. Haldol

50. The medicine that Laurie's psychiatrist said she was going to give to her was what type of medication?

   a. Antipsychotic   c. Antidepressant

   b. Antihypertensive   d. Anticholinergic

51. What song played at the end of the film?

   a. "Love Hurts"   c. "Mr. Sandman"

   b. "Teenage Frankenstein" d. "Love is a Lie"

52. On the sign at the Rabbit in Red, who was photographed in the picture as a way of advertising?

   a. Deborah Myers   c. Laurie Strode

   b. Annie Brackett   d. Judith Myers

53. What name did Lou Martini go by?

   a. Bad Lou   c. Bitchy Lou

   b. Baby Lou   d. Big Lou

54. Who was interviewing Lou Martini when he was dressed as Frankenstein?

   a. Holly West   c. Harriet West

   b. Helen West   d. Hillary West

55. Who played the role of Nurse Daniels?

   a. Viola Davis   c. Octavia Spencer

   b. Oprah Winfrey   d. Mary Birdsong

56. Lou's riddle to Howard was: "What does a stripper do with her asshole before she dances?" What was the answer to his riddle?

   a. She gives him five bucks and tells him to take out the trash

   b. She gives him ten bucks and tells him to take out the trash

   c. She gives him two bucks and tells him to take out the trash

   d. She gives him twenty bucks and tells him to take out the trash

57. What was the temperature on the news Lou was watching?
    a. 49°
    b. 42°
    c. 45°
    d. 40°

58. On the sign at the bookstore where Dr. Loomis' books were being sold, what did it say about Michael Myers?
    a. He was born to kill
    b. He was born to destroy
    c. He was born to demolish
    d. He was born to massacre

59. On the sign promoting Dr. Loomis' book that Michael was looking at, what was the book's tagline above Dr. Loomis' head?
    a. The true story of America's most iconic serial murderer
    b. The true story of America's most legendary serial murderer
    c. The true story of America's most notorious serial murderer
    d. The true story of America's most mythological serial murderer

60. On the billboard promoting Dr. Loomis' book, what was the question being asked?
    a. Why am I alive?
    b. Why am I killing?
    c. Why am I here?
    d. Why am I famous?

61. When was Dr. Loomis' books set to hit the shelves in bookstores everywhere, according to his billboard?
    a. October 30th
    b. October 25th
    c. October 31st
    d. October 29th

62. What channel did Lou's interview air on?
    a. Channel 13 News
    b. Channel 21 News
    c. Channel 18 News
    d. Channel 6 News

63. Who played the role of Coroner Hooks?
    a. Richard Riehle
    b. Dayton Callie
    c. Howard Hesseman
    d. Duane Whitaker

64. What was the name of the stripper shown at the Rabbit in Red?
    a. Misty Dawn
    c. Minnie Dearie
    b. Mimi Dynasty
    d. Missy Dynamo

65. What was the name of the fan during Dr. Loomis' book signing?
    a. Chett Johns
    c. Chett Jacobs
    b. Chett Jefferies
    d. Chett James

66. Why did Chett say Michael Myers is different from the other serial killers?
    a. Because he eats at the center of the victim's soul
    b. Because he eats at the core of the victim's soul
    c. Because he eats at the vulnerable parts of the victim's soul
    d. Because he eats at the insecure parts of the victim's soul

67. What kind of crust did Annie tell her dad she wanted on the pizza?
    a. Thin Crust
    c. Whole Wheat Crust
    b. Gluten Free Crust
    d. Double Stuffed Crust

68. What was Sheriff Brackett's response to Annie regarding the crust that she wanted to eat on the pizza?
    a. Why don't we just have them take the cheese and put it on cardboard
    b. Why don't we just have them take the cheese and put it on Styrofoam
    c. Why don't we just have them take the cheese and put it on aluminum foil
    d. Why don't we just have them take the cheese and put it on a sponge

69. What did Laurie say she did not want on the pizza?

   a. Onions   c. Cheese

   b. Veggies   d. Meat

70. When Dr. Loomis was watching back his interview on *The Newman Hour* (2009), the host sarcastically asked Dr. Loomis if there is no difference between Michael Myers and what?

   a. A bear   c. A shark

   b. A dinosaur d. A Yeti

71. Who sings "Love Hurts" at the end of the film?

   a. Nan Verno   c. Nazareth

   b. The Cranberries d. Cher

72. At the end of the film when Laurie is sitting in a white room, what does Deborah Myers have with her when walking toward Laurie?

   a. Black Dragon   c. White Horse

   b. Fiery Phoenix d. Gold Lion

73. What was the word Michael Myers first spoke at the end of the film?

   a. Suffer   c. Rot

   b. Leave   d. Die

74. What color car does Laurie drive?

   a. Black   c. Orange

   b. White   d. Red

75. Who played the role of Gary Scott?

   a. Adam Boyer   c. Mark Boone Junior

   b. Jeff Daniel Phillips d. Richard Brake

76. When Laurie was dreaming of killing Annie, what was she dressed up as?

    a. A Clown

    b. A Witch

    c. A Vampire

    d. A Skeleton

77. What event from *Halloween* (2007) did Laurie imitate when she was dreaming of killing Annie?

    a. Michael Myers killing Judith Myers

    b. Michael Myers killing Steve Haley

    c. Michael Myers killing Ronnie White

    d. Michael Myers attacking the nurse at Smith's Grove Sanitarium

78. What was Chett's nickname?

    a. The Bringer of Death

    b. The Bringer of Life

    c. The Bringer of Evil

    d. The Bringer of Murder

79. Which two famous serial killers did Chett say Michael Myers is much better than?

    a. Jeffrey Dahmer and Charles Manson

    b. Jeffrey Dahmer and Ted Bundy

    c. Jeffrey Dahmer and OJ Simpson

    d. Jeffrey Dahmer and Drew Peterson

80. Who played the role of Barbara Collier?

    a. Margot Kidder

    b. Betsy Rue

    c. Mary Birdsong

    d. Caroline Williams

81. What was inside Kyle's copy of Dr. Loomis' book that he brought to the book signing?

   a. A picture of Michael Myers

   b. A picture of his daughter, Lynda

   c. A picture of Laurie

   d. A picture of his family together

82. Who did Harley David dress up as for Halloween?

   a. A chick who is dressing up like a dude who wants to be a chick

   b. A dude who is dressing up like a chick who wants to be a dude

   c. A dude who is dressing up like a chick

   d. A chick who is dressing up like a dude

83. Which two people did Laurie tell first about her being Michael Myers' sister?

   a. Annie Brackett and Sheriff Brackett

   b. Dr. Loomis and Sheriff Brackett

   c. Annie Brackett and Mya Rockwell

   d. Mya Rockwell and Harley David

84. What did the host of *The Newman Hour* (2009) say Dr. Loomis is infamous for when introducing him to the audience?

   a. For being the psychologist of America's leading serial killer

   b. For being the psychologist of America's most evil serial killer

   c. For being the psychologist of America's most vile serial killer

   d. For being the psychologist of America's famous serial killer

85. What was the question that the host of *The Newman Hour* (2009) asked Dr. Loomis in which Weird Al answered as a joke?

   a. You were criticized and outright accused of profiteering off the misery of others, how do you even respond to that criticism?

   b. You were criticized and outright accused of profiteering off the massacres that have happened, how do you even respond to that criticism?

   c. You were criticized and outright accused of profiteering off the misfortune of others, how do you even respond to that criticism?

   d. You were criticized and outright accused of profiteering off the heartbreak and agony that Michael has caused, how do you even respond to that criticism?

86. What was Dr. Loomis' answer to the above question after responding to Weird Al's sarcastic humor?

   a. Actually, I take great issue with that statement. Besides, I might say that I have endured quite a lot of pain and agony of my own in order to tell this story.

   b. Actually, I take great issue with that statement. Besides, I might say that I have endured quite a lot of misery of my own in order to tell this story.

   c. Actually, I take great issue with that statement. Besides, I might say that I have endured quite a lot of heartbreak of my own in order to tell this story.

   d. Actually, I take great issue with that statement. Besides, I might say that I have endured quite a lot of misfortune of my own in order to tell this story.

87. During the Halloween party, where did Wolfie take Harley to have sex?

   a. The Woods
   b. A Barn
   c. His Truck
   d. His Van

88. What did Wolfie name the answer to the above question?

   a. The Shaggin' Wagon
   b. The Hideout
   c. The Pimp Mobile
   d. The Truck Fuck

89. The host of the Halloween party told the joke: "What is the difference between a Jack-o'-lantern and a blonde?" What was the answer?

   a. There is no difference. They both have a dumb expression and are hollow inside.

   b. There is no difference. They both have a perplexed expression and are hollow inside.

   c. There is no difference. They both have a blank expression and are hollow inside.

   d. There is no difference. They both have a dazed expression and are hollow inside.

90. When Laurie told Mya and Harley about being Michael's sister, what did Harley think Laurie was doing?

   a. Playing a Halloween trick
   b. Insane
   c. Joking
   d. Confused

91. What did Wolfie ask was real on Harley's body?

   a. Her boobs
   b. Her hair
   c. Her tattoos
   d. Her face

92. When Wolfie and Harley are having sex in the van, what song was playing in the background?

　a. "I Just Want to Make Love to You" by Foghat

　b. "Love Hurts" by Nana Vernon

　c. "I Fell in Love" by The Frank and Friends Big Band

　d. "The Chase is Better Than the Catch" by Motorhead

93. What is the name of the band performing at the Halloween party?

　a. The Frank and Friends Big Band

　b. Motorhead

　c. Captain Clegg and the Night Creatures

　d. Diamond Head

94. When Wolfie said he had to pee, what was Harley's response?

　a. Who said I don't want to watch?

　b. Who said I wasn't into watersports?

　c. Who said you can go pee?

　d. Who said you can just leave a girl alone in a van?

95. How did Laurie find out she is Michael Myers' sister?

　a. She heard Dr. Loomis tell Sheriff Brackett

　b. She read a note from her birth mother

　c. She saw it on the news

　d. She read it in Dr. Loomis' book

96. Who played the role of Nancy McDonald?

　a. Mary Birdsong　　c. Nicky Whelan

　b. Sylvia Jefferies　　d. Diana Ayala Goldner

97. When Laurie is being held down by Michael Myers as a kid, what did Dr. Loomis tell Laurie so she can fight it?

   a. It is all in her mind c. It is all a hoax

   b. It is all make believe d. It is all an illusion

98. What were Dr. Loomis' last words of the film?

   a. Michael, for God in Heaven

   b. Michael, don't let evil consume you

   c. Michael, think about what you're doing

   d. Michael, don't do this

99. Why was Laurie shot at the end of the film?

   a. Because she was helping Michael after being shot

   b. Because she had a gun

   c. Because she was reaching for Michael's knife

   d. Because she bent down next to Dr. Loomis

100. Who played the role of Mya Rockwell?

   a. Margot Kidder   c. Brea Grant

   b. Angela Trimbur   d. Nicky Whelan

Halloween (2018)

1. *Halloween* (2018) takes place how many years after the original events occurred?

    a. Twenty Years   c. Thirty Years

    b. Fifty Years   d. Forty Years

2. Which of the following films in the *Halloween* (1978) franchise does this film ignore in the storyline?

    a. *Halloween 4* (1988) to *6* (1995)

    b. *Halloween III* (1982)

    c. *Halloween 7* (1998) and *8* (2002)

    d. All of them except the original

3. Which star from the original *Halloween* (1978) film returns in the leading role?

    a. Charles Cyphers   c. Kyle Richards

    b. Brian Andrews   d. Jamie Lee Curtis

4. Who directed *Halloween* (2018)?

    a. John Carpenter   c. Malek Akaad

    b. Danny McBride   d. David Gordon Green

5. What was the budget of *Halloween* (2018)?

    a. $5 million   c. $7 million

    b. $2 million   d. $10 million

6. Which past Michael Myers actor returns to don the mask again for only one scene with Jamie Lee Curtis, as well as the breathing sound effects during post-production in *Halloween* (2018)?

    a. George P. Wilbur   c. Nick Castle

    b. Dick Warlock   d. Christopher Durand

7. Who portrays Michael Myers for a majority of the film, excluding the one scene with Jamie Lee Curtis?

    a. Omar J. Dorsey   c. Jefferson Hall

    b. James Jude Courtney d. Toby Huss

8. How much did *Halloween* (2018) gross at the box office?

    a. $91.8 million   c. $91.4 million

    b. $91.1 million   d. $91.9 million

9. When was *Halloween* (2018) released theatrically?

    a. October 19, 2018   c. October 31, 2018

    b. October 30, 2018   d. October 23, 2018

10. Who portrayed Karen Strode?

    a. Judy Greer   c. Virginia Gardner

    b. Andi Matichak   d. Rhian Rees

11. What job title did Aaron Korey and Dana Haines have?

    a. True-Crime British Journalists

    b. True-Crime British News Anchors

    c. True-Crime British Podcasters

    d. True-Crime British Meteorologists

12. Which actor/actress from the original *Halloween* (1978) film returned as the voice of the teacher?

    a. Nancy Loomis   c. PJ Soles

    b. Charles Cyphers   d. Kyle Richards

13. What was the name of the psychiatrist that took over for Dr. Sam Loomis when he died as Michael's psychiatrist?

    a. Dr. Cameron Elam   c. Dr. Frank Hawkins

    b. Dr. Ranbir Sartain   d. Dr. Aaron Korey

14. Who portrayed Vicky?
    a. Virginia Gardner
    c. Judy Greer
    b. Rhian Rees
    d. Andi Matichak

15. Which of the following characters from the original *Halloween* (1978) film is Cameron's father?
    a. Lonnie Elam
    c. Ben Tramer
    b. Tommy Doyle
    d. Bob Simms

16. What was the name of the boy that Vicky was babysitting?
    a. James
    c. Julian
    b. Josiah
    d. Jarrod

17. What was the working production title on set for the film?
    a. *Uncle Black Cat* (2018)
    c. *Uncle Witch* (2018)
    b. *Uncle Orange* (2018)
    d. *Uncle Pumpkin* (2018)

18. Which of the following from the original timeline is no longer in effect in this film?
    a. Michael killed his sister Judith
    b. Michael's psychiatrist was Dr. Sam Loomis
    c. Michael and Laurie are siblings
    d. Michael kills on Halloween

19. Which of the following *Halloween* films had an identical bus crash to this film?
    a. *Halloween 5: The Revenge of Michael Myers* (1989)
    b. *Halloween: The Curse of Michael Myers* (1995)
    c. *Halloween: Resurrection* (2002)
    d. *Halloween 4: The Return of Michael Myers* (1988)

20. What did Michael drop onto the floor in the stall that Dana Haines was using?

   a. Bloodied Fingernails   c. Bloodied Eyeballs

   b. Bloodied Teeth   d. Bloodied Hair

21. Who portrayed Sheriff Frank Hawkins?

   a. Will Patton   c. Jefferson Hall

   b. Miles Robbins   d. Drew Scheid

22. When did filming begin for *Halloween* (2018)?

   a. January 10, 2018   c. January 13, 2018

   b. January 4, 2018   d. January 21, 2018

23. Which two actresses were in talks of portraying Allyson?

   a. Abigail Breslin and Billie Lourd

   b. Scout-Taylor Compton and Danielle Harris

   c. Emma Roberts and Lucy Hale

   d. Carlson Young and Willa Fitzgerald

24. Among Aaron's collected files on Michael Myers was an illustration of whom?

   a. Annie Brackett   c. Dr. Sam Loomis

   b. Michael Myers as a boy   d. Marion Chambers

25. When Oscar sees Michael Myers, who does he call him in reference to *Halloween II* (1981)?

   a. Gary Hunt   c. Mr. Elrod

   b. Jimmy   d. Ben Tramer

26. What did Roth Cornet nickname the movie after watching the first trailer?

   a. *Friday the 31st* (2018)   c. *Samhain* (2018)

   b. *Grambo* (2018)   d. *The Babysitter Murders* (2018)

27. In Julian's bedroom, what was featured on the rotating lamp?

   a. Michael Myers' mask   c. Clown with a knife

   b. Rabbit in Red logo   d. Silver Shamrock Masks

28. What was the body count of *Halloween* (2018)?

   a. Eighteen   c. Twenty

   b. Nineteen   d. Twenty-One

29. Where did Ray say he accidentally got some peanut butter?

   a. The floor   c. The counter

   b. His penis   d. The dog bowl

30. After the end credits, what do you hear?

   a. Laurie's scream from the original film

   b. Michael breathing through his mask

   c. Dr. Sam Loomis' screams from parts 4 and 6

   d. Silver Shamrock's commercial song

31. Whose corpse did Michael put under the bedsheet as a ghost, symbolizing his entrance to the bedroom before he killed Lynda in *Halloween* (1978)?

   a. Dave   c. Oscar

   b. Vicky   d. Ray

32. What made Allyson pissed off at her boyfriend, Cameron?

   a. He was drunk and dirty dancing with three other girls at the dance

   b. He was drunk and passed out

   c. He was drunk and verbally abusing her

   d. He was drunk and making out with another girl at the dance

33. How much money did Aaron and Dana give Laurie for their interview with her regarding Michael Myers?

    a. $2000   c. $4000

    b. $3000   d. $5000

34. Who convinced Jamie Lee Curtis to reprise her role in the film?

    a. Channing Tatum   c. Oliver Hudson

    b. John Carpenter   d. Jake Gyllenhaal

35. Who portrayed Cameron Elam?

    a. Dylan Arnold   c. Drew Scheid

    b. James Jude Courtney   d. Will Patton

36. Where does Michael recover his mask?

    a. The trunk of Aaron's car

    b. A bag inside the bathroom stall

    c. A room inside Smith's Grove Sanitarium

    d. The medical bag of his psychiatrist

37. Who was mentioned as first on the scene to arrest Michael Myers after he was shot six times by Dr. Loomis?

    a. Sheriff Frank Hawkins   c. Deputy Gary Hunt

    b. Sheriff Leigh Brackett   d. Sheriff Ben Meeker

38. What two men does the cemetery caretaker say are buried in another cemetery not far from the one she is at now?

    a. Michael Jackson and Prince

    b. Abraham Lincoln and Edgar Allan Poe

    c. Patrick Swayze and Donald Pleasence

    d. Bernie Mac and Muddy Waters

39. Before Laurie is thrown off the balcony by Michael, what was Michael hiding behind before he jumped out to attack her?

   a. A rack of clothes

   b. A collection of Halloween masks

   c. A gun rack

   d. Mannequins

40. Where did Laurie tell Allyson she can go with the money to be safe?

   a. Canada

   b. Mexico

   c. Europe

   d. Hawaii

41. Why did Laurie break into Ray and Karen's house?

   a. To tell them about Michael's escape

   b. To tell them about her story 40 years ago

   c. To demonstrate the lack of security their house has

   d. To show them how much she actually loves them

42. Who portrayed Oscar?

   a. Drew Scheid

   b. Toby Huss

   c. Dylan Arnold

   d. Jefferson Hall

43. At the end of the film, who is holding the knife in the back of the pickup truck?

   a. Laurie Strode

   b. Allyson

   c. Karen Strode

   d. None of the Above

44. When Michael is engulfed in flames at the end of the film, what is particularly noticeable after Laurie leaves the burning house?

   a. Michael is screaming in pain and agony

   b. Michael is trying to climb out of the room he was trapped in

   c. Michael takes off his mask

   d. Michael has disappeared from the room he was in when the house was set on fire

45. How does Laurie become aware of Michael's whereabouts when she was patrolling the streets in her truck?
    a. She saw Michael's shadow walking behind a house
    b. Sheriff Frank Hawkins told Laurie that Michael was seen heading towards her daughter's house
    c. She remembered that he goes after babysitters on Halloween night and remembered that Allyson's best friend, Vicky, was babysitting a kid named Julian
    d. She heard a dispatch call on her truck's CB radio after Julian fled the house where Michael was attacking Vicky and called 911
46. How does Allyson attempt to trick Dr. Sartain to her go?
    a. She said that Michael is starting to wake up
    b. She said that she knows why Michael is evil and intended on killing her grandmother
    c. She said that Dr. Loomis has files in her grandmother's house that she can get him
    d. She said that Michael spoke to her
47. What is the name of Cameron's best friend?
    a. Oscar
    b. Allyson
    c. Dave
    d. Vicky
48. Who portrayed Dave?
    a. Toby Huss
    b. Jibrail Nantambu
    c. Dylan Arnold
    d. Miles Robbins
49. Why were Aaron and Dana so interested in Michael Myers?
    a. They wanted to see why he committed the murders in 1978
    b. They wanted to see what was possessing him to be evil
    c. They wanted to know more about why the Cult of Thorn drives him to kill
    d. They wanted to know if he really heard a voice the night he killed his sister, Judith

50. What was the date of birth on Judith's tombstone?

   a. November 10, 1947   c. November 15, 1947

   b. November 5, 1947   d. November 25, 1947

51. Before Michael breaks into a lady's house to retrieve his signature kitchen knife, what does he kill her with?

   a. Screwdriver   c. Hammer

   b. Saw   d. Nail Gun

52. Regarding question 51, what in particular does this lady have that is made evident after her death?

   a. She has a newborn baby

   b. She is pregnant due to a positive pregnancy test

   c. She is a newlywed

   d. She is a widow

53. Which of the following is not something Laurie did in *Halloween* (2018) that Michael originally did in *Halloween* (1978)?

   a. Laurie broke into a closet to attack Michael

   b. Laurie fell off a balcony and landed onto the grass, as Michael looked over the balcony, Laurie was gone

   c. Laurie lurked in the shadows and attacked Michael when he didn't expect it or see her

   d. Laurie was standing outside of the schoolhouse and Allyson saw Laurie standing there and watching her while she was in class

54. What did Laurie do every night for forty years and why did she do it?

   a. She trained every night, so she can be prepared for Michael when he comes for her

   b. She meditated every night, so she was mentally prepared for her final battle with Michael

   c. She would build the fortress she currently lives in for extra protection against Michael

   d. She prayed every night that Michael would escape so she can kill him

55. Who portrayed Dana Haines?

   a. Rhian Rees   c. Judy Greer

   b. Virginia Gardner   d. Andi Matichak

56. Where did Vicky, Oscar, and Cameron all go together?

   a. A Halloween Rave

   b. A 40th Anniversary Halloween Party

   c. A Halloween Dance

   d. A Halloween Satanic Ritual

57. What did Oscar do to Allyson before he was killed?

   a. Hugged her   c. Asked her on a date

   b. Kissed her   d. Asked to hookup

58. What did Laurie's trauma cost her in life?

   a. Her sanity and freedom

   b. Two marriages and custody of her daughter, Karen

   c. Three jobs

   d. Her friendship with Dr. Loomis

59. What was Ray doing in the kitchen?

    a. Cooking breakfast   c. Setting mouse traps

    b. Doing the dishes   d. Cleaning the countertops

60. Where is Laurie's "safe place" located?

    a. In a hidden door behind her closet

    b. In a hidden bunker underneath her kitchen island

    c. In a hidden passage behind a bookcase

    d. In a hidden alcove under her bed

61. When Allyson is running through the woods, she comes across a bunch of mannequins and targets shown earlier in the film during which of the following scenes?

    a. When Laurie had her daughter training for the moment Michael would escape

    b. When Laurie was shooting her guns for practice in preparation for Michael's impending escape

    c. When Aaron and Dana were heading to Laurie's house to conduct an interview with her

    d. When Sheriff Frank Hawkins was patrolling the streets

62. When the bus crashed, who was wandering the streets?

    a. The doctors of Smith's Grove Sanitarium

    b. The patients of Smith's Grove Sanitarium

    c. The injured driver

    d. Michael Myers

63. Who portrayed Ray?

    a. Haluk Bilginer   c. Drew Scheid

    b. Will Patton   d. Toby Huss

64. Who kills Sheriff Frank Hawkins and kidnaps Michael to take him to Laurie?

   a. Officer Richards   c. Aaron Korey

   b. Dr. Ranbir Sartain   d. Warden Kuneman

65. When Michael breaks through the glass of the door and grabs Laurie, what does Laurie shoot to free herself from his grasp?

   a. His face   c. His chest

   b. His shoulder   d. His hand

66. How did Karen know which gun to use when Michael found the hidden bunker?

   a. Karen's initials were on the gun

   b. Karen remembered which gun she always practiced with as a child

   c. Laurie told Karen that it was the gun to use if Michael found her

   d. Karen intuitively just chose that gun

67. How does Aaron try to get Michael to speak at Smith's Grove Sanitarium?

   a. He mentioned the morbid details of how he killed his sister, Judith

   b. He mentioned how Dr. Sam Loomis tried to stop Michael from his killing spree

   c. He shows Michael the mask he wore and mentioned Laurie's name

   d. He explains the significance of Halloween and why Michael chose that day to kill his sister

68. Where does Laurie shoot Michael when she sees him in an upstairs window?

   a. His head
   c. His stomach
   b. His heart
   d. His shoulder

69. What does Karen shoot Michael with?

   a. A shotgun
   c. A pistol
   b. A rifle
   d. A machine gun

70. When Laurie found Ray's body on the closet shelf, which character's corpse from *Halloween* (1978) did it resemble?

   a. Annie Brackett
   c. Lynda Van Der Klok
   b. Bob Simms
   d. Judith Myers

71. While Laurie is hunting down Michael in her home, what does she do after leaving each room?

   a. Presses a button to barricade the room, so she knows she checked it and Michael is not in it
   b. Fires a warning shot into the wall to let Karen know where she is located, and Michael isn't there
   c. Grabs another weapon or more ammo to be prepared for the next room she is about to enter
   d. Rapidly shoots her gun in case Michael is hiding outside of the room she is leaving

72. Which television show and movie were playing on the television sets in *Halloween* (2018)?

   a. *Voyagers* (1982) and *The Exorcist* (1973)
   b. *Voyagers* (1982) and *Repo Man* (1984)
   c. *Voyagers* (1982) and *The Thing from Another World* (1951)
   d. *Voyagers* (1982) and *Friday the 13th* (1980)

73. Which of the following actors expressed interest in playing Michael Myers?

   a. Chris Evans
   b. Robert Downey Jr.
   c. Jason Momoa
   d. Leigh Whannell

74. What does Laurie stab Michael with to allow Karen and Allyson to escape?

   a. A knife
   b. A fireplace poker
   c. A cleaver
   d. A syringe

75. Who portrayed Dr. Ranbir Sartain?

   a. Jibrail Nantambu
   b. Haluk Bilginer
   c. Jefferson Hall
   d. Miles Robbins

76. What is the name of Vicky's boyfriend?

   a. Oscar
   b. Dave
   c. Cameron
   d. Julian

77. What does Dr. Ranbir Sartain tell Aaron and Dana about Michael at Smith's Grove Sanitarium?

   a. He is planning his escape
   b. He is recovering from the six shots he received from Dr. Sam Loomis
   c. He can speak but refuses to do so
   d. He stares at the picture of Laurie Strode every day for hours

78. When Laurie discovers Michael Myers in an upstairs bedroom, who are noticeable from a past *Halloween* (1978) film roaming the streets?

   a. Trick-or-Treaters wearing Silver Shamrock Halloween masks
   b. Druids from the Cult of Thorn
   c. Patients from the Smith's Grove Sanitarium
   d. The Silver Shamrock Androids

79. How does Karen trap Michael in the safe room as it is filled up with gas?

   a. By closing the passageway using the kitchen island

   b. By putting a heavy sofa to cover the safe room's entry/exit

   c. By flipping the switch and having the metal bars close the exit from the room

   d. By barricading the room's entry/exit with heavy furniture and equipment

80. Who portrayed Allyson?

   a. Andi Matichak   c. Rhian Rees

   b. Jamie Lee Curtis   d. Judy Greer

81. Where is Michael being transferred to?

   a. Smith's Grove Sanitarium's solitary confinement

   b. A state prison

   c. A mental institution

   d. A maximum security prison

82. When talking to Vicky on the phone, Allyson mentioned that Halloween is on a what?

   a. Weekend   c. School night

   b. Friday   d. Family game night

83. On the television, the newscaster is heard describing the events of *Halloween* (2018) as what?

   a. The Haddonfield Slaughtering

   b. The Monster Mash

   c. The Halloween Massacre

   d. The Babysitter Murders

84. At Smith's Grove Sanitarium, which of the following indicates the most dangerous patients?

   a. Yellow-Lined Checkered Squares

   b. Black-Lined Checkered Squares

   c. Red-Lined Checkered Squares

   d. Blue-Lined Checkered Squares

85. While the father and his son are driving, before they see the crashed bus, the son tells his father he enjoys his what?

   a. Halloween costume   c. X-Box One

   b. New Bedroom   d. Dance Classes

86. What is the address of the disturbance that came across the police band?

   a. 707 Meridian   c. 15 Lampkin

   b. 1428 Elm   d. 21 Dayta

87. Who portrayed Aaron Korey?

   a. Nick Castle   c. Jefferson Hall

   b. James Jude Courtney   d. Toby Huss

88. What does Laurie say to Michael when she sets him on fire in the safe room?

   a. Happy Halloween, Michael   c. Burn in Hell, Michael

   b. Trick-or-Treat, Michael   d. Rest in Peace, Michael

89. What does Allyson say to Vicky regarding Michael being Laurie's brother?

   a. It was a rumor that circulated for a while but was found to be untrue

   b. It was true until a DNA test proved otherwise

   c. It was a bad storyline that people told when discussing the murders

   d. It was a story that people just made up

90. What was Michael trying to do to Laurie when he smashed through her door

    a. Break her neck

    b. Break down the door to gain access to her home

    c. Take her gun away

    d. Strangle her to death

91. On which date did Jamie Lee Curtis announce via Twitter that she was returning to play Laurie Strode?

    a. September 19, 2017   c. September 9, 2017

    b. September 15, 2017   d. September 17, 2017

92. Which of the following were the original working titles for *Halloween* (2018)?

    a. *Halloween Returns* (2018) and *Halloween: The Origin of Michael Myers* (2018)

    b. *Halloween Returns* (2018) and *Halloween: The Shape of Michael Myers* (2018)

    c. *Halloween Returns* (2018) and *Halloween H40: 40 Years Later* (2018)

    d. *Halloween Returns* (2018) and *Halloween: The Evil of Michael Myers* (2018)

93. The gas station is the same, exact replica as the gas station in which previous *Halloween* film?

    a. *Halloween 3: Season of the Witch* (1982)

    b. *Halloween 4: The Return of Michael Myers* (1988)

    c. *Halloween 5: The Revenge of Michael Myers* (1989)

    d. *Halloween H20: 20 Years Later* (1998)

94. Who portrayed Julian?

    a. Rhian Rees   c. Jefferson Hall

    b. Haluk Bilginer   d. Jibrail Nantambu

95. What does Aaron and Dana ask Laurie to do with Michael?
   a. Meet with him as a last attempt to get him to speak
   b. Meet with him and see if his rage occurs again
   c. Meet with him and see if there is a pattern in his attack on her like there was with Judith
   d. Meet with him and see if she can make a connection with him

96. Why can't Karen and Ray get in contact with Allyson?
   a. Because her phone died
   b. Because Cameron put her phone in food causing it to malfunction
   c. Because she forgot her phone at the Halloween dance
   d. Because she dropped her phone when she was running after seeing Oscar's dead body

97. What was the date of death on Judith's tombstone?
   a. October 31, 1957   c. October 31, 1978
   b. October 31, 1972   d. October 31, 1963

98. Danny McBride, when appearing on Empire Film Podcast to promote *Alien: Covenant* (2017), was jokingly asked if he'd be playing Michael Myers due to his large build, to which Danny responded by saying what?
   a. Oh God no! Michael's supposed to be a terrifying creeper with good posture, not Peter Griffin!
   b. Oh God no! Michael's supposed to be a terrifying creeper with good posture, not Homer Simpson!
   c. Oh God no! Michael's supposed to be a terrifying creeper with good posture, not Elmer Fudd!
   d. Oh God no! Michael's supposed to be a terrifying creeper with good posture, not Winnie the Pooh!

99. Who portrayed Laurie Strode?

    a. PJ Soles

    b. Jamie Lee Curtis

    c. Judy Greer

    d. Scout-Taylor Compton

100. What has Laurie been dealing with for the past forty years?

    a. Post-Traumatic Stress Disorder

    b. Schizophrenia

    c. Multiple Personality Disorder

    d. Drug Addiction

Halloween Kills (2021)

1. What does the mob keep chanting about Michael Myers?

    a. Evil burns tonight

    b. Evil ends tonight

    c. Evil loses tonight

    d. Evil dies tonight

2. Which five original characters from *Halloween* (1978) return in *Halloween Kills* (2021), excluding Laurie Strode and Michael Myers?

    a. Tommy Doyle, Lindsay Wallace, Marion Chambers, Leigh Brackett, and Morgan Strode

    b. Tommy Doyle, Lindsay Wallace, Marion Chambers, Leigh Brackett, and Lonnie Elam

    c. Tommy Doyle, Lindsay Wallace, Marion Chambers, Leigh Brackett, and Dr. Wynn

    d. Tommy Doyle, Lindsay Wallace, Marion Chambers, Leigh Brackett, and Richie

3. What mask was Marion Chambers wearing after she was killed by Michael?

    a. Silver Shamrock witch mask

    b. Silver Shamrock skeleton mask

    c. Silver Shamrock Jack-o'-Lantern mask

    d. Silver Shamrock android mask

4. Which character from *Halloween* (1978) returned in a flashback in *Halloween Kills* (2021)?

    a. Dr. Sam Loomis   c. Lynda Van Der Klok

    b. Annie Brackett   d. Bob Simms

5. Who was killed by Michael Myers at the film's cliffhanger ending?

    a. Laurie Strode   c. Allyson Nelson

    b. Lindsay Wallace   d. Karen Nelson

6. What holiday sweater was Karen wearing the entire movie?

    a. Valentine's Day   c. Saint Patrick's Day

    b. Christmas   d. Easter

7. Which character from *Halloween* (2018), thought to have died, was revealed to have survived?

    a. Frank Hawkins   c. Dr. Ranbir Sartain

    b. Ray Nelson   d. Vicky

8. Which iconic actress returned for the role she originated in *Halloween* (1978)?

    a. PJ Soles   c. Jamie Lee Curtis

    b. Nancy Kyes   d. Debra Hill

9. What did Laurie Strode scream from the back of a truck as firefighters went to extinguish her burning home with Michael Myers trapped inside?

    a. Let him burn   c. Let him die

    b. Let him rot   d. Let him alone

10. What are the names of the new occupants of the Myers home?

    a. Big James and Little James   c. Big John and Little John

    b. Big Jordan and Little Jordan   d. Big Josh and Little Josh

11. When Michael was killing Karen, the death was portrayed as a death in which iconic slasher film?

   a. *Friday the 13th* (1980)

   b. *Peeping Tom* (1960)

   c. *Psycho* (1960)

   d. *The Town That Dreaded Sundown* (1976)

12. What does Marion Chambers say before she attempts to shoot Michael Myers?

   a. Hey, Michael. This is for Haddonfield!

   b. Hey, Michael. This is for Laurie!

   c. Hey, Michael. This is for Dr. Loomis!

   d. Hey, Michael. This is for Judith!

13. What was the body count of *Halloween Kills* (2021)?

   a. Twenty-Eight
   c. Thirty
   b. Twenty-Nine
   d. Thirty-One

14. What was the budget of *Halloween Kills* (2021)?

   a. $25 million
   c. $18 million
   b. $20 million
   d. $31 million

15. For the first time in the franchise's history, *Halloween Kills* (2021) was released on October 15, 2021, in theaters and one streaming platform. Which streaming platform was it viewable on?

   a. Netflix
   c. Peacock
   b. Hulu
   d. Shudder

16. Which weapon did Tommy Doyle grab in the bar to kill Michael?

   a. Kitchen knife
   c. Beer bottle
   b. Metal tray
   d. Baseball bat

17. Which film, although no-longer a canon in this timeline, had archive footage shown?

   a. *Halloween 4: The Return of Michael Myers* (1988)

   b. *Halloween III: Season of the Witch* (1982)

   c. *Halloween: The Curse of Michael Myers* (1995)

   d. *Halloween II* (1981)

18. Who took over the role of Dr. Sam Loomis in the flashback scenes?

   a. Tom Kane
   c. Tom Jones Jr.

   b. Malcolm McDowell
   d. Tom Atkins

19. What does Karen stab Michael in the back with?

   a. Pitchfork
   c. Sword

   b. Scythe
   d. Meat cleaver

20. What did Lindsay put in the bag to hit Michael with at the park?

   a. Rocks
   c. Sticks

   b. Bricks
   d. Leaves

21. When was *Halloween Kills* (2021) released into theaters?

   a. October 13, 2021
   c. October 31, 2021

   b. October 15, 2021
   d. October 14, 2021

22. Who directed *Halloween Kills* (2021)?

   a. Jason Blum
   c. Cody Carpenter

   b. David Gordon Green
   d. Tommy Lee Wallace

23. Which actor in *Halloween Kills* (2021) passed away before the release of the film?

   a. Ross Bacon
   c. Lenny Clarke

   b. Giselle Witt
   d. Brian Mays

24. Although killed in Haddonfield by Michael Myers, what was the incorrectly listed location of death on the toe tag of Dr. Ranbir Sartain's corpse?

   a. Ismir, Turkey
   b. Stockholm, Sweden
   c. Berlin, Germany
   d. Turin, Italy

25. What was seen in the background from the original *Halloween* (1978) film in the flashback scene of *Halloween Kills* (2021)?

   a. The hardware store Michael broke into
   b. Bob's van
   c. Dr. Loomis' station wagon
   d. Annie's corpse on a stretcher

26. What item that Michael stole from the hardware store in the original *Halloween* (1978) film did he use to attack Pete McCabe in the flashback scene?

   a. Rope
   b. Lead Pipe
   c. Knife
   d. Wrench

27. In the flashback scenes, what is listed on the police officers' shoulder patches?

   a. Haddonfield P.D.
   b. Warren County
   c. Smith's Grove
   d. Russellville Township

28. During the *Halloween Kills* (2021) movie premiere, Jamie Lee Curtis went dressed as which of the following characters from a classic slasher film?

   a. Mrs. Voorhees
   b. Angela Baker
   c. Sally Hardesty
   d. Marion Crane

29. *Halloween Kills* (2021) is the first film to feature Michael Myers killing what type of people?

   a. Firefighters
   b. Children
   c. Police Officers
   d. Women

30. Which surviving character from a past *Halloween* (1978) film was almost brought back, but the idea was scrapped?

   a. Busta Rhymes as Freddie Harris

   b. Marianne Hagan as Kara Strode

   c. Josh Hartnett as John Tate

   d. Lance Guest as Jimmy Lloyd

31. What object did Michael Myers kill the first firefighter with?

   a. Halligan Bar   c. Oxygen Tank

   b. Fire Hose   d. Fire Axe

32. Which character from *Halloween (2018)* returned in a small cameo as an interviewee on the news in *Halloween Kills* (2021)?

   a. Guard Haskell   c. Warden Kuneman

   b. Julian   d. Sheriff Barker

33. Which two characters from *Halloween* (2018) with small roles in Halloween costumes returned as named characters in *Halloween Kills* (2021)?

   a. Brian Gregorie as Father and Vince Mattis as Lumpy

   b. Jonathan Bruce as News Reporter and Kurt Deimer as Teller

   c. Miguel Macario Mata as Cowboy Kid and Jacob M. Arnold as Pirate Kid

   d. Michael Smallwood as Hunky Doctor and Carmela McNeal as Sexy Nurse

34. Which character did the mob mistake for Michael Myers?

   a. Brian the Bartender c. Big John

   b. Marcus   d. Tivoli

35. Which character killed in *Halloween* (2018) returned as a corpse and was seen by his mother, just like Nancy Kyes in *Halloween II* (1981) where Sheriff Brackett saw her corpse?

   a. Dave
   b. Ray Nelson
   c. Aaron Korey
   d. Oscar

36. Who voiced Dr. Sam Loomis in the flashback scenes?

   a. Tom Jones Jr.
   b. Tom Kane
   c. Colin Mahan
   d. Damien Lee

37. What were Phil and Sondra playing with before they were killed by Michael Myers?

   a. Drone
   b. Paper Airplane
   c. Remote Controlled Car
   d. Silly Putty

38. What song was playing when Cameron and Allyson discovered the corpses of Big John and Little John?

   a. "Sexual Healing" by Marvin Gaye
   b. "Could I Have This Dance" by Anne Murray
   c. "Always & Forever" by Heatwave
   d. "We Go a Long Way Back" by Bloodstone

39. What mask was Marcus wearing after she was killed by Michael?

   a. Silver Shamrock witch mask
   b. Silver Shamrock skeleton mask
   c. Silver Shamrock Jack-o'-Lantern mask
   d. Silver Shamrock Michael Myers mask

40. What is Sondra's job, as shown in *Halloween* (2018)?

   a. Caretaker at the Haddonfield Cemetery
   b. Clerk at the Hardware Store
   c. Nurse at the Haddonfield Memorial Hospital
   d. Bartender at the local bar

41. What movie was Big John and Little John watching?
    a. *The Thing from Another World* (1951)
    b. *Brokeback Mountain* (2005)
    c. *Night of the Living Dead* (1972)
    d. *Love Streams* (1984)
42. Who found an injured Frank Hawkins in the streets?
    a. Allyson Nelson
    b. Cameron Elam
    c. Sheriff Barker
    d. Leigh Brackett
43. Who played a young Frank Hawkins in the flashback scenes?
    a. Airon Armstrong
    b. Ryan Lewis
    c. Jim Cummings
    d. Thomas Mann
44. What item did Karen use to lure Michael Myers into her trap and have him surrounded by the mob?
    a. His mask
    b. Judith's tombstone
    c. A picture of Laurie
    d. Silver Shamrock mask
45. Which character thought she saw Michael Myers in her car when leaving the bar?
    a. Marion Chambers
    b. Sondra
    c. Lindsay Wallace
    d. Vanessa
46. Who played Lonnie Elam in *Halloween Kills* (2021)?
    a. Scott MacArthur
    b. Robert Longstreet
    c. Lenny Clarke
    d. Omar J. Dorsey
47. What happened to Laurie once she arrived at the Haddonfield Memorial Hospital?
    a. She was given a proper physical examination
    b. She had surgery due to the stab wound she sustained
    c. She was given an injection of pain medication
    d. She was allowed to see her son-in-law, Ray's, corpse in the morgue

48. How did Laurie find out that Michael escaped the fire in her home and is still alive?

   a. Tommy Doyle entered her hospital room and told her that Marion was killed

   b. Lindsay Wallace entered her hospital room and requested her assistance

   c. Allyson blurted out his escape so Laurie can join the mob in the fight against Michael

   d. Frank told her when she was brought to her room to be treated for his injuries

49. Who played the role of Sondra in both *Halloween* (2018) and *Halloween Kills* (2021)?

   a. Carmela McNeal   c. Salem Collins

   b. Holli Saperstein   d. Diva Tyler

50. Kyle Richards returned to *Halloween Kills* (2021) as her character from the original *Halloween* (1978) film, Lindsay Wallace. In which reality show is Kyle Richards part of the main cast?

   a. *Real Housewives of Beverly Hills* (2010)

   b. *America's Next Top Model* (2003)

   c. *Project Runway* (2004)

   d. *Love & Hip Hop Atlanta* (2012)

51. Who played Michael Myers in the flashback scenes?

   a. Michael McDonald   c. J. Gaven Wilde

   b. Airon Armstrong   d. Nick Castle

52. Where did Tommy, Lonnie, Cameron, and Allyson find the corpses of Marcus and Vanessa?

   a. On the merry-go-round   c. On the slide

   b. On the swings   d. On the basketball court

53. What does Leigh Brackett say to Michael before he shoots him?

   a. Hey, Michael! It's Halloween. And evil will die tonight.

   b. Hey, Michael! It's Halloween. It's time you pay for killing my daughter.

   c. Hey, Michael! It's Halloween. Haddonfield will finally be at peace.

   d. Hey, Michael! It's Halloween. Everyone's entitled to one good scare.

54. David Gordon Green confirmed in an interview that *Halloween Ends* (2022), the finale of this timeline, takes place how many years after *Halloween Kills* (2021)?

   a. Four Years
   c. Two Years
   b. Seven Years
   d. Five Years

55. Who played Tommy Doyle, replacing the original actor, Brian Andrews?

   a. Paul Rudd
   c. Michael Smallwood
   b. Tristan Eggerling
   d. Anthony Michael Hall

56. What was Tommy Doyle celebrating at the local bar?

   a. Fortieth anniversary of Michael Myers' arrest

   b. Commemoration of Michael Myers' victims and those who survived him

   c. Forty years of Michael Myers' imprisonment

   d. All of the Above

57. When Leigh Brackett tells Tommy that Tivoli isn't Michael after he killed himself, Tommy thinks it still might be him. What does Tommy say is the reason he believed it was Michael?

   a. Because he was wearing a mental hospital uniform

   b. Because Michael always wore a mask and he never saw his face

   c. Because he looked like a man that would've been burned in the fire

   d. Because he is the same age and size that Michael was

58. What was the name of the charity that Tommy donated to in the local bar?

   a. Love Lives Today   c. Evil Dies Tonight

   b. Haddonfield Memorial Fund   d. Warren County Police Fund

59. Who were the three kids in Silver Shamrock masks that played a prank on Big John and Little John?

   a. Julian, Oscar, and Phil

   b. Dennis, Mindy, and Christy

   c. Sondra, Vanessa, and Lynda

   d. Marcus, Brian, and Annie

60. Who played Big John in *Halloween Kills* (2021)?

   a. Michael McDonald   c. Scott MacArthur

   b. Mike Dupree   d. Charlie Benton

61. What did Marcus try strangling Michael Myers with before he was killed?

   a. His hands   c. Some rope

   b. His scrubs   d. A stethoscope

62. Where did Tommy, Lonnie, Cameron, and Allyson find Marion's corpse?

   a. On the merry-go-round

   b. Hanging from the swing set

   c. On the teeter totter

   d. Stuffed in a basketball hoop

63. What movie did Michael McDonald direct Anthony Michael Hall in, yet in *Halloween Kills* (2021), they do not share any scenes together?

   a. *Leprechaun 4: In Space* (1996)

   b. *A Bucket of Blood* (1995)

   c. *Candyman 2: Farewell to the Flesh* (1995)

   d. *Children of the Corn 3: Urban Harvest* (1995)

64. How many pumpkins are featured in the opening title sequence?

   a. Twelve

   b. Ten

   c. Thirteen

   d. Eleven

65. Which actor that was never in a *Halloween* (1978) film had their photograph used in a yearbook to be Bob Simms so that they didn't have to use the picture of John Michael Graham from the original *Halloween* (1978) film?

   a. Kevin Spacey

   b. Leonardo DiCaprio

   c. Tom Hanks

   d. Bob Odenkirk

66. The mob in *Halloween Kills* (2021) is similar to that of the smaller mob in which *Halloween* (1978) film that is not in canon to this timeline?

   a. *Halloween H20: 20 Years Later* (1998)

   b. *Halloween 4: The Return of Michael Myers* (1988)

   c. *Halloween 5: The Revenge of Michael Myers* (1989)

   d. *Halloween: Resurrection* (2002)

67. Who recorded the sounds of Michael Myers breathing in *Halloween Kills* (2021)?

    a. Nick Castle

    c. James Jude Courtney

    b. John Carpenter

    d. Tony Moran

68. What did the children say was in the candy given to them from Big John and Little John?

    a. Paper

    c. Razor Blade

    b. Poison

    d. Peanuts

69. Who played Phil in *Halloween Kills* (2021)?

    a. Dylan Arnold

    c. Lenny Clarke

    b. Drew Scheid

    d. James Northrup

70. What mask was Vanessa wearing after she was killed by Michael?

    a. Silver Shamrock witch mask

    b. Silver Shamrock skeleton mask

    c. Silver Shamrock Jack-o'-Lantern mask

    d. Silver Shamrock Michael Myers mask

71. Who lobbied for Danielle Harris to cameo in *Halloween Kills* (2021), but the idea was immediately vetoed?

    a. Ryan Freimann

    c. Jamie Lee Curtis

    b. John Carpenter

    d. Danny McBride

72. The name Gamby was on one of the firefighter's helmets. Danny McBride played a character with that name on which television show?

    a. *Tarantula* (2017)

    c. *Vice Principals* (2016)

    b. *Good Vibes* (2011)

    d. *The Righteous Gemstones* (2019)

73. Which act was at the local bar before Tommy Doyle took the stage?

   a. Magic Show
   b. Puppet Show
   c. Ventriloquism
   d. Juggling

74. How did Tivoli kill himself when he was mistaken for Michael Myers?

   a. He shot himself in the head
   b. He hung himself
   c. He slit his wrist with a razor blade
   d. He jumped out of a window from the top floor of the hospital

75. When musing on the fact that Michael becomes more powerful the more fear he instills, what phrase does Laurie utter?

   a. The true curse of Michael Myers
   b. The true personification of evil
   c. The true power of thorn
   d. The true embodiment of the supernatural

76. Which city in Illinois is on the 2-D map that Lonnie shows to Cameron and Allyson?

   a. Chicago
   b. Bloomington
   c. Peoria
   d. Springfield

77. How did Vanessa accidentally shoot herself in the eye?

   a. She shot at Michael and the bullet ricocheted into her eye
   b. Michael kicked the car door into her, and she pulled the trigger into her eye
   c. She held the gun the wrong way and pulled the trigger into her eye instead of at Michael
   d. She pointed the gun at Michael, he twisted her arm towards her so the gun is facing her face, and she accidentally pressed the trigger

78. What was the original ending of the film that was cut from the theatrical version of the film, but was included in the film's Blu Ray?

   a. Laurie calls Karen's cell phone and Michael answers it. Laurie hears Michael breathing, knowing that Karen has been killed by Michael.

   b. Laurie shows up at the Myers House and calls out Michael's name as he was stabbing Karen.

   c. Laurie and Michael are both staring out of their respective windows and Allyson shows up to where her mom is lying dead and utters a wicked scream.

   d. Michael finishes stabbing Karen, looks out the window, as Laurie looks out her hospital window, and Karen's eyes open as she still has life in her.

79. What was Tivoli called in the credits of *Halloween* (2018)?

   a. Psych Ward Patient   c. Sanitarium Bus Passenger

   b. Escaped Mental Patient   d. Umbrella Man

80. What does the stuntman playing Michael Myers in the scene on top of the car have strapped to his hand to break the glass of the passenger side door that Marion is leaning against?

   a. Smaller Hammer   c. Thumbtacks

   b. Screwdriver   d. Wrench

81. Who played Little John in *Halloween Kills* (2021)?

   a. Will Patton   c. Michael McDonald

   b. Scott MacArthur   d. Troy Rudeseal

82. When Laurie and Frank were reminiscing about their past together, what did Laurie and Frank say they did with each other one night?

   a. Got married drunk   c. Shared a kiss with each other

   b. Had sex after the prom   d. Made a child together

83. Michael McDonald got killed by Michael Myers in *Halloween Kills* (2021) and by actor Mike Myers, in which *Austin Powers* (1997) movie?

   a. *Austin Powers: The Spy Who Shagged Me* (1999)

   b. *Austin Powers in Goldmember* (2002)

   c. *Austin Powers: International Man of Mystery* (1997)

   d. *Austin Powers: Welcome to My Underground Lair* (2000)

84. Which Halloween mask did Michael Myers hold up to show he killed the child who was wearing it?

   a. Silver Shamrock Jack-o'-Lantern mask

   b. Silver Shamrock witch mask

   c. Silver Shamrock skeleton mask

   d. Silver Shamrock Conal Cochran mask

85. When Tommy grabbed the baseball bat, what did he say when asked why he is using a baseball bat as his weapon?

   a. I've been waiting 40 years to beat Michael Myers' brain in

   b. Tonight, I have batting practice and Michael's head is the ball

   c. If I'm going down, I'm going down swinging

   d. Evil dies tonight, and it'll go down by my hands and this bat

86. Why was *Halloween Kills* (2021) postponed a full year for its release?

   a. Due to the COVID-19 pandemic

   b. Due to a delay in post-production editing

   c. Due to a scheduling conflict with Jamie Lee Curtis and filming got pushed back

   d. Due to a contract dispute with airing in theaters and streaming platforms simultaneously

87. When asked by a nurse of his pain level on a scale of 1 to 10, with 10 being the worst, Frank Hawkins responded with what number?

   a. One Hundred
   c. Ten
   b. Twenty
   d. Eleven

88. When Karen tricks Michael in *Halloween* (2018) and again in *Halloween Kills* (2021), what word does she say both times?

   a. Goodbye
   c. Die
   b. Gotcha
   d. Sucker

89. Before Lonnie goes into the Myers House to confront Michael, what does he say to his son, Cameron?

   a. I'll be back soon. I promise.
   b. I'll see you at the finish line.
   c. I'll be okay. Don't worry. I waited forty years for this moment.
   d. This place doesn't scare me. I'm not a kid anymore.

90. Who does Karen see in Judith's bedroom before she is killed by Michael?

   a. Michael Myers as a boy in a clown costume
   b. Judith Myers as a ghost
   c. Her husband, Ray, asking her to join him in the afterlife
   d. Allyson screaming outside of the window to look out behind her

91. In the flashback scenes, where did the sheriff's deputy instruct the other police officers to search for Michael?

   a. Chestnut North to the bypass
   b. Chestnut West to the bypass
   c. Chestnut South to the bypass
   d. Chestnut East to the bypass

92. When Laurie found out that Michael was still alive, what did she do for the pain?

   a. Took a bunch of pain pills

   b. Drank a swig of alcohol from her flask

   c. Said a prayer

   d. Injected herself with a syringe

93. Lindsay Wallace actress, Kyle Richards, broke what body part when filming her fight scene with Michael?

   a. Nose   c. Pinky Finger

   b. Ankle   d. Three Ribs

94. Lindsay finally found out that Lonnie didn't do what as a kid?

   a. Confront Michael Myers

   b. Go nosing around inside the Myers House

   c. Bullied Tommy

   d. Stole Judith's tombstone from the cemetery

95. Malek Akkad didn't want Paul Rudd back as Tommy Doyle because of what reason?

   a. He was asking for too much money due to his success on *Friends* (1994) and in *Ant-Man* (2015)

   b. He regretted being in *Halloween 6: The Curse of Michael Myers* (1995)

   c. He would be too distracting to the viewing audience due to his success, taking away from the other characters and actors in the film

   d. He isn't the look or size he wants Tommy Doyle to be in this film

96. Where was *Halloween Kills* (2021) filmed?

   a. South Pasadena, California

   b. Vancouver, British Columbia, Canada

   c. Wilmington, North Carolina

   d. Atlanta, Georgia

97. In the flashback scenes, when Frank Hawkins and his deputy are standing in the living room, what animal's carcass was revealed to be half-eaten by Michael?

   a. Dog

   b. Cat

   c. Skunk

   d. Rat

98. Which actor and stuntman, who previously played Michael Myers in a *Halloween* (1978) film, returned as Michael Myers in *Halloween Kills* (2021)?

   a. George P. Wilbur

   b. Don Shanks

   c. Dick Warlock

   d. James Jude Courtney

99. Who played Cameron Elam in *Halloween Kills* (2021)?

   a. Dylan Arnold

   b. Drew Scheid

   c. Miles Robbins

   d. Jefferson Hall

100. Before *Halloween Kills* (2021) was released, Jamie Lee Curtis stated that *Halloween Ends* (2022) will do what to a lot of fans?

   a. Make them happy

   b. Make them angry

   c. Make them uncomfortable

   d. Make them confused

Halloween Mashup

Part 1: Word Scramble

Unscramble the following *Halloween* (1978) franchise words, terms, or characters.

1. CRMSAE NEUEQ _____ _____
2. OEIDHLDNDAF _____
3. ROTNH _____
4. LLOEWHEAN _____
5. MCLHIEA SMRYE _____ _____
6. LEIV _____
7. VESIRL HKCRSOAM _____ _____
8. CHTBUER NIKEF _____ _____
9. BBRIAT NI DRE _____ _____
10. DTTMAAENRNIGNEN _____
11. TOBCORE _____
12. OONBMYEGAM _____
13. YITBASTBIIGN _____
14. HET PSEHA _____ _____
15. ETH NIICCL _____ _____

Part 2: Who Am I?

16. I am the niece of a serial killer. I survived my first two ordeals with him, but later was killed after giving birth. I tried to protect my baby after foreseeing my death and hid him well. Who am I?

_____

17. I am a mother who loved her son. I couldn't believe he killed Ronnie, Judith, and Judith's boyfriend in cold blood. I worked as a stripper at the Rabbit in Red. After my son was locked up and I figured there'd be no way to protect him, I put a bullet in my head while watching a slideshow of him as a boy. Who am I?

_____

18. I am the brother of a real estate owner and took over his company. I also bought the Myers House for my family to live in at a very cheap price without telling them and am the reason they got butchered by Michael. I tend to be a jackass and come off as an asshole to my family. I don't believe in the Boogeyman but found out the hard way that he exists. Who am I? _____

19. I am the head nurse at Haddonfield Memorial Hospital. I tend to be a bit of a prude, but I am just doing my job. I kept checking on Laurie Strode after she was brutally attacked by Michael Myers. I also yelled at Nurse Karen Bailey. Who am I? _____

20. I am the owner of a factory called Silver Shamrock. I make Halloween masks and plan to use my "innovation" to kill children worldwide. I got rich off cheap gags and Halloween masks. I am also an Irishman. Who am I? _____

21. We are a dysfunctional family. We consist of a father, Buddy, a mother, Betty, and our son, Buddy Jr. We are looking to refill our purchase order of the Silver Shamrock masks. We all died as a family during the demonstration to Dr. Challis on how these masks plan on killing children worldwide when they wear them during the giveaway. Who are we? _____

22. I am the annoying best friend of Rachel. I went to the Tower Farms Halloween party despite being told my life was in danger. I'm close to Jamie and sacrificed my own life to protect hers. Who am I?

_____

23. I am the stepmother of Jamie and mother of Rachel. I went out on Halloween night to my husband's work dinner. I got home and Rachel and Jamie weren't home before curfew. I later found out why, and, when getting Jamie ready for her bath, I was stabbed with a pair of scissors. I did survive the ordeal. Who am I?

_____

24. I am the reason Michael escaped from Smith's Grove Sanitarium. I also kidnapped Jamie and broke Michael out of the jail cell. I work at Smith's Grove Sanitarium and control Michael with the Curse of Thorn. I also taught Michael how to drive. Who am I?

_____

25. I am Rachel's love interest. I got mad that Rachel blew me off and went out with Kelly Meeker, the sheriff's daughter. I later tried to make it up to Rachel by protecting her, but I failed. I also work at the Discount Mart. Who am I? _____

26. I am evil. I have the eyes of the devil according to my psychiatrist. I am provoked by the Curse of Thorn. As a kid, I killed my sister and was locked up. Now, I am wanting to kill my other sister, Laurie. Who am I? _____

27. I babysat Michael on Halloween in 1963 when he killed his sister in cold blood. I am a member of the cult that rages Michael into a killing machine. Who am I? _____

28. I always use the word "totally." I am a cheerleader and best friends with Laurie and Annie. I am also dating Bob. Who am I?

_____

29. I was looking after Michael for years after both he and Dr. Loomis burned to death. I then handed him over to the state. I also

told Dr. Loomis about an ambulance accident and followed him to the scene of the crash. Who am I? _____

30. I am not a real person, but I was in someone's dream. I worked at the hospital and drove a truck. I got an axe in my back in front of this young, scared girl named Laurie. Who am I? _____

Part 3: Fill in the Blank

31. What was the type of dance that Laurie, Annie, and Lynda were going to go to? _____

32. What was the name of Rachel and Jamie's dog in *Halloween 4: The Return of Michael Myers* (1988)? _____

33. Who was the actor that the Michael Myers mask was molded from? _____

34. What was the name of Lindsay's dog in *Halloween* (1978)? _____

35. What was the name of Rachel's dog in *Halloween 5: The Revenge of Michael Myers* (1989)? _____

36. What condiment did Mr. Elrod decline to have put on his sandwich in *Halloween II* (1981)? _____

37. What did Michael use to kill Wesley in *Halloween* (2007)? _____

38. What year did Michael kill his sister as a boy? _____

39. What state is Haddonfield located in? _____

40. In the production cut of *Halloween 6: The Curse of Michael Myers* (1995), whose baby was Michael the father of? _____

41. What was sticking out of Dr. Mixter's eye in *Halloween II* (1981)? _____

42. The *Halloween* (1978) theme song was created by John Carpenter on what instrument? _____

43. What color was Rachel's robe in *Halloween 5: The Revenge of Michael Myers* (1989)? _____

44. What was Samantha Thomas dressed as for the Halloween party? _____

45. Besides Freddie, who helped Sara survive Michael Myers? _____

Part 4: Hidden Character

Find the hidden character by filling in the quotes below. Once completed, the bubbles will spell out the hidden character.

46. That was the _ _ _ _ _ _ O _ _.
47. Behind that boy's eyes was purely and simply _ _ O _.
48. You're looking a little O _ _ _ _ _ there Mikey.
49. I'll see you in O _ _ _.
50. Trick or _ _ _ O _.
51. The only bastard I see in this _ _ _ _ O is you.
52. He was doing very well last night. Maybe someone around here gave him O _ _ _ _ _ _.
53. He's come _ _ O _.
54. Both of them _ _ _ _ _ O burned to death.
55. _ _ _ _ O ' _ an orphan.
56. Death has come to your little town, _ _ _ O _ _ _.
57. It's Halloween. Everyone is entitled to one good O _ _ _ _.

Hidden Character: _____ _____

Part 5: True or False

58. Deborah Voorhees was the stepmother of Michael Myers.

    a. True   b. False

59. Laurie Strode is the adopted daughter of John and Debra Strode.

    a. True   b. False

60. Harley dressed as a dude who wants to be a chick for Halloween?

    a. True   b. False

61. Josh Hartnett, who played John Tate, also starred in the movie *Pearl Harbor* (2001)?

    a. True   b. False

62. Skyler Gisondo, who played Tommy Doyle in *Halloween* (2007), had a role in Season 3 of *Once Upon a Time* (2011) as Devin?

    a. True   b. False

63. Before discovering Samantha and Spitz's corpses, Tina saw a cat with blood on its fur?

    a. True   b. False

64. In *Halloween 5: The Revenge of Michael Myers* (1989), Mike was driving a Dodge Viper?

    a. True   b. False

65. Dr. Loomis survived the explosion with Michael Myers at the end of *Halloween II* (1981)?

    a. True   b. False

Part 6: This or That

66. Michael Myers killed his sister or his brother?

    a. His Sister		b. His Brother

67. Is Michael Myers evil or holy?

    a. Evil		b. Holy

68. Michael Myers wrote on the chalkboard in *Halloween II* (1981) the word Halloween or Samhain?

    a. Halloween		b. Samhain

69. Per Dr. Loomis, Samhain means Day of the Dead or All Hallows' Eve?

    a. Day of the Dead		b. All Hallows' Eve

70. Laurie Strode is the original final girl or the original victim?

    a. Original Final Girl		b. Original Victim

71. Lester only hates Lynda or only hates Annie?

    a. Lynda		b. Annie

72. Is Conal Cochran from Scotland or Ireland?

    a. Scotland		b. Ireland

73. Jamie Lee Curtis, who plays Laurie Strode, is a true Scream Queen or a true Killing Machine?

    a. Scream Queen		b. Killing Machine

74. Is Will the boarding school's principal or guidance counselor?

    a. Principal		b. Guidance Counselor

75. The boarding school's class trip was to Yellowstone National Park or Yosemite National Park?

    a. Yellowstone National Park		b. Yosemite National Park

76. In *Halloween H20: 20 Years Later* (1998), Laurie Strode/Keri Tate liked drinking merlot or chardonnay?

   a. Merlot   b. Chardonnay

77. Is Deckard a high school student or a college student?

   a. High School Student   b. College Student

78. Dr. Mixter goes to a country club or a strip club?

   a. Country Club   b. Strip Club

79. Nurse Karen Bailey is always on time or always late?

   a. Always on time   b. Always late

80. By the end of the *Halloween* (1978) franchise, before the reboot from Rob Zombie and Blumhouse, does Laurie Strode survive or die?

   a. Survives   b. Dies

Part 7: Matching

Match the actor/actress to the character he/she played by putting the correct letter on the line.

81. Nancy Stephens ___   a. Sheriff Ben Meeker

82. PJ Soles ___   b. Marion Chambers

83. Nancy Kyes ___   c. Jimmy

84. Hunter Von Leer ___   d. Dr. Sam Loomis

85. Beau Starr ___   e. Michael Myers

86. Wendi Kaplan ___   f. Annie Brackett

87. Donald Pleasence ___   g. Freddie Harris

88. Busta Rhymes ___   h. Lynda Van Der Klok

89. George P. Wilbur ___   i. Deputy Gary Hunt

90. Lance Guest ___   j. Tina Williams

Part 8: Who Said It?

Put on the line who said each of the listed quotes.

91. "You can't have the baby, Michael!" _____

92. "They're all going to kill us!" _____

93. "Yeah. I'm fine baby. The bullet just grazed me!" _____

94. "It's almost time to come home, Angel!" _____

95. "I bet she wears crotch less panties and barks like a dog!" _____

96. "Hello, dear!" _____

97. "Leigh, they found three bodies. Across from the Doyle house. Three kids. Leigh, one of them was Annie!" _____

98. "I'm getting my nipples pierced" _____

99. "Michael Myers, get your ass over here" _____

100. "Fuck off, Wade" _____

Part 9: Who Played Who?

101. Who played Rachel Carruthers? _____
102. Who played Samantha Thomas? _____
103. Who played Ellie Grimbridge? _____
104. Who played John Tate? _____
105. Who played Brady? _____
106. Who played Nurse Jill Franco? _____
107. Who played Becks? _____
108. Who played Danny Strode? _____
109. Who played Will Brennan? _____
110. Who played Kelly Meeker? _____
111. Who played Rudy Grimes? _____
112. Who played Mrs. Alves? _____
113. Who played Billy Hill? _____
114. Who played Dr. Hoffman? _____
115. Who played Wolfie? _____
116. Who played Nora Winston? _____
117. Who played Dr. Terrence Wynn? _____
118. Who played Alice Martin? _____
119. Who played Lonnie Elam? _____
120. Who played Kyle Van Der Klok? _____
121. Who played Jenna Danzig? _____
122. Who played Norma Watson? _____
123. Who played Ismael Cruz? _____
124. Who played Nurse Mary? _____

125. Who played Tim Strode? _____
126. Who played John Strode? _____
127. Who played Marge Guttman? _____
128. Who played Spitz? _____
129. Who played Linda Challis? _____
130. Who played Budd Scarlotti? _____
131. Who played Mrs. Elrod? _____
132. Who played Jackson Sayer? _____
133. Who played Dr. Frederick Mixter? _____
134. Who played Mrs. Blankenship? _____
135. Who played Deputy Logan? _____
136. Who played Marshal Terrence Gummell? _____
137. Who played Jimmy Howell? _____
138. Who played Nurse Janet Marshall? _____
139. Who played Aron? _____
140. Who played Debra Strode? _____
141. Who played Kara Strode? _____
142. Who played Nurse Karen Bailey? _____
143. Who played Deckard? _____
144. Who played Starker? _____
145. Who played Teddy? _____
146. Who played Nurse Agnes? _____
147. Who played Uncle Meat? _____
148. Who played Paul Freedman? _____
149. Who played Nurse Daniels? _____
150. Who played Darlene Carruthers? _____

Part 10: Multiple Choice

151. Which dream film was always being discussed about Michael Myers in a crossover, but is just rumors and may never happen?

    a. Michael vs. Freddy   c. Michael vs. Jason

    b. Michael vs. Pinhead   d. Michael vs. Ghostface

152. Excluding the Blumhouse timeline, which of the *Halloween* (1978) films did Jamie Lee Curtis star in, either as a main star or a minor role?

    a. *Halloween* (1978), *Halloween II* (1981), *Halloween 4: The Return of Michael Myers* (1988), *Halloween H20: 20 Years Later* (1998), *and Halloween: Resurrection* (2002)

    b. *Halloween* (1978), *Halloween II* (1981), *Halloween 6: The Curse of Michael Myers* (1995), *Halloween H20: 20 Years Later* (1998), *and Halloween: Resurrection* (2002)

    c. *Halloween* (1978), *Halloween II* (1981), *Halloween III: Season of the Witch* (1982), *Halloween H20: 20 Years Later* (1998), *and Halloween: Resurrection* (2002)

    d. *Halloween* (1978), *Halloween II* (1981), *Halloween 5: The Revenge of Michael Myers* (1989), *Halloween H20: 20 Years Later* (1998), *and Halloween: Resurrection* (2002)

153. What was the approximate budget of all the *Halloween* (1978) films combined?

    a. $72,350,000   c. $72,325,000

    b. $72,375,000   d. $72,300,000

154. What instrument was used to create the *Halloween II* (1981) theme song?

    a. Synthesizer Piano   c. Synthesizer Cello

    b. Synthesizer Violin   d. Synthesizer Organ

155. What was the original title for *Halloween* (1978)?

   a. *The Babysitter Killers* (1978)

   b. *The Babysitter Stalkers* (1978)

   c. *The Babysitter Murders* (1978)

   d. *The Babysitter Obsession* (1978)

156. What was the name of the *Halloween* documentary released on July 25, 2006?

   a. *20 Years of Terror*   c. *30 Years of Terror*

   b. *25 Years of Terror*   d. *35 Years of Terror*

157. Who narrated the above documentary?

   a. Nancy Kyes   c. Jamie Lee Curtis

   b. PJ Soles   d. Danielle Harris

158. Which slasher film inspired the creation of *Halloween* (1978)?

   a. *Friday the 13th* (1980)

   b. *A Nightmare on Elm Street* (1984)

   c. *The Texas Chainsaw Massacre* (1973)

   d. *Psycho* (1960)

159. In 1983, *Halloween* (1978) was released as a video game on which gaming console?

   a. NES   c. Atari

   b. Super Nintendo   d. Sega Genesis

160. Over a four-month period, who wrote a total of three young adult novels on *Halloween*, albeit unrelated to the films?

   a. Kelly O'Rourke   c. Curtis Richards

   b. Nicholas Grabowsky   d. Jack Martin

161. Where did the 25-year anniversary of *Halloween* (1978) convention take place?

   a. Pasadena, California   c. Los Angeles, California

   b. Anaheim, California   d. San Francisco, California

162. Which actor, who played an iconic killer in a horror franchise, was a guest speaker during the *Halloween* (2010) documentary?

   a. Kane Hodder   c. Robert Englund

   b. Brad Dourif   d. Clive Barker

163. On February 9, 2017, John Carpenter stated that the next *Halloween* (1978) film will be released on which date and be a direct sequel to the original film?

   a. October 31, 2018   c. October 30, 2018

   b. October 19, 2018   d. October 13, 2018

164. On February 9, 2017, John Carpenter said which of the following will be directing the next film in the *Halloween* (1978) franchise?

   a. Malek Akkad   c. Danny McBride

   b. David Gordon Green d. Rob Zombie

165. Premiering on The Biography Channel on October 28, 2010, what was the name of the *Halloween* (2010) documentary?

   a. *Halloween: The Inside Scoop* (2010)

   b. *Halloween: The Inside Story* (2010)

   c. *The Making of Halloween* (2010)

   d. *Halloween: The Original Slasher* (2010)

166. What was the month and year of the 25th anniversary convention of *Halloween* (1978)?

   a. October 2005   c. October 2003

   b. October 2001   d. October 1999

167. *Halloween* (1978) is the fourth highest ranked grossing horror film franchise, with the *Hannibal Lecter* (2001) series third and *A Nightmare on Elm Street* (1984) second. Which horror film franchise ranks first in highest-grossing?

   a. *Scream* (1996)   c. *Friday the 13th* (1980)

   b. *Saw* (2004)   d. *The Texas Chainsaw Massacre* (1974)

168. Who did John Carpenter receive help from in performing the *Halloween* (1978) theme song?

   a. Debra Hill   c. Dan Wyman

   b. Rob Zombie   d. Alice Cooper

169. Which instrument was used to create the theme song for *Halloween* (1978)?

   a. Organ   c. Piano

   b. Violin   d. Cello

170. Which previous film of John Carpenter's inspired Moustapha Akkad and Irwin Yablans to have John Carpenter write and direct *Halloween* (1978)?

   a. *The Thing* (1982)   c. *The Fog* (1980)

   b. *Assault on Precinct 13* (1976)   d. *Dark Star* (1974)

171. How many days did it take to film *Halloween* (1978)?

   a. 20 Days   c. 30 Days

   b. 18 Days   d. 21 Days

172. The first *Halloween* (1978) comic book was simply titled *Halloween* (2000). What was the first sequel titled?

   a. *Halloween: The Blackest Eyes* (2001)

   b. *Halloween: The Devil's Eyes* (2001)

   c. *Halloween: The Origin of Michael Myers* (2001)

   d. *Halloween: The Devil Walks Among Us* (2001)

173. The first *Halloween* (1978) comic book was simply titled *Halloween* (2000). What was the second sequel titled?

a. *Halloween: The Origin of Michael Myers* (2001)

b. *Halloween: The Blackest Eyes* (2001)

c. *Halloween: The Devil Walks Among Us* (2001)

d. *Halloween: The Devil's Eyes* (2001)

174. What was the approximately amount of box office sales for the *Halloween* (1978) franchise only in the United States?

a. $308,189,322 c. $308,824,329

b. $308,774,929 d. $308,522,645

175. What was the name of the first *Halloween*-related book, yet unrelated to the film's timeline, that was released on October 1, 1997?

a. *The Scream Queen* (1997) c. *The Scream Factory* (1997)

b. *The Scream Demon* (1997) d. *The Scream of Death* (1997)

176. In the novelization of the *Halloween* (1978) film, what two things did the novel expand on?

a. The festival of Samhain and the legend of Michael Myers

b. The festival of Samhain and Michael's time at the sanitarium

c. The festival of Samhain and Michael's childhood

d. The festival of Samhain and the history of Halloween

177. Who wrote the novelization of the *Halloween* (1978) film?

a. Nicholas Grabowsky c. Jack Martin

b. Kelly O'Rourke d. Curtis Richards

178. How much did all the *Halloween* (1978) films approximately make in the box office combined?

a. $396,122,771 c. $396,122,778

b. $396,122,773 d. $396,122,377

179. In the novelization of the *Halloween II* (1981) film, what was added to the novel?

   a. An additional storyline   c. An additional victim

   b. An additional killer   d. An additional survivor

180. In 2003, a comic with which title featured Lindsay Wallace as the main character?

   a. *One Final Battle* (2003)   c. *One Last Chance* (2003)

   b. *One Good Scare* (2003)   d. *One Crazy Night* (2003)

181. Michael Myers is one of several horror icons to be included in the 2009 version of the Universal Studios Hollywood's Halloween Horror Nights event as part of a maze titled what?

   a. *Halloween: The Curse and Vengeance of Michael Myers* (2009)

   b. *Halloween: The Myth and Legend of Michael Myers* (2009)

   c. *Halloween: The Life and Crimes of Michael Myers* (2009)

   d. *Halloween: The Resurrection and Return of Michael Myers* (2009)

182. Who wrote the novelization of the *Halloween II* (1981) film?

   a. Curtis Richards   c. Kelly O'Rourke

   b. Jack Martin   d. Nicholas Grabowsky

183. What was the name of the second *Halloween*-related book, yet unrelated to the film's timeline, that was released on December 1, 1997?

   a. *The Old Myers House* (1997)

   b. *The Old Myers Town* (1997)

   c. *The Old Myers Place* (1997)

   d. *The Old Myers Sanitarium* (1997)

184. Michael Myers makes an appearance as a playable character in which video game?

   a. *Mortal Kombat* (2017)
   b. *Dead by Daylight* (2016)
   c. *Street Fighter* (2016)
   d. *Grand Theft Auto* (2013)

185. Michael Myers can be downloaded as a playable character in which video game?

   a. *WWE 2K17* (2016)
   b. *Mortal Kombat* (2017)
   c. *Call of Duty: Ghosts* (2013)
   d. *Call of Duty: Black Ops* (2010)

186. Who voiced Michael Myers in the nineteenth episode of *Robot Chicken* (2005)?

   a. Joe Filippone
   b. John Rhys-Davies
   c. Seth Green
   d. Giancarlo Esposito

187. In a survey of the psychological appeal of movie monsters, it was published in the Journal of Media Psychology that Michael Myers was considered what?

   a. Embodiment of Horror
   b. Embodiment of Terror
   c. Embodiment of Pure Evil
   d. Embodiment of Pure Torture

188. What type of dog was Lester in *Halloween* (1978)?

   a. Pitbull
   b. Rottweiler
   c. German Shepherd
   d. Chocolate Lab

189. Which killer is Michael Myers associated with?

   a. Charles Manson
   b. Jack the Ripper
   c. OJ Simpson
   d. The Zodiac Killer

190. What garage did the truck driver work for who Michael killed in *Halloween* (1978)?

   a. Phillips Garage
   b. Pats Garage
   c. Phelps Garage
   d. Peters Garage

191. What medicine did Dr. Loomis tell Marion to give to Michael when they took him before the judge in *Halloween* (1978)?

    a. Thorazine   c. Morphine

    b. Codeine   d. Motrin

192. In *Halloween* (1978), what two movies did Tommy and Lindsay watch over the night?

    a. *The Thing from Another World* (1951) and *The Fog* (1980)

    b. *The Thing from Another World* (1951) and *Psycho* (1960)

    c. *The Thing from Another World* (1951) and *Alien* (1979)

    d. *The Thing from Another World* (1951) and *Forbidden Planet* (1956)

193. In *Halloween II* (1981), what movie were the Elrod's watching?

    a. *Halloween* (1978)   c. *The Thing from Another World* (1951)

    b. *Night of the Living Dead* (1968)   d. *Friday the 13th* (1980)

194. What was the novelty store that Dr. Loomis passed when in the Marshal's car in *Halloween II* (1981)?

    a. The Keepsake   c. Jonathan's Boutique

    b. Jeepers Creepers   d. Larry's Prank Store

195. When Nurse Karen Bailey went into the hospital, what movie was Mr. Garrett watching in *Halloween II* (1981)?

    a. *Dracula* (1931)

    b. *Abbott and Costello Meet Frankenstein* (1948)

    c. *Dementia* (1955)

    d. *20,000 Leagues Under the Sea* (1954)

196. What year was Santa Mira founded as told in *Halloween III: Season of the Witch* (1982)?

    a. 1885   c. 1888

    b. 1887   d. 1882

197. In *Halloween III: Season of the Witch* (1982), what type of community was Santa Mira?

a. Irish Potato Patch

b. Irish Amish Community

c. Irish Farming Town

d. Irish Ghetto

198. Who wrote the novelization of the *Halloween 4: The Return of Michael Myers* (1988) film?

a. Jack Martin
c. Nicholas Grabowsky

b. Curtis Richards
d. Kelly O'Rourke

199. Approximately how much did the *Halloween* (1978) franchise gross in the box office through international sales?

a. $87,600,126
c. $73,343,992

b. $91,228,341
d. $66,332,787

200. What was the name of the third *Halloween*-related book, yet unrelated to the film's timeline, that was released on February 1, 1998?

a. *The Funhouse* (1998)
c. *The Haunted House* (1998)

b. *The Greenhouse* (1998)
d. *The Mad House* (1998)

Part 11: Word Search

Find the words located in the word bank in the puzzle below.

```
R E B H A D D O N F I E L D P
D E H S G H C L I N I C N C S
K A A G S A M H A I N R F O A
H T N L B U T R U F D M J S N
C M M G T A Z B K U R P Y T I
R A B H E O B H X Q W E E U T
P C O P H R R Y O D N Y V M A
A F O U V A T F S S X C I E R
R J G M L T L A A I P G L S I
T I E P B H M L I I T I R O U
I Y Y K E O A W O N K T T T M
E C M I W R S F U W M F E A K
S L A N L N K P G Y E E N R L
V W N S A R S B O J M E N A Y
K I D J O Z N A S X L M N T A
```

Dangertainment	Babysitter	Haddonfield	Sanitarium
Halloween	Pumpkins	Costumes	Hospital
Samhain	Clinic	Realtor	Boogeyman
Parties	Masks	Thorn	Evil

Part 12: Crossword Puzzle

Complete the crossword puzzle using the correct answers from the clues below.

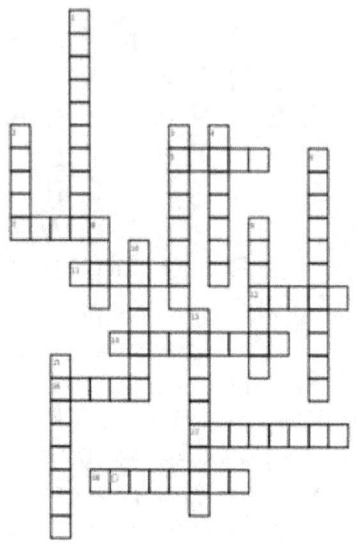

Down:
1. The occupation that Aaron and Dana have in Halloween (2018).
2. The nationality of Conal Cochran.
3. The occupation of Deborah Voorhees in Halloween (2007).
4. The word Lynda always says.
6. The hometown of Michael Myers.
8. What Dr. Loomis refers to Michael as.
9. The objects the drawing on the convenient store had covering her boobs in Halloween 5: The Revenge of Michael Myers.
10. The Celtic word written on the chalkboard in Halloween 2 (1981).
13. What Tommy refers to Michael Myers as.
15. The state that Smith's Grove Sanitarium is located in.

Across:
5. The name of the cult that Michael Myers was part of.
7. The white animal that the spirit of Deborah Voorhees had with her in Halloween 2 (2009).
11. The costume Billy wore in Halloween 5: The Revenge of Michael Myers.
12. Michael Myers' signature weapon.
14. The holiday Michael Myers kills people on.
16. The name of the deputy that Kelly Meeker found dismembered in Halloween 4: The Return of Michael Myers.
17. The place John's class was going to in Halloween H20: 20 Years Later.
18. Rudy's major in college in Halloween: Resurrection.

Answer Key

Halloween (1978)

1. B	26. D	51. C	76. A
2. D	27. A	52. D	77. B
3. A	28. B	53. B	78. B
4. A	29. C	54. A	79. C
5. C	30. B	55. A	80. C
6. C	31. B	56. A	81. D
7. C	32. A	57. B	82. A
8. B	33. C	58. C	83. D
9. D	34. A	59. C	84. A
10. C	35. A	60. B	85. D
11. B	36. B	61. D	86. A
12. A	37. C	62. D	87. B
13. A	38. A	63. D	88. B
14. A	39. A	64. D	89. C
15. C	40. A	65. C	90. C
16. C	41. B	66. C	91. B
17. A	42. B	67. A	92. D
18. C	43. D	68. C	93. D
19. C	44. C	69. B	94. B
20. D	45. C	70. A	95. C
21. B	46. B	71. C	96. A
22. B	47. A	72. A	97. C
23. C	48. A	73. C	98. D
24. C	49. C	74. D	99. A
25. C	50. C	75. B	100. C

Halloween II (1981)

1. C	26. A	51. B	76. A
2. C	27. A	52. C	77. A
3. C	28. B	53. C	78. D
4. C	29. C	54. A	79. C
5. C	30. C	55. D	80. C
6. A	31. D	56. B	81. C
7. B	32. B	57. B	82. B
8. D	33. C	58. C	83. B
9. B	34. A	59. B	84. B
10. C	35. A	60. C	85. C
11. B	36. C	61. A	86. C
12. B	37. B	62. C	87. C
13. D	38. B	63. C	88. C
14. A	39. C	64. D	89. A
15. A	40. C	65. B	90. A
16. C	41. A	66. B	91. B
17. D	42. A	67. B	92. D
18. C	43. D	68. C	93. D
19. D	44. B	69. A	94. B
20. B	45. A	70. B	95. C
21. C	46. B	71. B	96. C
22. C	47. B	72. D	97. A
23. B	48. A	73. C	98. B
24. C	49. A	74. C	99. C
25. D	50. B	75. C	100. C

Halloween III: Season of the Witch (1982)

1. D	26. D	51. C	76. D
2. A	27. B	52. A	77. C
3. B	28. C	53. A	78. B
4. C	29. C	54. C	79. A
5. C	30. A	55. D	80. A
6. C	31. A	56. D	81. A
7. A	32. D	57. A	82. A
8. A	33. D	58. C	83. A
9. D	34. B	59. A	84. C
10. C	35. B	60. C	85. D
11. B	36. A	61. A	86. D
12. D	37. D	62. C	87. A
13. A	38. C	63. A	88. B
14. B	39. B	64. A	89. C
15. A	40. B	65. B	90. C
16. C	41. C	66. C	91. B
17. C	42. C	67. A	92. D
18. D	43. D	68. A	93. C
19. B	44. D	69. B	94. B
20. B	45. C	70. B	95. A
21. C	46. A	71. A	96. A
22. C	47. B	72. A	97. C
23. D	48. C	73. B	98. C
24. B	49. A	74. D	99. C
25. A	50. C	75. C	100. C

Halloween 4: The Return of Michael Myers (1988)

1. D	26. D	51. C	76. D
2. A	27. B	52. A	77. C
3. B	28. C	53. A	78. B
4. C	29. C	54. C	79. A
5. C	30. A	55. D	80. A
6. C	31. A	56. D	81. A
7. A	32. D	57. A	82. A
8. A	33. D	58. C	83. A
9. D	34. B	59. A	84. C
10. C	35. B	60. C	85. D
11. B	36. A	61. A	86. D
12. D	37. D	62. C	87. A
13. A	38. C	63. A	88. B
14. B	39. B	64. A	89. C
15. A	40. B	65. B	90. C
16. C	41. C	66. C	91. B
17. C	42. C	67. A	92. D
18. D	43. D	68. A	93. C
19. B	44. D	69. B	94. B
20. B	45. C	70. B	95. A
21. C	46. A	71. A	96. A
22. C	47. B	72. A	97. C
23. D	48. C	73. B	98. C
24. B	49. A	74. D	99. C
25. A	50. C	75. C	100. C

Halloween 5: The Revenge of Michael Myers (1989)

1. D	26. D	51. C	76. B
2. D	27. C	52. B	77. C
3. B	28. B	53. B	78. C
4. B	29. D	54. C	79. C
5. D	30. A	55. D	80. C
6. C	31. B	56. B	81. D
7. A	32. C	57. C	82. A
8. C	33. C	58. C	83. B
9. C	34. A	59. A	84. A
10. A	35. A	60. A	85. B
11. D	36. B	61. C	86. C
12. D	37. C	62. C	87. B
13. B	38. B	63. B	88. B
14. B	39. A	64. D	89. B
15. B	40. B	65. D	90. D
16. B	41. D	66. C	91. A
17. A	42. D	67. B	92. A
18. C	43. B	68. C	93. A
19. C	44. C	69. C	94. D
20. A	45. C	70. C	95. C
21. C	46. A	71. D	96. A
22. A	47. A	72. A	97. A
23. C	48. C	73. D	98. A
24. C	49. C	74. D	99. D
25. C	50. C	75. D	100 C

Halloween 6: The Curse of Michael Myers (1995)

1. A	26. C	51. A	76. B
2. C	27. A	52. C	77. D
3. C	28. D	53. B	78. A
4. B	29. D	54. A	79. A
5. C	30. D	55. B	80. A
6. C	31. D	56. B	81. A
7. C	32. B	57. C	82. C
8. B	33. D	58. A	83. B
9. D	34. A	59. D	84. C
10. A	35. A	60. C	85. C
11. A	36. C	61. A	86. A
12. D	37. B	62. A	87. D
13. B	38. C	63. A	88. D
14. C	39. B	64. A	89. A
15. B	40. B	65. B	90. A
16. A	41. D	66. C	91. A
17. A	42. C	67. A	92. B
18. D	43. C	68. B	93. D
19. B	44. B	69. B	94. C
20. A	45. C	70. B	95. C
21. C	46. C	71. B	96. C
22. A	47. C	72. C	97. D
23. C	48. B	73. C	98. A
24. B	49. D	74. D	99. A
25. B	50. B	75. C	100. B

Halloween H20: 20 Years Later (1998)

1. C	26. A	51. B	76. A
2. C	27. B	52. B	77. B
3. C	28. C	53. B	78. D
4. C	29. D	54. C	79. D
5. C	30. A	55. D	80. D
6. A	31. B	56. B	81. D
7. B	32. A	57. A	82. A
8. D	33. B	58. A	83. C
9. C	34. A	59. B	84. D
10. C	35. C	60. D	85. C
11. D	36. C	61. A	86. A
12. B	37. B	62. B	87. C
13. A	38. C	63. B	88. A
14. B	39. C	64. C	89. A
15. B	40. C	65. D	90. A
16. C	41. C	66. C	91. B
17. C	42. C	67. B	92. C
18. C	43. B	68. D	93. D
19. C	44. D	69. A	94. A
20. B	45. D	70. B	95. B
21. B	46. C	71. B	96. A
22. A	47. A	72. C	97. D
23. A	48. C	73. D	98. A
24. A	49. A	74. A	99. A
25. D	50. C	75. A	100. A

Halloween: Resurrection (2002)

1. D	26. C	51. D	76. C
2. C	27. B	52. B	77. B
3. A	28. D	53. C	78. B
4. A	29. A	54. A	79. A
5. D	30. D	55. C	80. A
6. C	31. A	56. A	81. C
7. B	32. A	57. D	82. D
8. A	33. A	58. B	83. D
9. D	34. C	59. C	84. B
10. B	35. B	60. B	85. C
11. C	36. C	61. A	86. A
12. C	37. C	62. B	87. C
13. C	38. A	63. C	88. A
14. A	39. D	64. C	89. D
15. C	40. B	65. B	90. C
16. A	41. A	66. C	91. C
17. D	42. C	67. A	92. C
18. B	43. A	68. C	93. B
19. B	44. B	69. B	94. C
20. B	45. A	70. A	95. A
21. C	46. C	71. D	96. B
22. C	47. A	72. C	97. C
23. C	48. B	73. C	98. C
24. A	49. D	74. B	99. C
25. C	50. D	75. C	100. D

Halloween (2007)

1. C	26. B	51. C	76. B
2. A	27. C	52. B	77. C
3. C	28. A	53. D	78. A
4. C	29. A	54. C	79. A
5. C	30. C	55. C	80. C
6. B	31. A	56. A	81. D
7. D	32. D	57. C	82. D
8. A	33. B	58. A	83. C
9. B	34. A	59. B	84. C
10. A	35. A	60. D	85. B
11. C	36. A	61. B	86. A
12. C	37. B	62. B	87. A
13. B	38. C	63. C	88. A
14. C	39. D	64. A	89. B
15. C	40. D	65. D	90. D
16. D	41. B	66. C	91. D
17. D	42. A	67. C	92. B
18. D	43. C	68. C	93. C
19. C	44. C	69. A	94. C
20. C	45. A	70. A	95. B
21. C	46. B	71. B	96. C
22. C	47. B	72. C	97. C
23. A	48. C	73. A	98. D
24. D	49. A	74. C	99. D
25. A	50. C	75. B	

Halloween II (2009)

1. D	26. C	51. A	76. A
2. D	27. A	52. A	77. C
3. D	28. D	53. D	78. A
4. D	29. A	54. A	79. B
5. D	30. D	55. C	80. A
6. A	31. C	56. B	81. B
7. A	32. C	57. B	82. A
8. B	33. B	58. A	83. D
9. B	34. B	59. C	84. A
10. A	35. C	60. C	85. A
11. C	36. A	61. C	86. B
12. C	37. C	62. C	87. D
13. D	38. B	63. B	88. A
14. A	39. C	64. A	89. C
15. B	40. A	65. A	90. C
16. A	41. C	66. B	91. C
17. C	42. C	67. C	92. A
18. C	43. B	68. A	93. C
19. C	44. C	69. D	94. B
20. A	45. C	70. C	95. D
21. B	46. C	71. A	96. A
22. A	47. C	72. C	97. A
23. A	48. B	73. D	98. A
24. D	49. D	74. B	99. C
25. B	50. A	75. D	100. C

Halloween (2018)

1. D	26. B	51. C	76. B
2. D	27. C	52. A	77. C
3. D	28. B	53. A	78. A
4. D	29. B	54. D	79. C
5. D	30. B	55. A	80. A
6. C	31. B	56. C	81. D
7. B	32. D	57. B	82. C
8. A	33. B	58. B	83. D
9. A	34. D	59. C	84. A
10. A	35. A	60. B	85. D
11. C	36. A	61. B	86. A
12. C	37. A	62. B	87. C
13. B	38. D	63. D	88. A
14. A	39. D	64. B	89. D
15. A	40. B	65. D	90. A
16. C	41. C	66. A	91. B
17. B	42. A	67. C	92. C
18. C	43. B	68. D	93. B
19. D	44. D	69. A	94. D
20. B	45. D	70. C	95. A
21. A	46. D	71. A	96. B
22. C	47. A	72. B	97. D
23. C	48. D	73. D	98. B
24. C	49. A	74. A	99. B
25. C	50. A	75. B	100. A

Halloween Kills (2021)

1. D	26. A	51. B	76. B
2. B	27. B	52. A	77. B
3. A	28. D	53. D	78. A
4. A	29. A	54. A	79. D
5. D	30. A	55. D	80. D
6. B	31. A	56. D	81. C
7. A	32. B	57. B	82. C
8. C	33. D	58. A	83. C
9. A	34. D	59. B	84. C
10. C	35. D	60. C	85. C
11. C	36. C	61. D	86. A
12. C	37. A	62. B	87. D
13. A	38. B	63. B	88. B
14. B	39. C	64. A	89. B
15. C	40. A	65. D	90. A
16. D	41. D	66. B	91. C
17. D	42. B	67. A	92. D
18. C	43. D	68. C	93. A
19. A	44. A	69. C	94. B
20. B	45. D	70. B	95. C
21. B	46. B	71. A	96. C
22. B	47. B	72. C	97. A
23. A	48. A	73. C	98. D
24. A	49. D	74. D	99. A
25. C	50. A	75. A	100. B

Halloween Mashup
Part 1: Word Scramble

1. Scream Queen
2. Haddonfield
3. Thorn
4. Halloween
5. Michael Myers
6. Evil
7. Silver Shamrock
8. Butcher Knife
9. Rabbit In Red
10. Dangertainment
11. October
12. Boogeyman
13. Babysitting
14. The Shape
15. The Clinic

Part 2: Who Am I?

1. Jamie Lloyd
2. Deborah Myers
3. John Strode
4. Mrs. Alves
5. Conal Cochran
6. The Kupfer Family
7. Tina Williams
8. Darlene Carruthers
9. Dr. Terrence Wynn
10. Brady
11. Michael Myers

12. Mrs. Blankenship
13. Lynda Van Der Klok
14. Dr. Hoffman
15. Budd

Part 3: Fill in the Blank

1. Homecoming
2. Sundae
3. William Shatner
4. Lester
5. Max
6. Mayonnaise
7. Tree Branch
8. 1963
9. Illinois
10. Jamie Lloyd
11. Syringe
12. Piano
13. Pink
14. Devil
15. Deckard

Part 4: Hidden Character

1. Boogeyman
2. Evil
3. Crispy
4. Hell
5. Treat
6. House
7. Lessons
8. Home

9. Nearly
10. Jamie's
11. Sheriff
12. Scare
Hidden Character: Michael Myers

Part 5: True or False

1. B
2. B
3. B
4. A
5. A
6. A
7. B
8. A

Part 6: This or That

1. A
2. A
3. B
4. A
5. A
6. B
7. B
8. A
9. B
10. B
11. B
12. A
13. A
14. B
15. B

Part 7: Matching

1. B
2. H
3. F
4. I
5. A
6. J
7. D
8. G
9. E
10. C

Part 8: Who Said It?

1. Jamie Lloyd
2. Harry Grimbridge
3. Ronnie
4. Deborah Myers
5. Barry Simms
6. Mrs. Blankenship
7. Deputy Gary Hunt
8. Will Brennan
9. Marion Chambers
10. Kelly Meeker

Part 9: Who Played Who?

1. Ellie Cornell
2. Tamara Glynn
3. Stacey Nelkin
4. Josh Hartnett
5. Sasha Jenson

6. Tawny Moyer
7. Sean Whalen
8. Devin Gardener
9. Adam Arkin
10. Kathleen Kinmont
11. Sean Patrick Thomas
12. Gloria Gifford
13. Jeffrey Landman
14. Michael Pataki
15. Matt Bush
16. Tyra Banks
17. Mitchell Ryan
18. Anne Bruner
19. Brent Le Page
20. Robert Curtis Brown
21. Katee Sackhoff
22. Janet Leigh
23. Danny Trejo
24. Susan Swift
25. Keith Bogart
26. Bradford English
27. Garn Stephens
28. Matthew Walker
29. Nancy Kyes
30. Leo Rossi
31. Lucille Benson
32. Carmen Filpi
33. Ford Rainey
34. Janice Knickrehm
35. George Sullivan
36. John Zenda
37. Joseph Gordon-Levitt
38. Ana Alicia

39. Haig Sutherland
40. Kim Darby
41. Marianne Hagan
42. Pamela Susan Shoop
43. Ryan Merriman
44. Jonathan Terry
45. Wendy Wessberg
46. Maidie Norman
47. Howard Hesseman
48. Max Van Ville
49. Octavia Spencer
50. Karen Alston

Part 10: Multiple Choice

1. C
2. C
3. C
4. D
5. C
6. B
7. B
8. D
9. C
10. A
11. A
12. D
13. B
14. B
15. B
16. C
17. C
18. C

19. C
20. B
21. D
22. A
23. C
24. D
25. C
26. B
27. D
28. A
29. C
30. B
31. C
32. B
33. C
34. B
35. C
36. C
37. C
38. C
39. B
40. C
41. A
42. D
43. B
44. A
45. C
46. B
47. C
48. C
49. A
50. D

Part 11: Word Search

```
R E B H A D D O N F I E L D P
D E H S G H C L I N I C N C S
K A A G S A M H A I N R F O A
H T N L B U T R U F D M J S N
C M M G T A Z B K U R P Y T I
R A B H E O B H X Q W E E U T
P C O P H R R Y O D N Y V M A
A F O U V A T F S S X C I E R
R J G M L T L A A I P G L S I
T I E P B H M L I I T I R O U
I Y Y K E O A W O N K T T T M
E C M I W R S F U W M F E A K
S L A N L N K P G Y E E N R L
V W N S A R S B O J M E N A Y
K I D J O Z N A S X L M N T A
```

Dangertainment   Babysitter   Haddonfield   Sanitarium
Halloween   Pumpkins   Costumes   Hospital
Samhain   Clinic   Realtor   Boogeyman
Parties   Masks   Thorn   Evil

Part 12: Crossword Puzzle

Down:
1. The occupation that Aaron and Dana have in Halloween (2018).
2. The nationality of Conal Cochran.
3. The occupation of Deborah Voorhees in Halloween (2007).
4. The word Lynda always says.
6. The hometown of Michael Myers.
8. What Dr. Loomis refers to Michael as.
9. The objects the drawing on the convenient store had covering her boobs in Halloween 5: The Revenge of Michael Myers.
10. The Celtic word written on the chalkboard in Halloween 2 (1981).
13. What Tommy refers to Michael Myers as.
15. The state that Smith's Grove Sanitarium is located in.

Across:
5. The name of the cult that Michael Myers was part of.
7. The white animal that the spirit of Deborah Voorhees had with her in Halloween 2 (2009).
11. The costume Billy wore in Halloween 5: The Revenge of Michael Myers.
12. Michael Myers' signature weapon.
14. The holiday Michael Myers kills people on.
16. The name of the deputy that Kelly Meeker found dismembered in Halloween 4: The Return of Michael Myers.
17. The place John's class was going to in Halloween H20: 20 Years Later.
18. Rudy's major in college in Halloween: Resurrection.

Acknowledgements

My Mom: Thank you to my mom for always believing in me and encouraging me to go for and live my dreams. Without your outpouring of love, patience, and acceptance, I don't think I would've have the courage to go through with becoming an author and a filmmaker.

My Dad: I always loved my dad and thank him for his belief in me and how he always encouraged me to pursue my dreams. I love and miss you daddy so much. RIP!

My Boyfriend: I want to thank my boyfriend, Kyle, for everything he has done for me and for being my biggest cheerleader. Even when I felt down and defeated, he was ALWAYS by my side and picked me up when I was down for the count. I couldn't ask for anyone better than him to be there for me. He has supported me no matter what and has encouraged me, even when I didn't believe in myself. I love you so much, Kyle, more than you'll ever even know!

My Family: Thanks to both the McCoy and Seitzinger families for believing in me as an author and never giving up on me.

My Friends: Thanks to my friends for the encouragement in becoming an author, as well as for helping me in all types of ways, whether it be to talk to me about my dad's cancer battle, helping me making movies through Gravestone Films, or otherwise just supporting my passions. You guys and gals rock!

My Agents: I want to thank my literary agent, Eric Lincoln Miller, and talent agent, Timothy Beal, for helping me get this book out there and believing in me, my writing, and my expertise as a horror fan to do the *Halloween* (1978) franchise justice with a trivia book that will do right by the fans.

My Editor: A special thank you to Charles F. Rosenay, who took the time out of his schedule to edit this book and make it stand out, following all grammatical and writing guidelines, so you, the readers, can enjoy this book as much as I do!

Jesus Christ: And I saved the best for last. Thanks to my Lord and Savior, Jesus Christ. Because of Him, I have succeeded in things I only thought were dreams with no reality. He helped restore my faith during my dad's cancer battle, as well, and has helped my family in more ways than I can ever count! I love you, my Lord!

Social Media Lounge

Follow me, Scotty McCoy, on Facebook at www.facebook.com/smccoyauthor.

You can also follow me on Twitter at www.twitter.com/smccoyauthor.

My Instagram handle is @smccoyauthor, so follow me over there too.

****

Check out my editor, Charles Rosenay's, book at www.BookOfTop10HorrorLists.com and like his book's page on Facebook at www.facebook.com/BookOfHorrorLists.

****

Fans of the Paranormal and Supernatural, check out: www.ParanormalCT.com.

Horror fans visit www.DracTours.com for information on the Annual Dracula Tours to Transylvania. Follow on Facebook at www.Facebook.com/DracTours or call (203) 795-4737 for more information.

Dracula Tour Promotional Poster

www.ingramcontent.com/pod-product-compliance
Lightning Source LLC
Chambersburg PA
CBHW070823250426
43671CB00036B/1841